SuburbiaNation

Additional praise for Beuka's *SuburbiaNation*:

"In his introductory remarks, Robert Beuka describes his argument presented in the ensuing pages, that the suburban landscape 'stands as the material counterpart to specific drives and tendencies in American culture apparent from the postwar years onward.' Those drives and tendencies include the massive expansion of the middle class, the elevation of the ideal of the nuclear family, and collapsing of the distinction between public and private spaces.

"There have been many books published on the development of suburbia in the twentieth century, but none as thorough, comprehensive, and illuminating as Beuka's, primarily because it is not a sociological treatise, but rather a sensitive examination of the impact of suburban development on American culture—from F. Scott Fitzgerald, John Cheever, and John Updike through films that address problems in suburban life, including matters of race and gender. For example, although Fitzgerald studies have addressed the meaning of the city in *The Great Gatsby* and other works, no other book has attempted to place the novel in the context of the first years in the development of a suburban culture.

"Beuka's new approach to the meaning of the 'American Dream,' as reflected in popular culture—notably in television and popular magazines—sheds new light on the contemporary scene, and our response to historical events, particularly in the aftermath of 9/11.

"Above all, his treatment of the meaning of 'place' as a dynamic element in our lives offers new insight into the study of fiction and film.

"This is an important book for everyone interested in American Culture, American Studies, and fiction and film affected by the growth of suburbia. After reading it, I cannot look at the suburban nation as I did before, and my understanding of contemporary events has been deepened and enriched by Beuka's work."

—Ruth Prigozy
Professor of English, Hofstra University
Executive Director, F. Scott Fitzgerald Society

SuburbiaNation

Reading Suburban Landscape in
Twentieth-Century American
Fiction and Film

Robert Beuka

palgrave
macmillan

SUBURBIANATION

First published 2004 by PALGRAVE MACMILLAN™
175 Fifth Avenue, New York, N.Y. 10010 and
Houndmills, Basingstoke, Hampshire, England RG21 6XS.
Companies and representatives throughout the world.

PALGRAVE MACMILLAN is the global academic imprint of the Palgrave Macmillan division of St. Martin's Press, LLC and of Palgrave Macmillan Ltd. Macmillan® is a registered trademark in the United States, United Kingdom and other countries. Palgrave is a registered trademark in the European Union and other countries.

ISBN 1-4039-6367-3 hardback
ISBN 1-4039-6340-1 paperback

Library of Congress Cataloging-in-Publication Data

PS374
.S82
B48
2004

Beuka, Robert A., 1965-
    SuburbiaNation : reading suburban landscape in twentieth-century American fiction and film / by Robert A. Bueka.
    p. cm.
    Includes bibliographical references and index.   I1403963673
    ISBN 1-4039-6367-3 (cloth) -- ISBN 1-4039-6340-1 (pbk.)
    1. American fiction--20th century--History and criticism. 2. Suburban life in literature. 3. Motion pictures--United States--History. 4. Landscape in motion pictures. 5. Landscape in literature. 6. Suburbs in mass media. 7. Suburbs in literature. I. Title: Suburbia nation. II. Title.

PS374. S82B48 2004
813'.509321733--dc21   2003054914

A catalogue record for this book is available from the British Library.

Design by Planettheo.com

First edition: January 2004
10 9 8 7 6 5 4 3 2 1

Printed in the United States of America.

For Nadine

Contents

Eight pages of photographs appear between pages 148 and 149.

Acknowledgments

One of the most enjoyable and fruitful aspects of this project has been discussing it with others; everyone has an opinion on the suburbs, it seems, and I have profited greatly from feedback I've received over the past several years from colleagues, students, and friends. I owe a particular debt of gratitude to those who helped me formulate and articulate my ideas in the early stages. This work began as a dissertation, and I wish to thank my dissertation committee from Louisiana State University, professors J. Gerald Kennedy, Elsie Michie, Richard Moreland, Robin Roberts, and John Rodrigue, for their advice, support, and insightful criticism. Jerry Kennedy, my director, has been a mentor and trusted friend, and I thank him for his guidance. I am indebted as well to the LSU Graduate School, whose award of a Dissertation Year Fellowship provided me with much needed time to focus on research and writing. Professors Sarah Liggett and John Lowe from LSU, Patrick Meanor from State University of New York-Oneonta, and Lt. Col. James Meredith from the U.S. Air Force Academy offered suggestions, materials, and timely encouragement. The friends I was fortunate enough to meet during my graduate school days, Daniel Gonzalez, Chris Rieger, Brian Arundel, and Chad Husted, helped me probably more than they know through their intelligence, good humor, and camaraderie.

I benefited greatly from feedback I received as I was revising and expanding this work over the past two years. In particular, I wish to thank professors Ruth Prigozy of Hofstra University and Branimir Rieger of Lander University for their willingness to read and respond to the manuscript with thoughtful and practical critiques. I also owe thanks to Bronx Community College and the City University of New York for allowing me the time this past year to complete final revisions. My students and colleagues at Bronx CC have been enthusiastic and supportive during these exciting and often hectic days, and I am grateful to them for making work such a pleasure.

Several sections in this book have previously appeared, in somewhat altered form, in scholarly journals, and I would like to thank the editors of those journals for allowing me permission to use this material. A portion of chapter 1 was first published in the Fall/Winter 1999/2000 issue of the *Journal of Film and Video* as "Imagining the Postwar Small Town: Gender and the Politics of Landscape in *It's a Wonderful Life*." My thanks to editor Suzanne Regan, not only for publishing the essay, but also for her kindness and encouragement. A portion of chapter 3 was first published as the essay "'Just One Word . . . *Plastics*': Suburban Malaise, Masculinity, and Oedipal Drive in *The Graduate*" in the *Journal of Popular Film & Television*, Vol. 28, pp. 12-21, Spring 2000. Reprinted with permission of the Helen Dwight Reid Educational Foundation. Published by Heldref Publications, 1319 18th St. N.W. Washington, DC 20036-1802. Copyright 2000. Some of the material in the conclusion first appeared in the essay "'Cue the Sun': Soundings From Millennial Suburbia," from the *Iowa Journal of Cultural Studies*, Vol. 3, Fall 2003.

I owe a tremendous debt of gratitude to the good people at Palgrave Macmillan who have shepherded this project along. Amanda Johnson and Matthew Ashford, my editorial team, have handled the manuscript, as well as my innumerable queries and concerns, with intelligence, wit, and care. Sonia Wilson and Rick Delaney have displayed similar patience and concern in steering me through the production process, and Debby Manette made my head spin, in a good way, with her fine copyediting.

Throughout the process of writing this book, I have been able to rely on the love and caring of my family. I would like to thank my parents, William and Helen Beuka, and my siblings, Mary and Bill, for their undying support and encouragement. I thank my parents also for raising me on the border of the suburban and the rural; I thought often, while researching and writing this book, of my childhood home in Yorktown Heights, New York—the last house on Ferncrest Drive, bordering a large expanse of woods that to a boy's eyes stretched on forever. I think of that place often, still. I wish also to thank the Araoz family for their love and support; more than in-laws, Dorita, Daniel, and Lee have been friends and advisors to me. I would be remiss if I didn't thank as well a little fellow named Malcolm Andrew Beuka, for making the sun rise every day.

Most of all, I want to thank my wife Nadine, without whose love, insight, patience, and grace this work would not have been possible.

Utopia, Dystopia, Heterotopia

The Suburban Landscape in Twentieth-Century American Culture and Thought

Poised at the beginning of a new century, American cultural critics will doubtless soon find occasion to look back on significant developments in U.S. society over the course of the past hundred years. Among the myriad changes that have fostered America's evolution from a largely unsettled and expanding country to the tightly interconnected, late-capitalist nation of today, certainly one profound development can be seen on the face of the American landscape itself. While the beginning of the twentieth century saw increasing urbanization across the land, the second half of the century witnessed the massive development of the suburban landscape, a new type of terrain that dissolved the urban/rural place distinctions that had, until that point, largely characterized American topography. That the expansion of the suburban environment—particularly in the post–World War II era—stands as a significant cultural development is evidenced by the fact that, at the dawn of the twenty-first century, the United States is primarily a suburban nation, with far more Americans living in the suburbs than in either urban or rural areas.[2]

But the postwar expansion of the terrain that has come to be known as suburbia has marked more than a mere revolution in demographics. With its instantly identifiable, uniform architectural styles and landscape designs, the American suburb has contributed toward a proliferating sense of placelessness and in turn the perceived homogenization of American life. In this manner, the explosion of suburbia over the past half century has immeasurably altered the ways Americans think about place and their individual and collective relationships to it. Indeed, the ubiquity of the suburban landscape has engendered profound enough collective cultural effects to lead one observer to note that "the experience of suburbia is central if we are to make sense of our everyday life . . . in the twentieth century."[3] This book is an effort to begin to understand the cultural significance of the suburb, the most significant landscape to emerge in twentieth-century America.

Specifically, in this study I examine representations of the suburbs in American fiction and film of the twentieth century. My founding assumption is that the suburban settings in the texts I discuss function as decidedly more than simple backdrop, instead emerging as dynamic, often defining elements of their narratives. Paying attention to place in these narratives helps to shed light on American culture's complicated relationship to the suburban landscape as it has developed over the course of the twentieth century. This is a relationship worth exploring, because the suburban landscape, I will argue, stands as the material counterpart to specific drives and tendencies in American culture apparent from the postwar years onward: a massive expansion of the middle class, a heightened valorization of the nuclear family and consequent reification of gender identities, a trend—both utopian and exclusionary in nature—toward cultural homogenization, and a collapsing of the distinction between public and private spaces. That is, the suburban landscape that developed in the decades following the end of World War II both reflected and facilitated these tendencies, emerging as a symbolic manifestation of the values and contradictions of dominant U.S. culture. Reading suburban fiction and film with an eye toward landscape concerns, then, serves to expose the manifold cultural practices and anxieties that helped to shape U.S. society in the second half of the twentieth century.

An examination of the relationships between landscape and culture, this study takes its cue from the insights offered in the field of humanistic geography over the past three decades. As contemporary geographers remind us, all lived places resonate with the energies of those who inhabit them. In J. Nicholas Entrikin's terms, "We live our lives in place and have a sense of being part of place, but we also view place as something separate, something external. . . . Thus place is both a center of meaning and the external context of our actions."[4] The dual nature of place Entrikin suggests—of inhabited place as an objective reality or physical landscape and as an intellectually and emotionally invested *chora,* a kind of landscape of the mind—provides an apt starting point for this study of the dynamics of place in suburban fiction and film, for a number of reasons.[5] To begin with, Entrikin's comment reminds us that place is more than simply the passive physical backdrop against which the stuff of life (or fiction) is played out, instead often emerging as a "center of meaning" in our lives. While this observation may seem commonsensical to anyone who has ever had the experience of feeling a "sense of place," it works toward suggesting the *dynamic* element of place, the notion that the identity of a lived environment is, as Entrikin notes, "a function of the unique experiences that individuals and groups associate with [it]."[6] This dynamic conception of place is not only a recognizable element of day-to-day living for most of us, but also, I believe (and hope to demonstrate), a potentially compelling factor in the study of fiction and film. And as the burgeoning prominence of ecocriticism indicates, environmental concerns have assumed increasing importance in literary studies in recent years. While this work shares philosophical affinities with much recent ecocriticism, my analysis tends more in the direction of cultural studies than do the majority of ecocritical works, which to this point have tended to focus more squarely on issues related to the "natural" environment.[7] By contrast, in the chapters that follow I seek to examine the ways in which the unique landscape of suburbia can be read, in geographer D. W. Meinig's words, as reflecting "cultural values" and "social behavior," as presenting "at once a panorama, a composition, a palimpsest, a micro-cosm" of the dominant culture.[8]

The broad-based understanding of place expressed in the field of humanistic geography is especially important in a study of fictional repre-sentations of the suburban landscape because of the unique and often vexing cultural perception of the American suburbs. As I hope to demon-strate, the development and subsequent massive expansion of suburbia entailed the construction of not only a new kind of physical landscape, but new psychic and emotional landscapes as well. Always as much an *idea* as a reality, the landscape of American suburbia has become and remained something of a symbolic minefield, the mirror (or, perhaps better put, the picture window) through which middle-class American culture casts its uneasy reflective gaze on itself. Mere mention of the word "suburbia," after all, will call to mind for most Americans a familiar string of images—the grid of identical houses on identical lots, the smoking barbecue, the swimming pool—loaded signifiers that, taken together, connote both the middle-class "American dream" as it was promulgated by and celebrated in popular culture in the postwar years and that dream's inverse: the vision of a homogenized, soulless, plastic landscape of tepid conformity, an alienating "noplace." That such images seem drawn from an increasingly distant past, with "suburbia" and "the 1950s" occupying a shared space in the collective cultural imagination, is neither accident nor coincidence; as a culture we retain a detached view of suburban place, relegating to the past a psychologically troublesome landscape that is nonetheless increas-ingly the dominant terrain of the nation.

The persistence of a reductive, two-dimensional vision of suburbia reflects the extent to which this insurgent landscape became, in the postwar years, invested with fixed symbolic meanings. While the rapid development and spread of suburbs was largely a matter of necessity, an inevitable response to a great demand for housing, nevertheless the timing of this phenomenon has symbolic merit as well. Arriving as it did in a period of economic optimism and celebratory nationalism, suburbanization constructed a new type of landscape, complete with its own set of symbols and iconography, which served as the visible manifestation of the American "way of life." That is, while the appearance of planned suburban developments may have in actuality been a matter of form following function—the identical houses on identical plots a result of the developers' having followed the quickest, easiest, and most profitable building methods—this new type of residential space quickly became the visual image of the typical, even stereotypical, "American Dream" itself. Various media of popular culture, especially television and popular magazines, contributed through their glowing images of suburban life to an emerging sense of the suburbs as the promised land of the American middle class.

The utopian ideals associated with postwar suburban living sprang from the very nature of this new landscape, an environment that emphasized the prospect of perfectibility through its precise, meticulous plotting and architecture. Architectural critic Clifford Clark has noted this aspect of the suburban landscape as it emerged in the years following World War II, arguing that the development of suburbia was "a central part of a larger perfectionist impulse that swept through postwar society. . . . [T]he postwar housing boom was part of a one-dimensional frame of mind that stressed the possibility of creating the perfect society."[9] Clark's observation points toward a crucial connection between landscape design and utopic visions of community: In suburbia, homogeneity of architectural and landscape styles bespoke a desire to elide the very notion of difference among suburban residents. With their uniform, unassuming architectural lines and uncluttered, contiguous, parklike landscapes, the postwar suburbs offered residents visual evidence of their similarity to their neighbors, thus suggesting the utopian ideal of perfect community not only through similar experience and social stature, but also through a sense of shared, communal space. The personalizing alterations to suburban lawns and houses over ensuing decades have certainly by now left only remnants of what was once a truly homogeneous landscape, but what does remain is the residue of a utopian dream of community figured through landscape and architectural design. Indeed, as one critic has noted, today's suburb might well be read as the "all-but-vanished sign of the utopian specter haunting the postmodern condition."[10]

Even as postwar suburbanization was cloaked in utopian ideals of community and neighborliness, a number of social critics quickly began to decry the dystopian aspects of suburban existence. At the height of suburban development and expansion, a series of sociological works emerged that castigated the new suburbanites, their landscapes, and their ways of living. Such influential texts as David Riesman's *The Lonely Crowd* (1950), William H. Whyte's *The Organization Man* (1956), Paul Goodman's *Growing Up Absurd* (1960), and Betty Friedan's *The Feminine Mystique* (1963) read the suburbs as, respectively, a hotbed of conformity; an emasculating, corporate environment; a breeding ground for misdirected and disaffected youths; and a psychologically disabling prison for women. Indeed, these works—considered alongside a string of sensationalistic, quasi-sociological novels chronicling the living hell of suburban existence, such as John Keats's *The Crack in the Picture Window* (1957) and John McPartland's *No Down Payment* (1957)—signaled a chorus of vehement reaction against the suburban environment, and their influence can still be felt in contemporary attitudes toward suburban life. Fueled by, among other things, cold-war era concerns over enforced conformity, these critiques saw the suburban endeavor as threatening to cherished ideals of individuality and self-determination. Typical in this regard is the analysis of architectural critic Ada Louise Huxtable, who in a *New York Times* piece in 1964 lamented the spread of "regimented hordes of split-levels lined up for miles in close, unlovely rows," arguing that suburban developers were responsible for the "standardization of America on a surprisingly low level."[11] As reactions against what by some were perceived as the utopian possibilities of suburban life, these critiques helped to contribute to a two-dimensional view of the suburbs that persists in the popular imagination to this day: Viewed from the outset as either utopian models of community or dystopian landscapes of dispiriting homogeneity, suburbs remain a contested, if only superficially understood, terrain.

A useful tool toward overcoming this binary way of thinking about the suburban landscape may be found in Michel Foucault's notion of heterotopic spaces. As Foucault argues in his influential essay "Of Other Spaces," all societies create what he calls "heterotopias," places that in their very existence serve to mirror the culture at large. He describes the heterotopia as a "kind of effectively enacted utopia in which the real sites, all the other sites that can be found within the culture, are simultaneously represented, contested, and inverted," concluding that heterotopias are "absolutely different from all the sites that they reflect and speak about."[12] Thus seeing heterotopic places as "mirrors" to the society that produced them, Foucault suggests that such places create "a space that is other, another real space, as perfect, as meticulous, as well arranged as ours is messy, ill constructed, and jumbled."[13] Noting that a utopian ideal of achieving "human perfection" leads such places to be rigorously "regulated," Foucault describes heterotopias with phrasing that puts one in mind of the suburban landscape that emerged in the postwar years—a meticulous, ordered, regulatory environment. The appeal of seeing suburbs as heterotopic spaces is that Foucault's formulation allows a way out of the impasse of the utopia/dystopia binary that has characterized our perception of suburbia throughout the latter half of the twentieth century.

Considered as a kind of heterotopic "mirror" to mainstream American culture, the suburb instead emerges as a place that reflects both an idealized image of middle-class life and specific cultural anxieties about the very elements of society that threaten this image. Indeed, the notion of suburbia as an American heterotopia suggests long-held utopian and dystopian views of suburban life to be really two sides of the same coin, evidence of our culture's uneasy relationship to a landscape that mirrors both the fantasies and the phobias of the culture at large. The visions of suburbia offered by postwar social critics and novelists indicate that the fantasy image of the suburb as a place of prosperity and "community" was from the outset beset with numerous social concerns; over the ensuing decades of suburban expansion, fears over antagonistic class, gender, and race relationships have further complicated our cultural vision of suburbia. As the suburb gradually became the dominant landscape in the United States, it also began to reflect increasingly complex cultural concerns, mirroring the anxieties of the culture at large.

As to how precisely a landscape becomes invested with such varied cultural ideals and contradictions, evidence abounds in the social dynamics of both postwar and contemporary environments. Consider, for example, the connections between the postwar suburban expansion and the motivations behind such late–twentieth-century landscape phenomena as the rise of the "gated community" or, for that matter, such "New Urbanist" neotraditional communities as the new Disney corporation "company town" of Celebration, Florida. In each of these cases, a strong utopian impulse toward establishing community—coupled, of course, with the profit potential for developers themselves—fuels the development of an environment predicated on exclusionary principles and the rigid control of both physical and social landscapes. In the case of the postwar suburbs, the classic example of this tendency can be found in the story of Levittown, New York, founded in 1947 and arguably the prototype of the preplanned suburbs that would spring up across the nation over the coming decades.[14] The architectural firm of Levitt and Sons, in creating this first embodiment of American "suburbia," exercised nearly complete control over the landscape; beyond their revolutionary decision to use assembly-line techniques to produce quickly some 17,000 essentially identical houses on identical plots of land, the company maintained stringent regulations on use of the land by new homeowners and, more tellingly, restricted sales to "acceptable" buyers, notably refusing to sell any Levittown homes to

African Americans.[15] Questioned about his selective selling practices, company head William Levitt famously opined, "As a company our position is simply this: We can solve a housing problem or we can try to solve a racial problem but we cannot combine the two."[16] Levitt's stance epitomized the exclusionary principles informing the development of postwar suburbia, and the legacy of such a philosophy lives on today.

While Levittown offered the first example of a new kind of landscape that would offer the opportunity of home ownership and "community" building to a massive segment of the population for whom such ideals were previously unattainable, it also offered evidence of the restrictive covenants that would, for decades to come, ensure that suburbia remained, at heart, lily white. A similar restrictive impulse continues to inform the latest mutation of the suburban impulse in American society, the gated community.[17] In name alone, this architectural and landscape phenomenon suggests that the exclusionary ethos of postwar suburbia is not only alive and well, but has in fact, among residents of such places, mutated into a full-blown environmental paranoia.[18] On the other side of the coin, a fully preplanned town such as Celebration—founded in 1995 as a commuter suburb for workers at Disney World and other attractions in nearby Orlando—touts as its main selling point the re-creation of an old-fashioned sense of community through a landscape manufactured to instill a sense of nostalgia and a kind of willed communal innocence among its inhabitants. A promotional video for Celebration describes the town as a place of "innocence," of "caramel apples and cotton candy, secret forts and hopscotch on the streets. . . . A new American town of block parties and Fourth of July parades. Of spaghetti dinners and school bake sales, lollipops and fireflies in a jar."[19] Trading on patriotic images of a bygone America and on the innocence of youth, Celebration proposes to create, out of thin air, a sense of place and "tradition" that will unite the community that comes to live there. At the same time, rigid control of landscape design by the Disney Corporation suggests the extent to which Celebration's image of community and proposed "sense of place" will spring from Disney's own

Louis Marin?

micromanagement of the environment. As journalist Russ Rymer notes, it seems that in Celebration, the Disney corporation is attempting to foster a sense of community through "curb heights, window dimensions, sidewalk placement, and a thousand other design elements."[20]

Such terrains as those of the gated community or Celebration may be alien to most Americans, but their social dynamics are likely not so. From the postwar years on, the drive to create a landscape apart from problematic social concerns—the building of a "suburbianation"—has served only to reinforce the prevalence of these concerns in our culture at large. At the same time, the dominant images of suburbia promulgated by popular culture have turned on a kind of willful ignorance of such contentious social issues. To see this point, one need only consider the visions of suburbia offered on popular television sitcoms in the late 1950s through the early 1960s. Standing in for their real-life counterparts, the suburban communities pictured on such programs as *Father Knows Best, Leave it to Beaver, The Donna Reed Show,* and others provided American culture at large with what would become its prevailing vision of suburbia; centered on harmonious family and community life, such programs envisioned the suburbs as both an idealized and insular landscape. In this sense the fledgling medium of television helped to invest the emergent landscape of suburbia with what has turned out to be an incredibly durable symbolic meaning, one that retains at least a residual resonance today.[21]

Indeed, critics such as Samuel Freedman are quite right in lamenting that popular culture continues to "peddle the same old cliché[d]" vision of suburbia as that offered on 1950s' television, often seeking out the "dark" underside of the televised image of suburbia as middle-class utopia in a reaction that has itself become all too familiar, the dystopian view being yet another "clichéd" vision of suburban life.[22] Freedman's apt observation reminds us of the pronounced and lasting power of fictive images in helping to shape our view of life in particular landscapes—a phenomenon that is most evident in the relationship between suburban life and its depiction on the small screen. That is, our continued cultural reliance on a restrictive, binary system in defining the suburban milieu—with suburbia emerging as either the harmonious model of community offered in Beaver Cleaver's Mayfield or the inversion of that dream vision as it appears in any one of a number of recent films set in the suburbs (Todd Solondz's *Happiness,* Sam Mendes's *American Beauty,* etc.)—reveals nothing so much as how televised images of suburbia formed an integral part of what sociologist Albert Hunter has termed the "symbolic ecology" of this particular landscape, or the collection of "processes by which symbolic meanings of . . . environment [are] developed."[23]

Given the density of suburbia's symbolic ecology, it remains surprising that, until quite recently, cultural and literary critics have paid very little attention to this landscape. As Catherine Jurca points out, while literary critics for decades have focused on the city as the "complex generative location of realism, modernism, and, more recently, ethnic and African American literatures," suburbia has remained essentially "uncharted literary territory" among such critics.[24] Similarly, the suburbs have remained underrepresented in the increasingly popular theoretical study of place. While critical attention seems equally divided between the urban milieu favored by humanistic geographers and postmodern place theorists and the rural/wild places studied by ecocritics, suburbia, with a few notable exceptions, has remained until quite recently a critically forgotten place.[25] A number of titles published in the past few years, however, suggest that suburbia is once again becoming a subject of critical concern. Recent histories of suburbanization include Rosalyn Baxandall and Elizabeth Ewen's *Picture Windows: How the Suburbs Happened* (Basic Books, 2000) and Ann Marie Cammarota's *Pavements in the Garden* (Farleigh Dickinson, 2001); Lorraine Kenny's *Daughters of Suburbia* (Rutgers, 2000) and Tom Martinson's *American Dreamscape* (Carroll & Graf, 2000) are among the recent ethnographic and cultural studies of suburbia; and two new critical works focus on narrative representations of suburbia: Lynn Spigel's *Welcome to the Dreamhouse* (Duke, 2001), a study of television's depiction of suburbia, and Jurca's *White Diaspora* (Princeton, 2001), an excellent examination of the suburb in the early-twentieth-century novel.]

While this very recent proliferation of critical interest in suburbia perhaps suggests the emergence of a cross-disciplinary movement in suburban studies (it seems the first time since the late 1950s–early 1960s that suburbia has captured such broad-based critical attention), still one wonders why it took so long for critical interest in the suburbs to rekindle. Among fiction and film critics, ambivalence toward the suburban setting may well have been fueled by a perceived lack of serious fictional and cinematic works set there. And, after all, this point has its merits: The most predominant strain of suburban fiction over the past half century has consisted of lightweight comedies of suburban manners, a breezy but forgettable "tradition" ranging from John Marquand's satirical country club sketches and Max Shulman's suburban spoofs of the 1950s to any number of recent titles that continue the surface-level satirizing of suburbia. Hollywood cinema has often produced similarly lightweight suburban satires, as any viewer of films such as [Joe Dante's *The 'Burbs* (1989) or Burt Kennedy's *Suburban Commando* (1991) knows well enough.] To judge by this unchanging tradition of lightweight suburban satire, it would seem almost as if the suburb—a preplanned, homogeneous, transparently symbolic place—was from the outset overdetermined with cultural meaning, a landscape so indelibly etched with the markers of white, middle-class, family-centered American life as to make serious reconsideration—either fictional or critical—seem superfluous at best, if not downright repugnant.

Indeed, even as Hollywood has dramatically turned its eye back to the suburbs in the last few years, the "new" representations offered have come up against the same impasse of the overdetermination of suburbia, a point perhaps worthy of a brief digression here. Consider the case of two popular and critically acclaimed films of recent years, [Peter Weir's *The Truman Show* (1998) and Gary Ross's *Pleasantville* (1998).] In both of these films—each a paranoid fantasy about the alienating homogeneity of suburban life—the medium of television emerges as the factor that defines the suburban landscape, confirming our larger cultural vision of the suburb as an imaged place, a two-dimensional network of signifiers as constricting as they are predetermined. In *The Truman Show*, the protagonist Truman Burbank (Jim Carrey) slowly comes to learn that his idyllic suburban life, which revolves around his home, wife, and friendly neighbors, not only seems to be the stuff of network television, but in fact is so: As Truman eventually discovers, every aspect of his life is controlled by the omnipotent television director Christof (Ed Harris), who nightly broadcasts to 50 million viewers worldwide his creation, a program chronicling Truman's "real life" called *The Truman Show*. The aptly named protagonist (a would-be "True Man" who finds himself instead controlled by the world of studio television, long centered in and around Burbank, California) eventually escapes his imprisoning suburban "world," presumably bound for somewhere where he *can* be a true man. Left behind at the end of the film is a vision of the suburb as not only an artificial by-product of television culture but indeed as a prison, a (nearly) inescapable grid of preprogrammed behavior.

Pleasantville presents a similar thematic message, as its young protagonists David (Tobey Maguire) and his sister Jennifer (Reese Witherspoon) find themselves transported through their television set–qua–time machine back into the world of David's favorite 1950s' TV sitcom, *Pleasantville*. The film tracks the siblings' efforts to bring some "color" (both literal and figurative) into the black-and-white world of the 1950s' suburb they find themselves in. Although they eventually succeed in breaking through the soulless conformity of Pleasantville—and the town's gradual awakening is rendered through a characteristically late-twentieth-century visual gesture, the colorization of a black-and-white text—the pair meet significant resistance from the local chamber of commerce—angry, reactionary men who engage in book burning and other like acts of desecration meant to terrorize the newly transgressive citizens of Pleasantville into resuming their former conformist identities. As Freedman notes, "The World War II veterans who thronged to actual suburbs in the 1950s might quibble ever so slightly" with the Nazi-esque identity Ross ascribes to the town fathers of Pleasantville.[26] But it is just such an over-the-top critique of programmatic social rigidity that unites *Pleasantville* with *The Truman Show:* In both films, the suburb is depicted less as a lived place than as a signifier of certain co-optive, even totalitarian impulses that lurk beneath the fabric of centrist, middle-class American culture. And yet the grand sociopolitical message that these two films share is compromised by their reliance on models of suburbia drawn from the two-dimensional imagery of situation comedy of the 1950s. The fact that both films position their critiques of suburbia (and in a larger sense of American culture as a whole) through the medium of television suggests not only TV's lasting influence on our view of suburbia but also, ultimately, the desire to displace any serious consideration of the suburban milieu, to view it instead through the safe and ultimately reassuring lens of hyperbolic fantasy.

Films such as *Pleasantville* and *The Truman Show* may well suggest a renewed cultural interest, at the end of the twentieth century, in the physical and social landscape of suburbia; nevertheless, these films also represent a perpetuation of the two-dimensional view of suburban life that has characterized the dominant perception of suburbia over the course of the second half of the twentieth century. That is, while both films offer something of a corrective response to the fantasy vision of suburban community as it was envisioned in the situation comedies of the 1950s, the very fact that they both defer to the *Father Knows Best* image of suburbia in constructing their critiques suggests the continued cultural dominance of the televised image of suburbia from that bygone era.[27] While *The Truman Show* envisions contemporary suburban life as a 1950s-style suburban sitcom rendered inescapable through modern technology of surveillance and entrapment, *Pleasantville* constructs a morality tale concerning the values of contemporary suburban America by holding that social landscape up against *both* the utopian and the dystopian visions of suburbia (each hopelessly, if intentionally, exaggerated) that emerged in the 1950s. Together these films suggest how little our cultural vision of suburbia changed over the course of the century—as if there had been no other efforts, artistic or critical, aside from the ubiquitous fantasy image of the suburbs proffered by network TV in the 1950s and early 1960s, to interpret and represent suburban life in a nonstereotypical, nuanced fashion.

But in fact there have been such efforts, and they are the subject matter of this study. From the 1920s to the present, such noted authors as F. Scott Fitzgerald, John Cheever, John Updike, Ann Beattie, and Gloria Naylor have explored the dynamics of suburban place in their works, contributing to a small but compelling subgenre of suburban fiction. At the same time, Hollywood has on occasion turned a serious eye to the suburbs, as evidenced by the telling visions of suburbia offered in films by Frank Capra, Frank Perry, Mike Nichols, Bryan Forbes, and Reginald Hudlin. In this work I examine more or less contemporaneous works of fiction and film set in the suburbs, with the goal of showing how these texts reflect an increasingly complex vision of life in the suburbs as the century progressed. A basic assumption of my study is that these narratives share more than merely a common "setting"; that is, suburban place in these texts emerges as something more, to use Entrikin's terms, than the "external context" for action, instead also serving as a "center of meaning" in the works themselves. More than mere comedies of suburban manners, or—as in the case of films such as *Pleasantville* and *The Truman Show*—didactic essays on the dystopian aspects of suburbia, these works explore the psychological and cultural construction of suburbia as an idea(l), revealing in the process the consequent tensions that underlie the suburban experience.

While the readings I offer are characterized by their attention to class, race, and gender dynamics, it is my primary intention to maintain focus on the suburban milieu itself as the "expressive space," in geographer E. V. Walter's terms, that fosters these dynamics.[28] As Barbara Ching and Gerald Creed astutely point out, often in contemporary literary and cultural theory, the representation of "social distinctions primarily in terms of race class and gender . . . masks the extent to which these categories are influenced by place identification."[29] By contrast, I will suggest that it is the often troubled nature of suburban place identification that fuels the contentious social dynamics of this century's major works of suburban fiction and film. That is, the suburban milieu—which, as I will argue, has for at least the past half century represented both the promise and the failure of mainstream, middle-class American culture—emerges as the prism through which, in these works, the social dynamics of American life are filtered.

A useful theoretical tool in situating this argument is Pierre Bourdieu's notion of the "habitus" of perception, which he defines as an "internalized disposition" that "generates meaningful practices and meaning-giving perceptions."[30] Cultural geographer Martyn Lee has extended Bourdieu's notion of the habitus to the realm of place studies, speculating that what he calls a "habitus of location" generates place-specific actions and cultural predispositions, contributing to the "cultural character" of specific places.[31] Borrowing Lee's terminology, then, the broad goal of this study is to work toward illuminating the cultural character of American suburbia, viewing the major works of suburban fiction and film with an eye toward assaying the "habitus" of suburban location. In this sense, I am looking toward fictive and cinematic images of the suburbs as reflections of our larger cultural sense of suburban place, reflections of the place-specific social dynamics of the landscape that, more than any other, has come to define middle-class American life in the twentieth century.

Chapter 1 lays the groundwork for the study as a whole in its analysis of what I consider to be two "proto-suburban" narratives, Fitzgerald's *The Great Gatsby* and Capra's *It's a Wonderful Life*. My readings of these two works focus on the sense of an imperiled landscape that drives both narratives. While in *Gatsby* the fear of urban and ethnic infiltration into a pristine exurban space anticipates the phobic exclusivity of the suburbia of a generation later, in *Wonderful Life* the suburban development itself is imagined as the answer to an environmental identity crisis, as it presents the promise of old-fashioned community, albeit in a highly regulated and tightly controlled social landscape. Considered alongside one another, these two works—the first published some two decades before the sudden and massive development of postwar suburbia, the latter released just at the very outset of this trend—prefigure what would be among the recurrent concerns of subsequent suburban fiction and film: contentious class relations, narrowly defined gender identities, visions of community defined by racial and ethnic homogeneity, and, most significant, the struggle to create meaningful attachments to a prefabricated or otherwise artificial place. Community by racial, ethnic homogenity

In the chapters that follow, I focus primarily on landscape concerns, while considering in turn class, gender, and race dynamics of suburbs as they are presented in stories, novels, and films. Chapter 2 focuses on economic and class issues in John Cheever's work, arguing that Cheever—the American writer most clearly linked to a fiction of the suburbs—created a vision of postwar suburban life governed by an unforgiving social structure based on distinctions of class and taste. Both in his story collection *The Housebreaker of Shady Hill* and in his most famous story, "The Swimmer," Cheever inscribes the suburban landscape with the markers of an upper-middle-class society undercut by its own elitist class affiliations. A consideration of Frank Perry's film adaptation of "The Swimmer" augments this discussion, while also focusing on Perry's redirection of Cheever's text as an exploration of the troubled gender dynamics of suburban life.

Chapter 3 continues the focus on suburban gender identity, considering the cultural perception of imperiled masculinity in the suburban sphere as it was expressed in Updike's *Rabbit Redux* and Nichols's *The Graduate.* Each of these texts, I argue, posits the suburbs as an emasculating sphere; while Updike's Rabbit Angstrom functions as an American Everyman displaced and alienated by his relocation to the "cookie-cutter" suburbs, Nichols's Benjamin Braddock, as a young man coming of age in the upper-middle-class suburbs of Southern California, is driven to social and sexual transgression by his need to escape the shallow, materialistic sensibilities of his parents and their generation, whose "plastic" existence is captured through the trappings of their suburban home and surroundings.

Chapter 4 expands this examination of gender dynamics in suburbia by considering two works—Beattie's *Falling in Place* and Forbes's *The Stepford Wives*—that highlight the limitations placed on suburban women. Following Betty Friedan's famous analysis of suburban gender politics laid out in *The Feminine Mystique,* I read these two texts as evidence of ongoing cultural concern over the plight of suburban housewives, whose sometimes stultifying existence was a matter bound up with their relationship to the landscape. While Beattie's work concerns a woman isolated in an unfulfilling suburban town and marginalized to the point of emotional paralysis, Forbes's film offers a dystopian fantasy of utter masculine control in the suburban sphere. Both works, I argue, situate critiques of the unrewarding life of the suburban woman—what Friedan had more than a decade earlier dubbed "the problem that has no name"—in the era when the women's movement was at its peak, suggesting that a tradition of gendered inequities continued to impact the experience of suburban women. In a broader sense, the works I discuss in chapter 4 throw into relief the male-centered sensibilities of previous suburban fiction and film.

Similarly, the works I address in chapter 5, Naylor's *Linden Hills* and Hudlin's *House Party,* in depicting the suburban experience of African Americans, suggest by contrast the extent to which the whiteness of suburban experience is taken as something of a given in our culture. Perhaps fittingly, then, both of these texts position racial matters as central to the experience of their protagonists. Naylor paints the all-black suburb of Linden Hills as a dystopian, Dantean landscape where residents' heightened materialistic sensibilities lead to the erosion not only of a sense of community, but indeed of racial identity itself. In Hudlin's *House Party,* the "half-white" protagonist is torn by his romantic and sexual desire for two young women—one from "the projects" and one from the affluent suburbs; his traversal of these contrasting landscapes throughout the film coincides with his own need to prove himself not just as a man, but as a black man. Both Naylor's and Hudlin's texts envision the suburban landscape as one of intense surveillance and control, and I argue that this presentation of landscape is part of the effort of both texts to imply the challenges and contradictions involved in maintaining a sense of racial identity in a landscape historically predicated on an aggressively defended ideal of whiteness.

In contrast to the more simplistic visions of suburbia from postwar television and the recent spate of antisuburban films, the works I discuss offer compelling evidence of the heterotopic nature of suburbia, the manner in which the suburb has come to reflect the phobias and insecurities of American culture. I have arranged my chapters chronologically, with the hope of highlighting what I feel to be increasingly complex fictional and cinematic representations of the suburbs over the course of the twentieth century. Consonant with my view of suburbia as a "mirror" to mainstream American society is the belief that representations of this landscape reflect historically specific social and cultural concerns. This is not to claim that race and gender politics, for example, represent in comparison to class issues relatively new concerns about the suburbs. Instead, I would suggest that major fictional and cinematic treatments of particular sociopolitical issues might be read as reflecting prevailing concerns of their time. In Frederic Jameson's terms, "the literary work or cultural object, as though for the first time, brings into being that very situation to which it is also, at one and the same time, a reaction."[32] Rather than an attempt to impose neat chronological order on the social evolution of a tumultuous terrain, then, the structure of my argument suggests that political and demographic developments in American society over the second half of the century shifted the terms of the suburban question; while the suburb remains a "mirror" to mainstream culture at large, evolving social concerns have positioned suburbia as an ever more con-

tested and conflicted terrain. The representations of the suburbs I consider tend, in their increasing social complexity, to reflect this
phenomenon.

The thematic direction of the narratives I discuss has everything to do
with the troubled nature of suburban place identification. For the suburb,
in breaking apart the urban/rural binary that had previously characterized
the American landscape, presents a third term in this equation, a space that
remains an enigma even to itself: economically linked to the city, the
suburb nevertheless resists urban identification; and if suburbia masquerades as the country, as a sort of plotted, ordered, endlessly repeating
pastoral landscape, its calculated, precise parceling of the natural landscape stands in stark contrast to the abiding contours of the rural terrain it
superseded.[33] Moreover, as opposed to the traditional American "small
town," the suburb, as it appears in the majority of the works I will consider,
is not a singular, specifiable place. Instead, suburbia is most noteworthy
for the planned homogeneity of its architecture and landscape. In that
sense, one might think of postwar suburban developments as prototypes
of what Jameson has called "postmodern hyperspace," that which "has
finally succeeded in transcending the capacities of the individual human
body to locate itself . . . and cognitively to map its position in a mappable
external world."[34] That is, the suburb presents what memoirist D. J.
Waldie has termed "the anxiety of the grid": the sense that the suburban
subdivision lacks its own, self-contained sense of place identity and
instead "opens outward without limits" to a landscape composed of like
grids.[35] And yet, despite these alienating features of the suburban landscape, for the characters in the works I will examine—and, indeed, for ever
increasing numbers of Americans—the suburb remains "home," the most
important and profound of places, in Gaston Bachelard's terms "our first
universe, a real cosmos in every sense of the word."[36] Hence the suburb,
neither urban nor rural and uniform enough to be rendered "placeless,"
stands as both a "place" and a "noplace," a paradox that, I believe, helps
shape the dynamics of suburban fiction and film.

These place-bound dynamics peculiar to the suburban terrain form the starting point for this study. My basic premise throughout is that the social structure of suburbia—itself an outgrowth of individual and communal relationships to the landscape—comes to dominate these works of fiction, that the particularities of suburban existence are inseparable from the meanings of these texts. I wish to challenge readings such as the following by critic Philip Nicholson, who laments the lack of a "bard" of the suburbs: "Who sings the song of the suburbs? Where is its poet? Where is the Woody Guthrie of Woodmere, the Sinclair Lewis of Levittown? Some fine novelists have set their stories and characters in suburban communities, but the setting is typically a backdrop, a tableau, for a look at characters and stories whose meaning transcends their place. John Updike, Philip Roth, John Cheever . . . [and] others depicted the dramas of people in suburbia, but in most cases the stories could as easily have unfolded in different non-suburban surroundings."[37] On the contrary, I claim that the works I examine are inextricably bound to the suburban landscape and community. Rather than being randomly or accidentally placed, these works are situated specifically and precisely in suburban communities that are themselves amalgams of various social and cultural anxieties—places that might be read, in geographer Yi-Fu Tuan's terminology, as "landscapes of fear."[38]

Ultimately, the value of studying fictional treatments of life in the suburbs lies in working toward discovering the cultural significance of a place that over the course of a half century has evolved from a revolutionary and emergent terrain to become the dominant landscape of the United States. While both the look of the suburbs and the dynamics of suburban experience have changed considerably over this span of years, the prevailing cultural vision of the suburbs has, I believe, remained relatively unchanged. This resistance toward a sustained and nuanced reconsideration of the cultural dynamics of the suburbs may derive from the perception of suburbia as a culturally flat, static place—but then that perception itself is what is countered by the depictions of suburban landscape and life in the works I consider in this study. For the authors and filmmakers I discuss, the suburbs present a reflection of both the values and the anxieties of dominant U.S. culture. Their various gazes into the heterotopic "mirror" of suburbia reveal a landscape both energized and compromised by manifold cultural aspirations and fears. Reading the emplacement of these narratives as a reflection of their cultural politics is a gesture that presumes that places in general, and in this case suburban places, are hybrid cultural constructions. Put another way, in radical geographer David Harvey's terms, "Place, in whatever guise, is like space and time, a social construct. . . . The only interesting question that can then be asked is: by what social process(es) is place constructed?"[39] This study, in examining the cultural dynamics of suburbia, attempts to posit a place-specific answer to Harvey's intriguing question.

"The hour of a profound human change"

Transitional Landscapes and the Sense of Place in Two Proto-Suburban Narratives

The landscape that Americans think of today as "suburbia" began to emerge rapidly in the years following World War II, with developers across the nation following the example set by the architectural firm of Levitt and Sons in their creation of Levittown, New York, an immensely popular preplanned suburb built in 1946-47. Nevertheless, the American suburban impulse did not begin with Levittown, but rather was evident as early as the first decades of the nineteenth century, with the founding of the nation's first commuter suburbs.[1] Over the course of the nineteenth and early twentieth centuries, suburbs continued to gain prominence across the country.[2] From the outset, American suburbs have occupied what environmental historian John Stilgoe aptly refers to as a "borderland" identity, a space situated both physically and philosophically between the urban and the rural.[3] Thus, while nineteenth-century suburbanization reflected the increasing importance of urban centers in American society, at the same time the suburb served as the physical embodiment of an ongoing agrarian impulse in the national culture. Tied to both the urban and rural spheres yet not fully identifiable with either, the early suburbs composed a new type of landscape, one that quickly became overlaid with symbolic meaning. From the outset, the suburb was viewed, alternately, as a landscape modeling democratic values and a pastoral retreat from the rush of urban culture.[4] Moreover, the nascent landscape of the suburbs signaled a heightened valorization of domesticity, as suburban home life represented an escape from what was seen as a corrupting urban sphere to an environment centered around the individual home and family.

In the first half of the twentieth century, American suburbs continued to reflect, in historian Margaret Marsh's terms, this "blend of domestic, pastoral, and democratic values."[5] At the same time, the rapidly expanding suburban sphere served as evidence of increasing class stratification in the United States, as home ownership in affluent suburbs became an ever more noticeable marker of success, at least throughout the 1920s.[6] While the Great Depression of the 1930s temporarily halted the expansion of the suburban landscape, New Deal initiatives such as the creation of the Federal Housing Administration (FHA) in 1934 laid the groundwork for the massive expansion of both the suburban landscape and the American middle class in the years following World War II.[7] And if postwar development towns such as Levittown suggested through homogeneity of design a utopian ideal of classless community, the same cannot be said of the suburban landscape as it developed earlier in the century. Despite the philosophical underpinnings shared by pre- and post–World War II suburbs—both valorized familial domesticity in an environment positioned as the antidote to the evils of city life—the contrast between the class-conscious suburbs of the early twentieth century and the (at least seeming) classlessness of postwar suburbia suggests the extent to which the cultural dynamics of the suburban experience changed as the century progressed.

Given the evolution of America's cultural vision of the suburban environment, representations of suburban life from fiction and film predating the rise of "suburbia" proper provide compelling perspective on developing notions of suburbanness. As Catherine Jurca argues, nowhere is this fact more apparent than in Sinclair Lewis's classic 1922 novel, *Babbitt.* Set in the nondescript city of Zenith and its equally unremarkable suburb, Floral Heights, *Babbitt* transpires in a mid-American anyplace; Jurca aptly notes that Lewis's "vision of a national neighborhood . . . anticipates the unprecedented homogeneity associated with the paths of suburbanization since World War II."[8] And *Babbitt* anticipates later fictional representations of suburbia in other ways as well: By using the trappings of the suburban setting to indicate his protagonist's immersion in a banal world of convention and creature comforts—describing Babbitt's house, the narrator informs us that "Though there was nothing in [it] that was interesting, there was nothing that was offensive"—Lewis fashioned a trope that would be repeated faithfully in virtually all subsequent suburban fiction.[9] Moreover, the struggles of Lewis's protagonist, George F. Babbitt—between conformism and rebellion, domesticity and adventure, civic pride and a sense of entrapment—set the blueprint for subsequent representations of male suburbanites, a point to which I will return later on. Ultimately, Lewis's depiction in *Babbitt* of a disaffected middle-class suburbanite—a reluctant member of Mencken's "booboisie"—in many ways set the standard for fictional treatments of the suburbanite. As Jurca concludes, Babbitt worked to "establish alienation as the authentic voice" of suburban culture, and Lewis's alienation theme has been reworked repeatedly in subsequent suburban fiction.[10]

While Lewis's social satire profoundly impacted subsequent representations of the middle-class yokel, his condemnation of the mindless middle American tended toward the one-sided, as did his treatment of landscape. That is, despite its indelible sendup of suburban manners, *Babbitt* provides little sense of a national landscape in transition, which was as much the case in the 1920s as it would be again in the post–World War II years. Two classic narratives from the first half of the twentieth century that illustrate both the aspirations and the contradictions of suburban living—while providing a sense of evolving local and national terrains—are F. Scott Fitzgerald's *The Great Gatsby* (1925) and Frank Capra's *It's a Wonderful Life* (1946). To be sure, these works chronicle vastly different experiences: While Fitzgerald portrays the exurban elite of 1920s New York, Capra focuses on the small-town middle class weathering the Great Depression and World War II. Although two decades separate the appearance of these texts, Fitzgerald's novel and Capra's film share a common concern over the evolution of their landscapes toward the suburban environment that would appear in the postwar years. Each text is set in an environment in transition, and each positions a nostalgia for landscapes of the past in the face of the onrush of modernity, figured in the form of suburbanization. These works serve as apt introductions to the issues encountered in the more specifically "suburban" literature of the second half of the century, for in treating the intimate connections between environment and experience, each text imagines the suburb as a contested terrain. And although they construct vastly different visions of suburban "community" (or lack thereof), both *The Great Gatsby* and *It's a Wonderful Life* imagine the suburb as a setting whose social dynamics hinge on the circumscribing of social roles and identities.

The social dynamics of both of these works stem from their precise historical and geographic placement, as both are set in environments in the process of evolving from higher-class enclaves to middle-class suburbs. As historian Kenneth Jackson notes, by the later nineteenth century, expansion of industry, coupled with the development of the commuter railroad, had made prosperous "main line" suburbs and elite exurban areas recognizable features of the American landscape and imagination.[11] Associated with stately "country living," such places as New York's Westchester County (later to be the setting for *It's a Wonderful Life*) and, more dramatically, Long Island's Gold Coast (later the setting for *The Great Gatsby*) provided imaginative models of the type of nonurban experience that the middle and working classes could at that time only dream of.[12] But by the time these works appeared, this was no longer entirely the case: By

1925, with the increasing popularity of the automobile, the population of Long Island was expanding rapidly, and middle-class newcomers were harbingers of the suburbanization to come.[13] This demographic shift on Long Island came at the expense of the dwindling power of Gold Coast millionaires, whose days of dominance on the landscape were numbered. Moreover, by 1946, an improved network of highways, along with the need for housing created by returning veterans and their growing families, threatened the genteel atmosphere of main-line suburbs such as those in Westchester County. Both *The Great Gatsby* and *It's a Wonderful Life* pay careful attention to matters of physical and social terrain, and their respective treatments of landscape provide compelling evidence that, even before the "age of suburbia" proper, suburbanization was beginning to shape the imaginative, as well as physical, landscape of the United States.

In their contrasting visions of exurban and suburban landscapes, these two proto-suburban narratives point toward many of the very issues that were to inform our vision of suburbia later in the century. Since its first appearance in the 1950s, the "suburban debate" in both the popular media and sociological circles has centered around certain diametrically opposed visions of the suburb—as both a self-sufficient space of the "good life" and an alienating "noplace"; both an inclusive model of old-fashioned "community" and a paranoid, exclusionary space; and both a matriarchal realm of female power and the worst sort of suffocating, male-dominated enclosure for women. One sees just these sorts of contrasts at work in Fitzgerald's novel and Capra's film: Whereas in *Gatsby* a disconnectedness from place opens out into a sense of alienation, in *Wonderful Life* small-town space is celebrated, even as it becomes so stultifying as to be seen by the central character as a kind of trap; in *Gatsby* a paranoid exclusivity drives much of the plot, in contrast to the utopian vision of inclusive community presented in *Wonderful Life;* and *Gatsby*'s drive to "domesticate" the lead female character within a hierarchical, male-dominated relationship gives way to *Wonderful Life*'s nod toward female empowerment, albeit in a scheme where female power is predicated on enclosure within the domestic sphere.

Beyond these broad social issues, both texts anticipate concerns about place identification that would characterize later suburban fiction and film. Specifically, both are infused with nostalgia, exhibiting a reverence for what Gaston Bachelard has compellingly termed "eulogized spaces," landscapes of memory whose idealization contrasts with the banality of contemporary, workaday landscapes.[14] Just this sort of nostalgia for "eulogized spaces" would become a recurring gesture in later suburban fiction and film, as the suburb itself continued to be rendered as a somehow less "genuine" environment than the country, the city, or even the traditional small town. Indeed, *Gatsby*'s vision of the expansion of the city into the countryside and *Wonderful Life*'s chronicling of the tenuous existence of the old-fashioned small town, considered together, anticipate the position of the suburbs somewhere in between these various realms, in the process reflecting a broad cultural awareness of the ways in which the American landscape was evolving to accommodate increasing suburban expansion. Finally, both of these works—intentionally or otherwise—highlight the malleable nature of *landscape* in its broadest sense, the idea that all places are fantasy creations and as such are subject to misconception, contention, and reinvention. This concept is something that would become of particular importance later, in the suburban age, when for perhaps the first time in U.S. history the meanings of brand-new, preplanned landscapes had to be created—much like the new homes that filled these landscapes—instantly, and from the ground up.

🏠 🏠 🏠

. . . for a transitory enchanted moment man must have held his breath in the presence of this continent, compelled into an aesthetic contemplation he neither understood nor desired, face to face for the last time in history with something commensurate to his capacity for wonder.[15]

The expansive, lyrical closing of Fitzgerald's *The Great Gatsby* is an unforgettable extended moment, a rumination on both the "transitory" nature of enchantment itself and our undying though futile compulsion to attempt a return to a time and place of wonder's fulfillment. The final paragraphs of the novel retrospectively reinforce the central importance of landscape throughout; as Nick Carraway lies "sprawled out on the sand" (181) of Gatsby's beach and looks out at the Long Island Sound, he couches his final thoughts on Gatsby and all he represents in terms of the West Egg landscape that surrounds him. In counterpoising the palatial yet "inessential" houses that dot the coast—houses that Nick senses beginning to "melt away"—with the "old island" that once revealed for Dutch sailors "a fresh, green breast of the new world" (182), Fitzgerald inscribes his multiform vision of the "American dream" and its inaccessibility onto a landscape rich with both evanescent and enduring symbolic meanings.

It is a fitting close for a novel that pays such careful attention throughout to issues of landscape and place. Indeed, it might be argued that the central drama of this novel involves a struggle for *emplacement,* the tragic, futile effort of five "Middle Westerners" to create for themselves a meaningful space within the gravitational circle of metropolitan New York.[16] Viewed in this light, the novel becomes something more than an examination of the "American dream" played out against a "Jazz Age" backdrop; instead, it emerges as an exploration of the nature of urban and exurban experience in an increasingly metropolitan and "rootless" era. All of the major characters face the dilemma of rootlessness: Jordan Baker remains in motion throughout the novel, untied to any landscape or place; Daisy seems entrapped within the Buchanan mansion, torn between the lure of Gatsby's gaudy monument to her and dreams of her "beautiful white girlhood" at the family home in Louisville; Gatsby, appropriately dubbed "Mr. Nobody from Nowhere" by Tom, attempts to create an identity primarily by manufacturing a place; and Tom Buchanan, the character most clearly in possession of a place of his own, can understand that place only in racial, hierarchical terms, all the while living in fear of the encroachment of racial and ethnic others on the landscape that surrounds him. As for Nick, he is a lost soul among lost souls. A proto-suburbanite, Nick lives a commuter's lifestyle, directing the motion of the narrative with his daily commutes between an inhospitable urban center and a "home" most notable for its incongruity and *placelessness*. Indeed, it is largely through Nick's struggles to understand and interpret the landscapes he traverses that we are introduced to the larger issues of the novel.[17] This is only appropriate, given that the social dynamics of *The Great Gatsby*— involving not only the pervasive feeling of rootlessness among the main characters, but also a repressive code of gender politics, an imperiled sense of class prerogative, and a reactionary and paranoid resistance to the incursion of racial and ethnic others—are themselves matters that revolve around and are born of the evolving physical and social landscape.

Fitzgerald's depiction of a changing and often alienating landscape is a function of the specific historic and geographical setting of the novel. Set in 1922, at the height of the Jazz Age, on Long Island's North Shore, or "Gold Coast," this novel draws heavily on the dynamics of setting to establish its larger meanings.[18] In the 1920s, Gatsbyesque parties were hardly a rarity on Long Island's North Shore, which at the time accommodated over 500 estates on the order of the Buchanan and Gatsby mansions.[19] Built by millionaires and industry tycoons, these palatial homes both utilized and reshaped the natural geography of the region, signifying social class through elaborate architecture and appropriation of the rural, seaside landscape.[20] The creation of these homes, which Gold Coast historian Monica Randall calls "an architectural phenomenon unparalleled both in excessiveness and originality," began shortly after the turn of the century and continued into the 1920s.[21] And more was at stake in the construction of these estates than merely building places to live: As Ronald Berman has argued, this phenomenon was most notable for its symbolic overtones, for the sense that "a new American history could be created in twenty-four hours, an illusion of ancestry long in the land."[22] Berman's observation is an apt one, for it is the very illusiveness of dreams of ancestry and connection to the landscape that provides much of the dramatic tension and carries much of the thematic weight of *The Great Gatsby*. Interestingly enough, as Jan Cohn has pointed out, the names of home designs in the postwar suburbs (in Levittown, models included the "Rancher" and the "Colonial") would similarly attempt to evoke historical connections to the American landscape.[23]

One need not look far to find the deep and often conflicted connections between landscape and a sense of history and belonging in *The Great Gatsby*. The paradigmatic connections between place and identity are set up in the opening pages, when Nick situates the Carraway family as "something of a clan," who have been anchored to the same "Middle Western city," a land of "wide lawns and friendly trees," for the past three generations (2-3). By contrast, Tom and Daisy Buchanan, whom we first meet a few pages later, are characterized by Nick as "drifters"; still, despite Nick's incredulity, Daisy has declared their move to East Egg a "permanent" one. And the carefully landscaped opulence of the Buchanan home suggests some sense of permanence or, in Berman's terms, a feeling of "ancestry long in the land." Nevertheless, this sense of permanence is manufactured and illusory, and as Tom stands on the porch showing Nick his estate, his proprietary ease seems to be undercut by a need to explain the orchestrated magnificence of the place:

> "I've got a nice place here," he said, his eyes flashing about restlessly.
> Turning me around by one arm, he moved a broad flat hand along the front
> vista, including in its sweep a sunken Italian garden, a half acre of deep,
> pungent roses, and a snub-nosed motor-boat that bumped the tide offshore.
> "It belonged to Demaine, the oil man." He turned me around again, politely
> and abruptly. "We'll go inside." (7-8)

In deferring to the previous owner of the estate at the end of this speech, Tom reveals the anxiety that has accompanied his purchase of an unreadable symbolic landscape.[24] This fact is underscored by Fitzgerald's use of cinematic technique in the passage: the reader here is offered the equivalent of a "panning shot" across the expanse of Tom's property, but no "voice-over" to explain the significance of the terrain. The primacy of the visual code in this passage (and, indeed, throughout the description of Tom and Daisy's home) suggests a partial reification of a landscape whose symbolic properties have exceeded interpretation.[25] As a homeowner once removed from his own landscape, Tom Buchanan quickly emerges as a character who is off balance and quite literally "out of place," one reason perhaps for his tenacious belief in whichever pseudoscientific theories he can find to help him explain his world.

Like Tom, Nick also finds himself "out of place" from the outset. As he confesses in the beginning of his narration, the "thing to do" on moving to New York would have been to "find rooms" in the city; instead, drawn by his longing for an environment at least superficially similar to that of his hometown, Nick settles in the "commuter town" of West Egg. Hence, although Nick and Tom have very different reasons for settling on the North Shore, both share a desire to create meaning and a sense of belonging through connection to the exurban landscape. While they both fail in this effort, they fail for different reasons, because these two characters represent different historical moments in the evolution of their common landscape: Tom represents the vulnerable second generation of a Gold Coast elite whose time was already on the wane, while Nick—whether he recognizes it or not—stands as a member of the new commuter class, the growth of which was already in this era beginning to turn Long Island into the suburban mecca that it still is today.[26] Indeed, thanks largely to the automobile, Long Island's Nassau County at the time of this novel was beginning this very transition, nearly tripling in population during the decade of the 1920s.[27] Such a rapid evolution in landscape and demographics leaves its mark on both of these characters; if Tom cannot read the symbolic excess of his landscape because it is already a part of the past, Nick's dilemma is that the landscape to which he should belong—the soon-to-be-born Nassau County suburbia—has not yet quite arrived. The incongruity of his lone "cardboard bungalow" sandwiched between numerous West Egg mansions is an image that perfectly captures this novel's larger sense of a landscape in transition.[28] It is perhaps the most visible manifestation of Fitzgerald's tendency to use landscape to look both forward and backward in time. As Richard Lehan argues, this is a novel that not only considers the lure of the past but also, at times, catches a "sense of the future."[29]

Gatsby himself embodies this sense of being caught in an insupportable present—situated, as Lehan argues, "between a dead past and an implausible future."[30] But Gatsby's dilemma is as much spatial as it is temporal, as his romantic quest is consistently played out in terms of landscape. From the first appearance of Gatsby in the novel—as Nick spies him peering longingly across the Sound, hands outstretched toward the green light on Daisy's dock—to his last appearance, when Nick describes him just before the murder as being in "a new world, material without being real, where poor ghosts, breathing dreams like air, drifted fortuitously about" (162), Gatsby's dream resides in landscapes. And though he may be one of the most conspicuous homeowners in American literature, Gatsby seems hardly *in possession* of his own home at all, and he is consistently portrayed throughout the novel as dislocated from place. When he first divulges his origins, telling Nick he comes from the "Middle Western" city of San Francisco, he hints at the type of distortion that will characterize his relationships to place throughout the novel. Indeed, from the recounting of his time with Dan Cody sailing the "West Indies and the Barbary Coast" to his own recollection of the war years, covering not only his time at Oxford but also his life as a "young rajah in all the capitals of Europe" (66), one wonders whether Tom Buchanan might have been more on the mark to call Gatsby "Mr. Nobody from Everywhere." His disconnection from a verifiable geography poses a dilemma for those like Tom who are trying to read Gatsby. Nick eventually associates Gatsby with his West Egg home, but does so in a way that effaces any real connections to place or landscape, insisting instead on the absolute autonomy of Gatsby's manufactured identity: "Jay Gatsby of West Egg, Long Island, sprang from his Platonic conception of himself. He was a son of God" (99).

If this observation confers on Gatsby a sort of idealized, Adamic status, at the same time it emphasizes the plasticity of Gatsby's identity, something he attempts to counter through the presentation of his West Egg landscape. Gatsby's manipulation of his own landscape draws attention to the malleable nature of the Gold Coast environment and in so doing emphasizes what Nick early in the novel refers to, somewhat mysteriously, as the "bizarre and not a little sinister contrast" (5) between East Egg and West Egg. For Gatsby's idea is to keep his home "always full of interesting people, night and day" (91), as a means of impressing his importance on Daisy. This attempt to keep alive a perpetual *tableau vivant* for Daisy's sake necessitates a constant flow of partygoers, whom Gatsby shuttles in from the city in his Rolls-Royce and from the train stations in his station wagon, and "whose cars from New York are parked five deep in the drive" (40) on a given Saturday night. Gatsby's need to populate his symbolic landscape—and the guests *are* the principal symbol of this landscape— accentuates the sense of West Egg as a transitory environment, a place quite literally filled with commuters.

The rush of activity Gatsby brings to the North Shore is abhorrent to an East Egger such as Tom Buchanan, a man who is attempting to shape exurban space in a different fashion, emphasizing an expansive rurality and the exclusive class identifications that go with it. Indeed, Tom not only bristles at the insurgent, democratic impulse of Gatsby's parties—as suggested by the ethnic family names on Nick's famous list of the partygo- ers—but fears the push of urban progress itself, recognizing that such progress involves expansion and intrusion, processes that are already imperiling his rural fantasy landscape. Tom so resists the inevitable encroachment of commuter society that he takes symbolic measures against "the auto age," becoming, to the best of his knowledge, "the first man who ever made a stable out of a garage" (119).[31] Daisy also shares in this disdain for Gatsby's parties and what they represent; Nick's recounting of her view of West Egg emphasizes her fear of the changing, increasingly mobile and urban, landscape: "She was appalled by West Egg, this unprecedented 'place' that Broadway had begotten on a Long Island fishing village—appalled by its raw vigor . . . and by the too obtrusive fate that herded its inhabitants along a short-cut from nothing to nothing" (108). In noting the "appalling" consequences of such an ill-planned, ad hoc merger of urban and rural environments, Daisy's analysis of West Egg resembles nothing so much as the chorus of negative reaction that would greet the emergence of preplanned suburbs some twenty years later.

The irony of Daisy's reaction to Gatsby's parties and what they represent lies in the fact that Gatsby is not trying to create a landscape of the *future*, but instead is seeking rather desperately—through the manipulation of landscape—to return to the *past.* The "Gatsby mansion" and all that comes with it are mere symbolic devices meant to lure Daisy away from East Egg and back to a relationship that is psychologically situated in the Louisville landscape of 1917. As Nick's narration repeatedly emphasizes, Gatsby's dream vision of Daisy is inextricably bound up with his memories of Louisville and more specifically of Daisy's girlhood home. In the early-morning conversation after the night of the accident—in what is to be their final meeting—Gatsby indicates to Nick that he wants to "talk about Daisy," and the fashion in which he mythologizes their brief courtship underscores his intriguing psychological ties to Daisy's family home:

> He found her exciting and desirable. He went to her house, at first with other officers from Camp Taylor, then alone. It amazed him—he had never been in such a beautiful house before. But what gave it an air of breathless intensity was that Daisy lived there. . . . There was a ripe mystery about it, a hint of bedrooms upstairs more beautiful and cool than other bedrooms, of gay and radiant activities taking place through its corridors, and of romances that were not musty and laid away already in lavender, but fresh and breathing and redolent of this year's shining motor-cars and of dances

whose flowers were scarcely withered. It excited him, too, that many men had already loved Daisy—it increased her value in his eyes. He felt their presence all about the house, pervading the air with the shades and echoes of still vibrant emotions. (148)

Remarkable for the way that it conflates romance, real estate, and conspicuous wealth, this passage goes a long way toward explaining the motivations behind the creation of what Nick calls "that huge incoherent failure of a house" that Gatsby maintains at West Egg. Driven by his complex fantasy image of Daisy's Louisville home—a vision informed by both the genteel lure of the Southern agrarian past and the "freshness" of Daisy's sexuality and conspicuous wealth—Gatsby attempts to create a simulacrum of the Louisville estate in West Egg. What he comes up with, instead, is a crass, clumsy pastiche of architectural styles and tastes, a place that reflects both the loftiness of his aspirations and his inability to reach them.

If Gatsby's gaudy home is the definitive evidence of his pursuit of a "vast, vulgar, and meretricious beauty" (99), it is also a tribute of sorts to Daisy, a fact that directly links her to the vulgarity of Gatsby's landscape. Indeed, Gatsby's home is the most visible symbol of the novel's tendency toward an alignment of the feminine with the material, a dynamic ultimately subsumed within a larger drive toward containment of the female. This sense of a dual positioning of female characters is evident from the first appearance of Daisy and Jordan in the Buchanan living room, as they are described by Nick as little more than "flighty" objects who are ultimately subject to the controlling will of Tom: "The only completely stationary object in the room was an enormous couch on which two young women were buoyed up as though on an anchored balloon. They were both in white, and their dresses were rippling and fluttering as if they had just been blown back in after a short flight around the house. . . . Then there was a boom as Tom Buchanan shut the rear windows and the caught wind died out about the room, and the curtains and the rugs and the two young women ballooned slowly to the floor" (8).

Rendered virtually equivalent to the furniture in this passage, the two women seem to function as mere adornments to the Buchanan home. And while Jordan goes on to remain a relatively unfettered, if ineffectual, character in the novel, this passage is an early indication of what will be an ongoing push to contain Daisy within the domestic sphere. This domestic impulse is tied to the novel's larger anxieties over the changing social landscape on the Gold Coast, for Daisy, as much or more so even then Gatsby, is aligned with a form of reckless commodification. Nick's narration at times suggests that he reads Daisy in this manner, but it is Gatsby who eventually fills in the blanks for Nick as he describes the seductiveness of Daisy's voice:

> "Her voice is full of money," he said suddenly.
>
> That was it. I'd never understood before. It was full of money—that was the inexhaustible charm that rose and fell in it, the jingle of it, the cymbals' song of it. . . . High in a white palace the king's daughter, the golden girl. . . . (120)

Here Daisy, as the "Golden Girl" who inspires Gatsby's acquisitive ways, is set up as the figure through which, in Brian Way's words, "money becomes socially desirable."[32] Positioned as the cause behind a form of crass materialism, Daisy is thus linked in a larger sense, as Roger Lewis has argued, to the commercial ethos of postwar suburban consumer society.[33] And in this regard, Daisy represents a disruptive force in a landscape still clinging to its illusions of a genteel, rural sensibility.

This confluence of the novel's landscape politics and sexual politics is played out in Daisy's travels between the Buchanan home in East Egg, a place of confinement, and Gatsby's home in West Egg, itself both an escape from East Egg and a monument to careless commercialization. But in Daisy's final appearance in the novel, captured by Nick as he peers through a "rift" in the drawn blinds of the Buchanan home, such motion ceases: "Daisy and Tom were sitting opposite each other at the kitchen table, with a plate of cold fried chicken between them, and two bottles of ale. He was talking intently across the table at her, and in his earnestness his hand had fallen on and covered her own. Once in a while she looked up at him and nodded in agreement" (146). This image of Tom's eventual dominance over Daisy, when considered alongside her ultimate departure with him, suggests the extent to which Daisy has become "domesticated" by the end of the novel. But this passage is also striking in its subversion of expected class roles: Seated around the kitchen table consuming their peasant fare, Tom and Daisy in their final appearance seem hardly the elites they once were. Nick's voyeuristic vision, then, yields an image that captures in miniature the changes in social landscape suggested by the Buchanans' abandonment of their home: the turn toward a more middle-class, suburban environment and the emergence of a social landscape that, as Daisy's fate suggests, involved an increasing drive to position the female within the domestic sphere.

In the end, such a transition toward a landscape of the future seems only fitting, even inevitable, as the logical conclusion to the drama of evolving landscape that persists throughout the novel. Still, there is a distinct irony in this sense of a coming transformation of the Gold Coast environment: In the face of the alienating and often unreadable landscape they inhabit, the characters of this novel have the tendency to look not *forward* but rather *back,* seeking refuge in imaginatively reconstructed visions of past environments. Consider, for example, the much-discussed "Jacob's Ladder" section that concludes chapter 6; here Fitzgerald's use of nearly cinematic technique conveys the acuity, even the tyranny, of Gatsby's memories of Daisy and the Louisville landscape of 1919 that retains for him an enduring symbolic resonance:

> One autumn night, five years before, they had been walking down the street when the leaves were falling, and they came to a place where there were no trees and the sidewalk was white with moonlight. They stopped here and turned toward each other. . . . The quiet lights in the houses were humming out into the darkness and there was a stir and bustle among the stars. Out of

the corner of his eye Gatsby saw that the blocks of the sidewalks really formed a ladder and mounted to a secret place above the trees—he could climb to it, if he climbed alone, and once there he could suck on the pap of life, gulp down the incomparable milk of wonder. (112)

It is no coincidence that this passage occurs just after Daisy's first visit to a party at Gatsby's; nor is it without significance that hearing the "Jacob's Ladder" story produces in Nick a sympathetic reaction, one in which he too is on the verge of remembering "something—an elusive rhythm, a fragment of lost words" (112) from his own past. Gatsby is not the only character in this novel who is in some sense trapped in landscapes of the past. Indeed if, as Berman suggests, the "*ur*-dream" of this novel is "the memory of Eden," it seems that all of the major characters maintain visions of their own personal Edens. Nick's "Middle West," Daisy's "beautiful white girlhood," Gatsby's Louisville of five years past, and Tom's "civilization" are all idealized, largely imaginary places, that, like the "old island here that flowered once for Dutch sailors' eyes—a fresh, green breast of the new world," are ultimately inaccessible and irretrievable.[34]

The disparity between such idealized images of past landscapes and the realities of the contemporary landscape is a recurring theme in the novel, nowhere more carefully portrayed or infused with the force of history than in the scene of Gatsby and Daisy's first reunion. Here, as Gatsby and Nick wait for Daisy and gaze over at Gatsby's house, the conversation is telling: "'My house looks well, doesn't it?' he demanded. 'See how the whole front of it catches the light?'" (91). In viewing the great symbol of his own house, Gatsby seems confident that it will shortly and finally do its symbolic work; however, after Gatsby has shown Daisy the house, a "bewildering" moment transpires. Nick describes the onset of night in West Egg: "Outside the wind was loud and there was a faint flow of thunder along the Sound. All the lights were going on in West Egg now; the electric trains, men-carrying, were plunging home through the rain from New York. It was the hour of a profound human change, and excitement was generating on the air" (96).

Fitzgerald's synesthetic pairing of the "flow of thunder along the Sound" with the "plunging home" of the commuter trains reminds us of the machine in Gatsby's garden: This is not Louisville, 1917, but Long Island, 1922—a bustling suburb in the making, a lapsed Eden character- ized by a merely illusory sense of rootedness, a stark contrast to the transcendent Louisville landscape that exists forever fixed in Gatsby's mind. It is little surprise when Nick observes, immediately following this passage, that "the expression of bewilderment had come back into Gatsby's face" (97); thrust into the present time and place, Gatsby at this moment realizes the incongruity between his dreams and reality. The hour of a profound human change, indeed.

This is not the novel's only moment involving specific mention of commuting. With its near-constant motion between New York and East and West Egg, the narrative is literally shaped by the act of commutation, and what the various commutes reveal is the sharp contrast between ways of living in urban and exurban spaces.[35] New York itself comes to be associated not only with glamour and excitement but also with violence, as in Tom and Gatsby's showdown at the Plaza and, more explicitly, in Tom's breaking of Myrtle's nose in the 158th Street apartment. Exurban East and West Egg, by contrast, are initially represented as havens, fantasy worlds seemingly protected from violence and decay by their very distance from the urban center. The third term in this equation is the "valley of ashes," the industrial Queens landscape that is traversed in the various commutes between the city and the exurbs. Rendered as an Eliotic "Waste Land," this setting is most notable for its two main images, the ash heaps themselves and the infamous eyes of Dr. T .J. Eckleburg that "brood over the solemn dumping ground" (23). Eckleburg's eyes underscore the notion of the Queens landscape as a primarily visual phenomenon, a visible record of the outward progress of urban blight. Indeed, this site/sight cannot be avoided; while the commuters' motor road and railroad run beside one another temporarily in an attempt to "shrink away" from this landscape, the effort is futile, for we are told that "passengers on waiting trains can

stare at the dismal scene for as long as half an hour" (24). Hence the very
visibility of this landscape is what gives the lie to the myth of commutation—that one can be a "city person" while at the same time maintaining a
rural identity. Instead, the surreal inversion of rurality in the valley's
landscape, which is likened to a "fantastic farm where ashes grow like
wheat into ridges and hills and grotesque gardens" (23), emphasizes the
corruptibility of landscape. By situating the killing of Myrtle in the valley,
Fitzgerald uses the setting to underscore the fear of urban violence and
decay spreading outside the bounds of the city center. Fittingly, Myrtle's
death occurs during—indeed, is caused by—a journey back from the city.
In subsequently making his final trip east to Gatsby's home, George
Wilson completes the movement of "urban" violence eastward into the
exurban landscape.

Allied to this gradual encroachment of violence into nonurban spaces
is the increasing presence of those of non-"Nordic" background in the
affairs of the novel. In much the same way that confrontation and physical
violence are initially situated in the city itself, visibly "ethnic" others also
are carefully and specifically placed in the city early in the novel. While
Meyer Wolfsheim, the stereotypical Jewish gangster, holds forth in his
midtown Broadway haunts, other ethnic figures seem to mark the boundaries of the city: While passing over the Queensboro Bridge into the city,
Nick spies a car full of mourners in a funeral procession who look at him
with "the tragic eyes and short upper lips of southeastern Europe," and
immediately afterward a limousine passes in which a white driver is
ferrying "three modish negroes, two bucks and a girl" (69). Nick's reaction
to his company on the bridge suggests his resistance to, even fear of, the
racial pluralism of the city: "'Anything can happen now that we've slid over
this bridge,' I thought; 'anything at all . . .'" (69). This observation, in its
emphasis on geographic and demographic boundaries, recalls in a gentler
fashion Tom Buchanan's paranoid fantasy about the "Rise of the Colored
Races," in that both ideas suggest that the exurban spaces of East and West
Egg are predicated on an ideal of whiteness, on an eastern extension of

Daisy's "beautiful white girlhood." But from the increasingly "ethnic" names on Nick's famous list of Gatsby partygoers to the heightened presence of Wolfsheim and his "people" as the novel proceeds, to the crucial eyewitness in the hit-and-run ("a pale well-dressed negro"), it is clear that Tom's ideal of racial "purity" is on the wane.

Indeed, it might be argued that the direct correlation between increasing violence and increasing "visibility" of race and ethnicity in this novel is itself a narrative underscoring of Tom Buchanan's own reactionary, racist philosophy. This is the stand taken by Felipe Smith, who argues that "race and ethnicity operate as hidden metaphors for difference in a narrative scheme that allows Fitzgerald to indulge in Manichean racial typing."[36] But whether or not Fitzgerald is, as Smith would argue, ultimately culpable in creating for the novel a racist agenda seems less verifiable than the fact that the novel's sense of racial paranoia does extend beyond the vilified character of Tom Buchanan. As the Queensboro Bridge passage demonstrates, Nick, as much as Tom, identifies ethnic others as a potentially disruptive force associated with the urban sphere.[37] Driven by the same reasoning that made "white flight" out of the city to the suburbs a reality not only in the 1920s but for generations to come, Nick's fear of the urban center and its inhabitants reflects a social phenomenon that would greatly influence suburbanization in the second half of the century.[38] As his moment on the Queensboro Bridge suggests, the presentation of race and ethnicity in the novel is inextricably bound to matters of landscape, with racial paranoia being part and parcel of the larger fear of urban expansion beyond such boundary lines as the East River.

The culmination of this fear of urban expansion comes, of course, with the killings of Myrtle and Gatsby. But even after the death of Gatsby and the subsequent disappearance of Tom and Daisy, actions that in their own right reveal the changing nature of the Gold Coast environment, two other moments transpire near the end of the novel that serve as reminders of the extent to which *The Great Gatsby* can be read as an examination of a landscape in transition. The first involves Gatsby's father, who excitedly shows Nick a prized possession: "It was a photograph of the house, cracked in the corners and dirty with many hands. He pointed out every detail to me eagerly. 'Look there!' and then sought admiration from my eyes. He had shown it so often that I think it was more real to him now than the house itself" (173).

While the irony of Mr. Gatz's action—being fixated on an old photograph of his son's house even as he stands inside the house itself—borders on the pathetic, he is really doing nothing more than others have done throughout the novel: confusing idealized representations of place with the "real thing," searching for place-bound connections to the past in the face of an alienating and unreadable present moment. Indeed, one of Nick's final actions carries the same symbolic message. In what may be, from the perspective of landscape and place, the most telling moment of the novel, Nick describes his final effort to preserve the idealized memory of Gatsby's landscape: "On the last night, with my trunk packed and my car sold to the grocer, I went over and looked at that huge incoherent failure of a house once more. On the white steps an obscene word, scrawled by some boy with a piece of brick, stood out clearly in the moonlight, and I erased it, drawing my shoe raspingly along the stone. Then I wandered down to the beach and sprawled out on the sand" (181). This action—which immediately precedes Nick's expansive, lyrical close to the narration—underscores the inevitability of the decay of this exurban landscape. But perhaps more significantly, Nick's erasure stands as a last effort to maintain an idealized vision of place, to freeze a living, evolving landscape into a fixed and permanent symbol. That such an effort is doomed to failure is one of the principal insights of this novel.

🏠 🏠 🏠

In contrast to Fitzgerald's vision of an imperiled exurban enclave characterized by artificiality and exclusivity, Capra, in *It's a Wonderful Life*, attempts to imbue the coming landscape of suburbia with what he portrays as the egalitarian values of the traditional small town. The film offers a contrasting vision to *The Great Gatsby* in terms of the dynamics of ethnicity, as it creates—through the subplot of Mr. Martini's move to the suburban development of Bailey Park—a fantasy vision of the inclusiveness of the new suburbs. And while in *The Great Gatsby* Fitzgerald highlights the acute class consciousness of elite exurbanites who fear the encroachment of the middle class, in *It's a Wonderful Life* Capra works hard at rendering the coming suburban landscape as home to a classless community. While both works are steeped in nostalgia, their portrayals of landscapes of memory differ crucially: Fitzgerald demonstrates the futility of the nostalgic impulse—"so we beat on, boats against the current, borne back ceaselessly into the past" (182)—in the face of an alienating modernity, while Capra suggests nothing short of the resurrection of the past as a model for landscapes of the future. That is, Fitzgerald represents the inexorable approach of the suburban landscape in fatalistic terms, while Capra—releasing his film on the eve of the suburban revolution—welcomes the emergence of the "new small town," but does so in a manner that reveals a plethora of insecurities over the direction in which this new kind of town will develop.

Released in December 1946, just over one year after the end of World War II, *It's a Wonderful Life* reflects the varied concerns of an unsettled American society in the booming postwar years. In many ways a testament to the cultural uncertainty underlying postwar optimism, the film offers a nostalgic vision as a means of reinforcing both traditional American values and, as Kaja Silverman has convincingly argued, the "dominant fiction" of male subjectivity, at a time when so many veterans were returning to a changed and unfamiliar social landscape.[39] Less frequently commented on is the extent to which *It's a Wonderful Life* expresses a profound trepidation over the future of the small-town landscape in the postwar era. This becomes apparent through the manipulation of the image of the town throughout the film, as George Bailey comes to inhabit both the traditional small town, Bedford Falls, and the dark urban nightmare world of Pottersville. In the contraposition of these two visions of the same town we get a sense of anxiety over the direction in which the small-town landscape is evolving. That is, while the happy ending works to reinforce the sense of old-fashioned community in Bedford Falls it also reminds us of how close this small town had come to devolving into seedy, urban Pottersville. And as the Pottersville sequence demonstrates, the film's landscape concerns are not limited to matters of evolving physical terrain, but also turn on the changing social landscape in the postwar era.

Historically, there was good reason for this concern over a landscape in transition, as the identity of the American small town was very much up in the air in this period. While the first half of the twentieth century saw increasing urbanization across America, the time of this film's release coincided with the beginning of a massive boom in new housing starts and the emergence of the suburban landscape.[40] The year 1946 was, after all, also the year that ground was broken on Levittown, New York, an event that signaled the coming age of suburbia. And in its own way, *It's a Wonderful Life* carefully addresses the emergence of the suburban landscape: The distinctly suburban-looking development of Bailey Park, which represents the future of Bedford Falls, also serves—through the subplot of Mr. Martini's move there—as a central symbol in a larger thematic pairing of new home construction and ownership with the rebuilding of traditional community values. Insofar as Capra's film focuses on matters of town and community building, it stands as a sort of primer on the potential for creating old-fashioned "small-town" communities in newfangled landscapes and in that sense as an early hint of the utopic vision of suburbia that was to be developed and propagated throughout American popular culture—most noticeably on television—in the coming decade. As Patrick McGee notes, Capra's George Bailey serves as a "symbolic father of the new suburbia for ordinary working-class people, a vision that will dominate the American landscape in the fifties and sixties."[41]

Indeed, visions of suburbia were already becoming more prevalent in films of the immediate postwar years. *It's a Wonderful Life* was only one of many postwar films—including dramas, comedies, and other holiday movies—that depicted the move to suburbia as the resolution to any number of conflicts and difficulties. In Peter Godfrey's comedy *Christmas in Connecticut* (1945), for example, a returned war hero eventually falls in love with his celebrity hostess, as the two of them learn the ropes of being true Connecticut exurbanites; William Wyler's postwar drama *The Best Years of Our Lives* (1946) concludes with an image of veterans dismantling bomber planes to be used as scrap metal for prefabricated housing; in the holiday comedy/romance *Miracle on 34th Street* (George Seaton, 1947), all is finally made right in the lives of each character with the "gift" of a suburban house in the film's closing frames; and in *Mr. Blandings Builds His Dreamhouse* (H. C. Potter, 1948), the protagonist's personal and professional crises vanish in one fell swoop with the completion of construction on his new family home in exurban Connecticut. As is the case in each of these films, in *It's a Wonderful Life* Capra puts a good deal of faith in the coming landscape of suburbia; however, his seemingly innocuous film presents a far more complex and uncertain vision of this new terrain.

Given the thematic centrality of the film's milieu, Capra's choice of geographic and historical setting is worth considering in some detail. The film is set in the fictional small town of Bedford Falls, New York, and it shows the changes Bedford Falls went through between the years of 1919 and 1946. The name of the town, along with several other clues, suggest that it is modeled on Bedford Hills, New York, a small town in Westchester County, a prosperous, established, and still-expanding suburban area.[42] The choice of locale warrants consideration; by using stately but expanding Westchester as a model for his fictional milieu, Capra lent a distinct historical relevance to the dramas of real estate development and community building that comprise so much of the focus of his film.[43] In addition to geographic placement, the historical time frame is equally important, for the rather broad historical purview provides Capra with the opportunity to present a landscape in transition.[44] In contrast to the idyllic small-town identity maintained by the Bedford Falls of George Bailey's youth, the town in later years must weather financial crises that threaten to tear apart the community. This threat is made explicit in the fantasy sequence near the end of the film that documents the "Pottersville" landscape, as this nightmarish, film noir travelogue throws into bold relief the close connections between landscape and community identity, as well as the very precariousness of the small-town identity of Bedford Falls. Ultimately, the film infuses the "new Bedford Falls" of the Bailey Park era with the values of the old small town, a move that can be read as, if not exactly an apology for suburbanization, at least an effort to envision the new suburban community in the image of the traditional small town.

And while "suburbia" itself is hardly the subject matter of this movie—indeed, the newer, recognizably "suburban" neighborhood of Bailey Park makes only one appearance in the film, though it is a memorable one—certainly an uneasiness over the changing nature of the small-town landscape in the postwar era is a factor that defines the film. This anxiety over a landscape in transition lends thematic resonance to the old-time small-town milieu that Capra creates in Bedford Falls proper. As Gilles Deleuze notes, a film's milieu embodies its fictive society's "illusions about itself, about its motives . . . about its values and its ideals: 'vital' illusions . . . which are more true than pure truth."[45] In the case of Capra's Bedford Falls, these illusions center on an old-fashioned sense of community in the town, revealed in the self-consciously nostalgic vision of Bedford Falls presented throughout much of the flashback portion of the film. And while many critics over the years have followed James Agee's critique of the film's milieu as being "backward," "Norman Rockwellish," and "essentially nineteenth century," it seems clear that Capra's dated representation of Bedford Falls was intentional.[46] If we can agree with critic George Toles that Capra was putting forth in this film the "fantasy premise . . . that a beloved place could be utterly obliterated, and then magically re-established," then it is precisely his overly romanticized vision of the Bedford Falls landscape of 1919 that lends such dramatic effect to the reaffirmation of community that occurs at the end.[47] That is, in a film that devotes so much of the narrative to shifting between different time frames and various incarnations of one town's landscape, the nostalgic sense of community is nothing less than the necessary illusion that holds together the milieu.

And it is apparent from the outset of the film that both the social and the physical landscapes of Bedford Falls are, primarily, imaginative creations. As several critics have noted, the opening cut from a panning shot of the landscape of Bedford Falls to the heavenly perspective of Joseph and Clarence—what Silverman refers to as the film's "celestial suture"—foregrounds the fictive, imaginary nature of the town's landscape.[48] That is, Joseph's role in projecting or screening, for Clarence and indeed for us, the viewers, certain visions of the townspeople and their history creates a narrative frame that emphasizes the sense of a selective, imaginative re-creation of landscape at work. Capra underscores his self-reflexive depiction of the town as an imaginary landscape through recurring reminders about the tenuous and transitional nature of the physical environment itself: (Appearing variously as the old-fashioned small town of Bedford Falls, the raucous, seedy, and quasi-urban Pottersville, the squalid ghetto of Potter's Field, and the site of the uniform, newfangled suburban subdivision of Bailey Park, the landscape of *It's a Wonderful Life* metamorphoses constantly.)

And if, as Toles argues, Bedford Falls "seems haunted in a trance by the forms that Pottersville will eventually assume," nonetheless a central drive of the film is to eradicate the specter of Pottersville by reimagining the "new town" of the postwar years in the image of the old town presented at the beginning of the story.[49] This compulsion to resurrect the values of the Bedford Falls of 1919 sets in motion the often-repressive social machinery of the film. As Raymond Carney astutely argues, "Bedford Falls represents a landscape of the imagination associated more with the repression of desire than with innocence and simplicity."[50] And the film does more than merely squash George Bailey's desire to escape his hometown; indeed, along the way to establishing its utopian vision of postwar community, *It's a Wonderful Life* engages much broader issues of desire and its relationship to ethnic, class, and sexual politics. Capra noticeably struggles with his positioning of socially volatile characters and themes, a fact that underscores both the problematic relationship between community building and personal liberty and the difficulties involved in imagining a new physical and social landscape in an old-fashioned manner.

In its compulsion to reject the modern, urbanist landscape vision of Potter—and, indeed, of the young George Bailey—the film engages matters of sexual, ethnic, and class position in a way that marks the eventually reestablished Bedford Falls landscape as a place fraught with anxieties and contradictions. The central importance of the embattled milieu is foregrounded early in the film, when we learn that George wants nothing more than to escape the confines of Bedford Falls; as he tells his father, Peter Bailey, at the dinner table on the night of Harry's dance (and the night of Peter's death), his dreams are aligned not with his rurally identified, sleepy small town but the modern, urban milieu: he explains that he wants to "build things . . . design new buildings—plan modern cities." He expands on this modernist, urban vision in the subsequent discussion with Mary after the dance. After they throw their rocks through the windows of the old Granville house, George explains the "wish" that he had made: "Well, not just one wish. A whole hatful, Mary. I know what I'm going to do tomorrow and the next day and the next year and the year after that. I'm shaking the dust of this crummy little town off my feet and I'm going to see the world. Italy, Greece, the Parthenon, the Colosseum. Then I'm coming back here and go to college and see what they know . . . and then I'm going to build things. I'm gonna build air fields. I'm gonna build skyscrapers a hundred stories high. I'm gonna build bridges a mile long."

Crucial to this scene is the way in which George's relationship toward place is linked to both his place in history and his status as a *builder:* While he does wish to immerse himself in the past by taking in the architectural treasures of the Old World, George views these historical artifacts primarily as models for his modern architectural ambitions. But in contrast to George's urban vision of creating monumental bridges and skyscrapers, the primary drive of the narrative is to harness George's constructive energies and put them to use in building the small town of Bedford Falls— both literally, in his role as financier of the Bailey Park subdivision and official town spokesman on the importance of home ownership, and figuratively, as the one person whose presence solidifies and unites the community. Hence, it is no surprise that George's elucidation of his "dreams" is set against the backdrop of the once-stately yet now decaying Granville house: Here Capra provides a visual cue as to the direction in which George's capacity as a builder will lead him. Just as he will be called on to "rebuild" the home he is then in the process of defacing, George will find himself not only building houses in Bailey Park but also, in a very real sense, "rebuilding" a sense of community, based on the values of the traditional, rurally identified small town, in postwar Bedford Falls.

That such an effort will not be accomplished without some difficulty is brought home by a telling sequence in the middle of the film that occurs after the wedding party for George's brother, Harry, and his wife, Ruth. Despondent that Harry's marriage and employment prospects represent the final nail in the coffin of his dreams of travel and adventure, George leaves the party and seems indecisive as to where to go. Temporarily resisting his mother's advice to go visit Mary Hatch, a "nice girl" who Mrs. Bailey feels will help George "find the answers," George instead heads for downtown Bedford Falls. Here he encounters Violet Bick, whose independence and overt sexuality mark her as the antithesis of the domestic Mary Hatch. Shot in dark, shadowy, almost film noir style, this scene—like the later Pottersville sequence—offers a glimpse of what Bedford Falls might be in the process of becoming: a quasi-urban landscape where the energies of sexuality and commerce, as represented by the independent and boisterous Violet, shape the town and its inhabitants. George, standing at the crossroads of Bedford Falls and, as we soon learn, at the crossroads of his own life, approaches Violet, who is in the process of extricating herself from the groping hands of two other would-be suitors. The subsequent exchange between George and Violet underscores the incongruity between George's vision of Bedford Falls, which remains a rural one, and that of Violet and the assembled crowd, who eventually mock George for his ludicrous proposition:

> "Are you game, Vi? Let's make a night of it."
>
> "Oh, I'd love it, Georgie. What'll we do?"
>
> "Let's go out in the fields and take off our shoes and walk through the grass."
>
> "Huh?"
>
> "Then we can go up to the falls. It's beautiful up there in the moonlight, and there's a green pool up there, and we can swim in it. Then we can climb Mt. Bedford, and smell the pines, and watch the sunrise against the peaks, and . . . we'll stay up there the whole night, and everybody'll be talking and there'll be a terrific scandal . . . "
>
> "George, have you gone crazy? Walk in the grass in my bare feet? Why, it's ten miles up to Mt. Bedford."

Shocked and embarrassed by Violet's rebuff, George snaps back at her to "just forget about the whole thing," as the gathered crowd laughs derisively. In this scene George has misread not only Violet but also the nature of the Bedford Falls landscape itself. Still clinging to his nostalgic vision of a primarily rural Bedford Falls, George and his idea of a good date are terribly out of place in what seems to have become, while George wasn't looking, a rather sophisticated, even racy town.

Crucial to the scene is the role that Violet Bick plays; here, as she does throughout, Violet serves as the locus of the film's anxieties over the changing social and sexual landscape of the town. Capra positions Violet as a central object of male sexual desire, a fact made clear not only in this scene but also in a previous "downtown" scene in which George, Bert the cop, and Ernie the taxi driver ogle her as she passes in the street. But like George, Violet possesses an energy that must be contained or suppressed in order to reestablish the social landscape. This point is brought home during the Pottersville fantasy sequence near the end of the movie when, in what is certainly one of the film's most aggressive and violent scenes, George witnesses Violet being dragged kicking and screaming from a "Dime-A-Dance" hall into a police wagon. Here Capra makes explicit connections among sexuality, feminine independence, exploitative capitalism, and social decay, and again Violet serves quite literally as the embodiment of Bedford Falls' sordid underside. Hence, in this scene Capra manipulates both the architecture of the town and the image of Violet to emphasize the tenuous and imperiled nature of both the physical and the social landscapes of Bedford Falls.

The symbolic use of Violet Bick can be fully understood only when it is considered in light of the portrayal of Violet's textual counterpart, Mary Hatch/Bailey. In every conceivable sense, the two are set up as polar opposites throughout the film. Indeed, even the visual code insists on the contrast: while Violet is featured most prominently in dark, noirish scenes, Donna Reed's Mary is consistently bathed in soft focus, a technique that emphasizes both her innocent sexuality and—inasmuch as soft focus itself was a technique of an earlier era of cinema—her ties to a nostalgic vision of small-town life. As opposed to Violet, an exemplar of female independence who is consistently shown in outdoor shots, walking the streets of downtown Bedford Falls on her own or in the company of men, Mary is shown mostly in indoor shots and almost never alone, but rather positioned beside or behind George or the children. Indeed, even in her one memorable outdoor scene, the walk to 320 Sycamore after Harry's dance, Mary winds up enclosed again, this time peeking over the top of the hydrangea bushes as George drives off to tend to his father. This consistent visual emphasis on Mary's enclosure suggests her identification with the domestic sphere. Even during the turbulent war years, Mary's agency in helping the town carry on is painted in domestic terms: as the voice-over of the World War II montage tells us that Mary "had two more babies, but still found time to run the

U.S.O.," we see a shot of Mary cheerily serving doughnuts to servicemen passing through town on the train. Most noteworthy as a mother and caregiver, Mary, while clearly the textual opposite of Violet, serves an equally ideological function in the sexual politics of the film.

The extent to which Mary is positioned as the object of a domesticated form of desire is made clear by her relationship to capital in the film. Mary is by no means inept with money or a stranger to it; on the contrary, she not only finances the bailout of the building and loan by turning over the $2,000 in wedding money, but also secretly arranges for the purchase of 320 Sycamore and collects the money that saves George and, in the process, resurrects the community's sense of identity at the end of the film. Indeed, in contrast to the once-shrewd but now-failing Potter and the well-intentioned but bungling Baileys, Mary seems the only character in the film who consistently engineers positive financial transactions. Nevertheless, Capra's relentless alignment of this character with the domestic sphere extends to Mary's financial capabilities as well. In each of her transactions, she functions as a sort of extension of George and his role as home-builder, twice saving his home-financing business and once purchasing—almost magically, it seems even to George—the home in which they will spend their lives together. In the end, it seems that despite her financial acumen, Mary would have virtually no identity at all were it not for her marriage to George Bailey. This is made clear in the climactic moment of the Pottersville fantasy sequence when George, after enduring all the other hardships of this nightmare world, comes face to face with Mary Hatch, a spinster, closing up the library. Particularly since we know that the library itself is symbolic of the futility, even impotence, of George's dreams (at one point Violet questions George's affinity for the library, asking him, "Don't you ever get tired of just reading about things?"), Mary's position here is indicative of her own lack of vigor and agency. Bespectacled and dressed in a plain gray suit, Mary—though certainly an independent woman—has been stripped of her only two pieces of cultural capital: her physical beauty and her status as Mrs. Bailey. As critic Randall

Fallows puts it, Mary in this scene represents "a caricature of the career woman—asexual, drab, without humor or compassion. In short, Mary's life has no meaning outside of the role that [George] can provide for her."[51]

What Capra comes up with, then, in the treatment of Mary and Violet is something akin to what Deleuze and Guattari would refer to as a "splitting" of the feminine object of desire into the polar opposites of the "rich woman" and the "poor woman."[52] Violet, as the base or "low" object of desire, is characterized by her poverty and increasingly lurid behavior, moving from merely borrowing money from George to get out of town fast, to "turning tricks" at the Dime-A-Dance club. Mary, on the other hand, as the "high" object of desire, has little problem generating capital, but does so at the cost of her identity, as she becomes increasingly enclosed within the domestic sphere. This splitting of the female object of desire serves a distinctly ideological function as Mary, who remains a central figure throughout, comes to embody the domestic ethos of the small-town milieu, while Violet is increasingly marginalized and remains most memorable as a figure of the Pottersville, rather than Bedford Falls, landscape. As counterpoised characters, then, Mary and Violet both illustrate the idea that the landscape is evolving toward an increasingly limited and circumscribed space for women.[53] And while Joseph McBride is quite right in arguing that this sort of sexual politics is emblematic of Capra's larger postwar political "regression," at the same time it is worth noting how Capra's handling of feminine sexuality turned out to be consonant with the larger, repressive political climate in postwar America: It was precisely the sort of independence and exuberance represented by a character like Violet that was reined in during the postwar era, in favor of the domesticated female role embodied in Mary.[54] This was to be particularly true in the 1950s, the decade of mass suburbanization, which was to become a most stultifying era for many previously active, socially engaged women.[55]

If the film demonstrates anxieties over the position of the female in the postwar social landscape, it also certainly struggles with the position of the male, as Silverman has noted. As she argues in *Male Subjectivity at the*

Margins, It's a Wonderful Life was one among a number of postwar films that dealt with the "historical trauma" of World War II by working toward reinstating the "dominant fiction" of male subjectivity.[56] Silverman points out that George, as the most conspicuous male to remain behind in Bedford Falls during the war, serves as a sort of "stand-in" for the missing phallic presence in the town; hence, his many struggles throughout the film are emblematic of the difficulties involved in revivifying a sense of masculine agency in the postwar era. And while Silverman notes that the film struggles in its efforts to reinstate the dominant fiction of male subjectivity, she concludes that in the end it "does not so much cancel as defer the phallic legacy," in that the sentimental reincorporation of George into the community at the close of the film stands as a "resounding reaffirmation of faith in male subjectivity, the family, and small-town American life."[57] Indeed, as Silverman suggests, George's struggle and eventual reintegration involve more than the drama of imperiled masculine presence; in addition, if we are to put any stock in the Pottersville sequence, it seems that the very identity of the town—its social, economic, and physical landscape—is dependent on a successful reintegration of George Bailey.

Hence one of the central dilemmas of this film: how to push the character of George Bailey into accepting, and even celebrating, the sense of entrapment he experiences in Bedford Falls. As Carney has argued, George is "relentlessly frustrated and trapped—formally, socially and psychologi-cally" throughout the film, and all of the important people in George's life—his parents and brother, Mary, Potter—continually work to position him in various ways.[58] Likewise George is eavesdropped on by nosy neighbors, jeered by onlookers such as Sam Wainwright, more than once encircled and pinned against the wall by angry crowds, spied on by Mrs. Hatch, and given over to the police by Potter. Of course, the ultimate entrapment for George is the domestic life he leads at 320 Sycamore with Mary and their children. The antithesis of his dreams of travel and adventure, George's home life is emblematic, as Robert B. Ray has noted, of a larger American cultural opposition between adventure and domesticity.[59] Carney takes this line of analysis a step further, arguing that Capra's film stands as another in a long line of American "Post-Romantic" texts that dramatize the competing pulls of frontierlike adventure and a more domesticated life of community involvement. As Carney notes, in George "Capra imagines the possibility of a life that cannot escape or repress these conflicting imaginative tendencies but must live within their contradictions."[60]

This is why the house at 320 Sycamore figures so prominently in the film: In its various stages of evolution, the house serves as a constant reminder of the ongoing battle between the forces of domesticity—feminized in the form of Mary Hatch, the homemaker—and adventurousness, which is ascribed to the masculine through both the men in town who go off to war and the freewheeling, unfettered capitalist Sam Wainwright. In its dilapidated state as the target of Mary and George's rock throwing early in the film, the 320 Sycamore house serves as the conduit for the enunciation of these very contrary desires; it is here that we learn of George's plans to "shake off the dust of this crummy little town and see the world" and here where Mary makes the all-important wish she will later reveal on their wedding night. In that scene, after bailing out the building and loan with their honeymoon money, Mary welcomes George "home" to 320 Sycamore in a most curious fashion. Referring to the house over the phone as the "Waldorf Hotel," Mary goes on, with the help of Bert the cop and Ernie the cab driver, to decorate the house with posters of far-off places. As George enters his new "home" for the first time, the camera pans across the living room, which features an assemblage of disparate images. Travel posters over the windows advertise the exotic pleasures of the "South Seas," while Hawaiian music plays on a jerry-rigged old record player. At the same time, we see two game hens roasting over the fire in the fireplace and Mary standing beside this image of warm domesticity, bathed in soft focus. It is in the midst of this maze of signifiers that Mary pronounces to George the weighty words "Welcome home, Mr. Bailey," before eventually disclosing to him the desire on her own part that lay behind the creation of this interesting new "home": "Remember the night we broke the windows in this old house? This is what I wished for."

And while George at that moment seems thrilled by Mary's wish and its coming to fruition, it is not difficult to see that 320 Sycamore is the prison house of George's dreams. His hopes for a life of adventure are finally put to rest entirely with the purchase of this house, a fact underscored by the evolution of the symbolism in the Bailey home: Both the travel posters that adorn the house in the wedding night scene and the model buildings and bridges that later sit atop a drawing table in the living room stand as empty signifiers, hollow reminders of George's yearning for adventure, which are far less real than the leaky roof or the loose banister knob, themselves more tangible reminders of the mundane, domestic duties that occupy George's time and energy. In essence, George's sense of entrapment in the 320 Sycamore house, a feeling he expresses vehemently before storming out on Christmas Eve, is indicative of his imperiled masculinity. Caught in the "feminized" domestic sphere at 320 Sycamore and overshadowed in the masculine world of finance by both the memory of his father and the gaudy success of his childhood friend Sam Wainwright, George lacks a space of his own in which to prove his masculinity.[61] But through its treatment of landscape, the film ultimately does offer George such a space, for the one way that he is able to prove his worth—and thereby reinstate the notion of male subjectivity—is through his battles with Potter over the future of the Bedford Falls landscape. That is, George proves his own worth and ability—if only to himself—by emerging as the person who saved the town from devolving into sleazy Pottersville, the nightmare world he visits courtesy of his guardian angel, Clarence. Hence it is precisely the film's self-conscious play with its own milieu, its insistent portrayal of Bedford Falls as an imagined, created, malleable landscape, that allows for the resolution of George's untenable dilemma of imperiled masculinity.

The ultimate proof of George's successful reintegration into the Bedford Falls community is the final scene, a richly ironic celebratory moment in which seemingly all the residents of Bedford Falls come to rescue George from his $8,000 debt, showering him with money and hailing him as "the richest man in town." That line, delivered by George's returning war hero brother, Harry, is doubly ironic in that everyone knows who the truly richest man in town is—the Scrooge-like villain, Mr. Potter. In finally conferring Potter's status on George, Harry's line may resolve the issue of George's vulnerable masculinity, but at the same time it retrospectively opens up thorny financial issues, reminding us of the fine line that the film has walked throughout with regard to money matters. If, as Robert Schultz argues, this film "functions ideologically to mitigate the cultural anxieties of a capitalist society," then surely the focal point for resolving this anxiety comes in the handling of the George/Potter relationship.[62] The cartoonish, self-consciously anachronistic characterization of Potter indicates the lengths Capra goes to distance his movie from the realities of bare-knuckle capitalism, even while he is championing what would become one of the greatest vehicles of capitalist expansion in the postwar period, the housing industry. The stark contrast between the Bailey and Potter and versions of capitalism becomes an integral part of a larger ideological project of imagining a benign capitalism at work in the town. And still, it is necessary to imperil the distinction between the two capitalisms, if only to throw it into even greater relief; Carney, who considers Potter as a "doppelganger" of George, notes this tactic of the film, arguing that it is "not accidental that halfway through the movie Potter's most threatening gesture to George is not an attempt to destroy him but an offer to merge with him."[63] This crucial scene—when George, after a moment of doubt, disgustedly refuses Potter's offer to make George his business manager—seals for good the economic distinction between the two and paves the way for the nearly utopic vision of Bedford Falls as a classless society.

The embodiment in George of a purely benevolent form of capitalism—a capitalist practice grounded on George's father's motto, which hangs on the wall of the office, "All you can take with you is that which you've given away"—resonates also throughout the town, which George continues to remake in his own image.[64] Bedford Falls resembles, as Agee notes, "a kind of Christian semi-socialism, a society founded on affection, kindliness, and trust."[65] The cooperative ethos of the Bedford Falls community is underscored visually throughout the film by the sheer prevalence of group shots and group activities; indeed, even the one opportunity for community discord, in the building and loan "run" scene, shows an angry mob being transformed into a cooperative community. What brings them around is George Bailey's most dramatic speech, one in which he makes clear the film's underlying utopian vision of classless community by contrasting it to Potter's monopolistic malice: "I beg of you not to do this thing. If Potter gets hold of this Building and Loan there'll never be another decent house built in this town. He's already got charge of the bank. He's got the bus line. He's got the department stores. And now he's after us. Why? Well, it's very simple. Because we're cutting in on his business, that's why. And because he wants to keep you living in his slums and paying the kind of rent he decides. . . . Now, we can get through this thing all right. We've got to stick together, though. We've got to have faith in each other."

By conflating not only a sense of community but indeed a kind of spiritual bond—a communal and reciprocal "faith in each other"—with the future of the landscape, George in this speech enunciates one of the central messages of the film: that capitalism, imagined in the form of a community of homeowners, can be purified of its negative connotations. Even the money that has disappeared from the building and loan in this scene—and money is constantly disappearing in the film, finally to reappear in one lump sum at the end—is not "dirty money" at all, but yet another symbol of community, as George explains when a patron demands his money: "No, but you . . . you . . . you're thinking of this place all wrong. As if I had the money back in a safe. The money's not here. Your money's in Joe's house, right next to yours. And in the Kennedy house, and Mrs. Macklin's house, and a hundred others. Why, you're lending them the money to build, and then, they're going to pay it back to you as best they can. Now what are you going to do? Foreclose on them?" George's rhetoric indicates how far the film goes in its efforts to distance itself from exploitative capitalism: in emphasizing the financial agency of the borrowers themselves—their power in decisions about lending and foreclosure—George effectively disappears altogether as a financier and offers the vision of an autonomous collection of homeowners, financing the construction of their community primarily through their "faith" in one another.

That such "faith" pays dividends is made apparent through the contrast between the two competing residential districts in the film, Bailey Park and Potter's Field. The former, a typical suburban development, nevertheless retains a particular resonance not only by virtue of its name, which signifies its creator's acceptance of the pastoral vision, but also because it was built on the site of the old cemetery. This locale suggests nothing less than the "resurrection" of the town, a point further emphasized by the funereal connotations in the name of Bailey Park's textual counterpart, the town "slum," Potter's Field. This play on death and rebirth alludes to the fact that, much as George is "reborn" at the end of the film through his eventual display of faith ("Please God, let me live again"), the old-fashioned sense of community in Bedford Falls is being reborn in Bailey Park, by virtue of the "faith" the residents have in one another. The subsuming of residents' economic interests as homeowners within this larger framework of faith and community reflects an effort to paint the new subdivision as a sort of classless community. Still, the film cannot elide class issues altogether, as the continuing existence of Potter's Field is a reminder of a persistent class structure in the town. A squalid, teeming environment, Potter's Field remains on the periphery of the film (it is only actually shown once), but still stands as a reminder of the poverty and social decay on the outskirts of Bedford Falls itself. With the slow but steady annihilation of Potter's Field (a process described by Potter's own rent collector, who at one point advises his boss, "Your Potter's Field, sir, is becoming just that"), the town works toward establishing a landscape free of such markers of social and economic difference.

The crowning achievement of this effort comes in the sequence chronicling Mr. Martini's move from Potter's Field to Bailey Park, a defining moment in terms of the film's concerns about landscape. The sequence begins with a shot of Martini's street in Potter's Field, a dirt road lined with broken-down, ramshackle houses and teeming with downtrodden and disheveled residents. Prompted by a neighbor who asks whether he has rented a new house, Martini celebrates his advancement: "Rent? I own the house. Me, Giuseppe Martini, I own my own house. No more we live like pigs in thisa Potter's Field." Clearly, Martini's jubilance supports Schultz's argument that in this film, the people's "happiness, self-worth and community concerns are based on their ability to have a degree of economic independence through property ownership."[66] But there is more to this scene than merely the conflation of home ownership and self-esteem, for Martini is also the most identifiably "ethnic" character to rise to the status of homeowner. And, as he suggests in his pidgin English, the move to Bailey Park also represents a step toward assimilation in the larger community and removal of the stigma of association with the base, lowly, even the animalistic ("No more we *live like pigs* in thisa Potter's Field").[67] While Martini's move works to emphasize the inclusiveness of the new subdivision of Bailey Park, at the same time the film cannot seem to resist an ethnic stereotyping of Martini: Immediately after his "live like pigs" speech, Martini loads the family goat, along with his children, into George Bailey's car. Judging from George's surprised reaction, this will likely be the first goat in Bailey Park. If the film seems anxious and contradictory in its treatment of Martini, the issue of ethnicity is eventually smoothed over altogether in the subsequent "moving in" scene in Bailey Park. As George and Mary ritualistically welcome the family to "the Martini Castle," a crowd of onlookers beams and applauds in support of their new neighbors. The well-wishers here represent nothing less than the utopic dream of the suburban subdivision, a place whose relative symmetry and homogeneity of landscape are emblematic of a larger spirit of community accord.

And yet the Bailey Park scene seems—even more so than the Pottersville sequence—a visual aberration, in that it depicts a landscape so markedly different from everything else we have seen in the film. In contrast to the well-worn stature of the 320 Sycamore house and the stately facades of downtown, the small, fairly uniform ranch houses of Bailey Park, with their distinctly postwar suburbia look, seem a step out of the film's time frame. But this jarring visual contrast only reinforces the fact that this film is looking forward in time as much as it is looking back. More than a simple-minded piece of "nostalgia" about a time and place from the past, *It's a Wonderful Life* stands as a very timely work, in that it captures the sense of the small-town American landscape in transition. The anxiety the film reflects over an evolving physical and social terrain was a matter of real concern in the postwar years; with the help of the newly passed GI Bill, World War II veterans and their families were in this period moving out of crowded cities and into both new suburbs and new subdivisions within established towns.[68] Given this historical context, it is little wonder that the film pays such careful attention to matters of home and community building. But perhaps most interesting about the film in terms of landscape is the struggle it goes through in an attempt to establish a utopian vision of the new, suburban small town as a classless, inclusive model of community. This thematic concern is worth noting precisely because, in the end, Capra's strained handling of ethnic, class, and sexual politics reveals the flip side of the utopian vision of the new suburban landscape. Indeed, the sorts of issues *It's a Wonderful Life* raises about the connections among landscape, community, and the individual were to become fodder for the "suburban debate" in both the popular media and intellectual circles in the 1950s—one indication that this "nostalgic" film may have been, in some sense, ahead of its time.

♠ ♠ ♠

In both *It's a Wonderful Life* and *The Great Gatsby,* "suburbia" as we know it today is referenced indirectly, and only through brief glimpses—Nick Carraway's "cardboard bungalow," Bailey Park's prefab homes. Nevertheless, these texts anticipate both representations of the suburbs in fiction and film of the second half of the century and indeed many social concerns of the suburban age. Fitzgerald portrays an environment characterized by exclusivity and fear of encroaching others, issues that would inform the suburban works of Cheever, Perry, Updike, and Naylor. Capra, attempting to depict the coming suburban environment as a model of community, nonetheless envisions a prohibitive and repressive social landscape, a view that would reemerge in the works of Nichols, Beattie, Forbes, and Hudlin. In a more general sense, both Fitzgerald and Capra express uneasiness over the evolution of their respective landscapes, and the closing gestures of both narratives—Fitzgerald's image of "boats against the current, borne back ceaselessly into the past" and Capra's shot of the gathered townspeople singing "Auld Land Syne"—are steeped in a similar brand of nostalgia. This connection, driven by the compulsion of each text to locate meaning in the "eulogized spaces," the landscapes of memory, also anticipates prevailing concerns in the suburban age. Such a sense of yearning for lost connections to landscape recurs throughout the major works of suburban fiction and film, testament to an ongoing perception of the suburb as a vexing, even alienating, environment.

Finding the Worm in the Apple

John Cheever, Class Distinction, and the Postwar Suburban Landscape

"How American is your way of living?"

So reads the outsized, bolded blurb atop a feature story in the September 1950 issue of *House Beautiful* magazine. Unremarkable in most respects, the article offers a predictable string of chides and blandishments aimed at encouraging young suburban housewives to buy the latest domestic accoutrements offered by the magazine's advertisers. An excerpt of the prose indicates how latent threats of exposure and humiliation are used to prod the reader into a striving, materialistic (or, in *House Beautiful*'s terms, *American*) relationship to home and surroundings: "What *is* your house saying about you? . . . Does it form a suitable background for you, your manners, your ambitions, and values? Or does it make you look ridiculous, as if you didn't quite belong, as though you'd strayed onto a stage set? Does your house express the serenity and self-assurance of a person living in a democratic society where Everybody is Somebody? Does it show that you are sure of yourself as a person of character and importance, or does it show you are worried because you're not somebody else?"]

In a number of ways, this odd bit of consumeristic journalism plays on social concerns facing an expanding American middle class at midcentury. Essentially defining (American democracy) as the freedom to contrive (or purchase) a [unique identity,] this string of invasive rhetorical questions is designed to encourage young homeowners to assert their claim to financial and class status through the [commodification of home and surroundings.] And while such an approach has always been the bread-and-butter of the "house and garden" magazine, the fluidity of both class lines and landscape in mid-twentieth-century America lends a bit more depth to *House Beautiful*'s aggressive positioning of its readers.[2] In 1950 the United States was in the early stages of several interlocking social/demographic trends that would permanently impact both the physical and social landscapes of the nation: [the postwar baby boom, a massive expansion of the middle class, the greatest housing boom to date in U.S. history, and the onset of mass suburbanization.] Together these trends helped to push to the forefront of national consciousness the relationships between physical and social place—a point not only suggested by *House Beautiful*'s rhetoric, but indeed borne out by a steady stream of both sociological and fictional accounts of middle-class suburbanites published in the postwar years and particularly in the 1950s.

The most notable shift in middle-class demographics in the postwar years sprang from the [explosive growth of the housing market,] as the prospect of home ownership, [long considered a marker of middle-class standing in American culture,] rapidly became available to a large segment of the population.[3] As a result of the relatively low cost of the new, mass-produced housing and easier financing terms made possible by the support of the Federal Housing Authority (FHA) and the Servicemen's Readjustment Act (or "GI Bill") of 1944, housing starts skyrocketed in the late 1940s and 1950s.[4] With the vast majority of FHA guarantee money earmarked specifically for new suburban housing projects, it was perhaps a fait accompli that the suburbs would, by the end of the 1950s, be well on the way to becoming the dominant landscape of the United States.[5] The bellwether for mass suburbanization was the construction and immediate success of the first Levittown, on New York's Long Island. Opened to the public in 1947, Levittown was an immediate hit with GIs, hundreds of whom lined up for days before the official opening of business, awaiting the chance to buy their own house and, in effect, purchase their place in the new American middle class. Following Levitt's lead, other merchant builders were soon constructing similar development towns across the nation; by 1950 such construction accounted for four fifths of all new housing starts.[6] As suburban historians Rosalyn Baxandall and Elizabeth Ewen note, the relatively modest price and size of most development homes did not negate the fact that the new suburbia was facilitating the emergence of a new, landed middle class: "Property, however small, transformed greenhorns into middle-class Americans. . . . [W]ho cared what Mr. Kilroy did during the day? What mattered was that his home bore the trappings of a middle-class life. . . . It was what one consumed— not what one produced—that was important."[7]

The new middle-class suburbanite quickly became the object of sociological scrutiny, as a stream of criticism in popular journals and books consistently tied the uniformity of the suburban landscape to a variety of detrimental effects on residents. Noted social critics such as Lewis Mumford decried the homogeneity of landscape and architecture in the new suburbs as environmentally and socially dispiriting. This point was echoed by David Riesman in his influential study *The Lonely Crowd* (1950), which argued that similarity of environmental and social experience was fostering the emergence of what Riesman called "other-directedness," or a kind of conformist groupthink. William H. Whyte, beginning in a series of articles in *Fortune* magazine and subsequently in his 1956 study *The Organization Man,* expressed concern over the corporatized nature of home life, seeing in the prefabricated, socially homogeneous suburbs a mirror image of the "gray flannel" corporate world. While the cultural critique of suburbia was many faceted—indeed, articles in popular journals blamed suburban living for everything from dysfunctional families (composed of "feminized" husbands, "overbearing" wives, and "rebellious" children) to ulcers, hypertension, and cardiovascular disease—the predominant recurring elements of the suburban critique were concerns over the unchecked spread of this new homogeneous environment.[8]

At the same time that popular magazines were abuzz with debate over the new suburbs and suburbanites, fiction writers were finding material for best-sellers amid the landscape of the new suburbia. In fact, as Catherine Jurca argues in her recent study *White Diaspora: The Suburb and the Twentieth-Century American Novel,* sociological and fictional renderings of suburbia and its inhabitants often were curiously intertwined, as postwar novelists "adopted quasi-sociological techniques in fiction dealing with the suburbs."[9] This approach is most evident in novels such as John McPartland's *No Down Payment* (1957)—later made into a motion picture directed by Martin Ritt—and John Keats's 1956 novel *The Crack in the Picture Window,* works that construct a sort of novelistic scaffolding as a means toward effecting a lay-sociological critique of the new suburbia. This is especially the case in Keats's novel, a hyperbolic, even frenzied attack on suburban sensibilities. Like many sociologists, authors such as Keats and McPartland saw in suburban homogeneity the environmental correlative to a sense of diminishing national character.[10] Other novelists continued the dissection of postwar suburbia: Both Sloan Wilson, in *The Man In the Gray Flannel Suit* (1955), and John Marquand, in *Point of No Return* (1949), portrayed advancement in the corporate and suburban worlds as alienating experiences; Marquand, in his lighter satirical sketches, and Max Shulman, in novels such as *Rally Round the Flag, Boys!* (1957), lampooned the mindlessness of Connecticut suburbanites; Philip Roth, in his debut novella *Goodbye, Columbus* (1959), presented the New Jersey suburb of Short Hills—as seen through the eyes of his working-class, urban protagonist—as both an idyllic paradise and an artificial, forbidding bourgeois enclave; and Richard Yates, in his first novel, *Revolutionary Road* (1961), depicted the move to the New York suburbs as representing the figurative—and in one case literal—death of his would-be urban-sophisticate protagonists.

But few American writers of the twentieth century remain more immediately or definitively associated with a fiction of the suburban middle class than John Cheever. Indeed, Cheever's fictional milieu is notable for its class-bound consistency, a world whose boundaries are marked by ubiquitous cocktail parties, swimming pools, and commuter trains. His tireless attention to the rites and trappings of post–World War II upper-middle-class life earned Cheever a good deal of unwarranted criticism as the chronicler of a superficial and even monotonous world. But in fact, beneath the veneer of his bourgeois universe, Cheever consistently draws attention to the fractures that compromise the structure of a seemingly placid suburban society. Unlike lesser writers such as Keats, McPartland, and Shulman, whose suburban critiques—whether light-hearted or vitriolic—were grounded in the presentation of an utterly homogeneous and vapid suburban experience, Cheever created socially and economically complex fictional communities. Typical of many of his best stories is the portrayal of characters existing on the fringes of suburban affluence, figures both enmeshed within and repulsed by the acute class hierarchy of their community. Presenting the suburban landscape as a symbolic field inscribed with the markers of social status—a terrain shaped by the kind of environmental self-consciousness *House Beautiful*'s editors hoped to inspire ("What *is* your house saying about you?")— Cheever offers in his stories of suburban life a complex critique of postwar class consciousness.

The economic and social dynamics of Cheever's stories of the late 1940s through early 1960s reflect larger societal concerns over the relationship between economic position and social "place," as the American middle class expanded and redefined itself in the postwar era. In some of his most powerful stories over the course of these years—"The Enormous

Radio" (1947), "The Housebreaker of Shady Hill" (1956), "The Swimmer" (1964), and others—Cheever offered a vision of class dynamics that grew increasingly complex as the booming postwar period gave way to the instability of the 1960s. In each, Cheever uses the tenuous class position of his protagonists to examine larger issues facing the American middle class, and particularly affluent suburbanites, in the post–World War II, pre-Vietnam era: issues of power, surveillance, alienation, and the breakdown of community. In these stories in particular, Cheever works to break apart his own seemingly homogeneous and self-contained middle-class world, exposing it as an "imagined community" (to borrow Benedict Anderson's phrase) relentlessly driven toward dissolution by its own internal class dynamics.

In one of his most famous stories, "The Country Husband" (1954), Cheever describes his fictional suburban village of Shady Hill as "hang[ing], morally and economically, from a thread," and one could say the same about many of the communities in Cheever's stories.[11] Financial uncertainty lurks beneath the lives of many of Cheever's characters; often, as is the case in both "The Enormous Radio" and "The Swimmer," the revelation of such financial difficulty works to dissolve communities, revealing their lack of cohesion, or what we might call their fictive nature. Cheever's suburban stories repeatedly depict a class structure based on a rigid, if tacit, hierarchy of class distinctions. His suburbanites signify their social standing through elaborate architecture and landscape design, evidencing an adherence to what C. B. Macpherson has termed "possessive individualism," or the valorization of property ownership as a nexus of individual social power.[12] To read the topography of Cheever's suburban stories, then, is to be immersed in a landscape defined by markers of class distinction. Indeed, landscape design becomes only one manifestation of the elite status maintained by Cheever's suburbanites; also signifying their class position through the display of refined cultural tastes—as the narrator of "The Housebreaker of Shady Hill" observes, "My neighbors are rich and they use their time wisely. They travel around the world, listen to good music, and given a choice of paper books at an airport, will pick Thucydides, and sometimes Aquinas" (258)—Cheever's characters maintain a position of superiority in what Pierre Bourdieu calls the "culture game."[13] Endowed with refined taste and the "cultural capital" it brings, these characters model an exclusive suburban experience where evidence of cultural distinction serves as the measure of social status.[14]

In his recurring focus on a subtle yet unforgiving social stratification, Cheever emerged as a critical observer of social standards among the postwar middle class—or, in Scott Donaldson's words, as "the Jeremiah of [the] suburban age."[15] This attention to matters of class conflict reflected contemporary changes taking place in the structure of the American middle class, changes that were paralleled by the evolution of the physical landscape of the United States at this time. The rapid spread of Levittown-like suburban development towns, a phenomenon that both reflected and helped to facilitate a massive expansion of the American middle class, resulted in a blurring of distinctions among social strata.[16] As sociologist Vance Packard asked in his influential study *The Status Seekers* (published in 1959, one year after the appearance of Cheever's suburban sequence *The Housebreaker of Shady Hill*): "What, actually, has happened to social class in the United States during the recent era of abundance?"[17]

The question had merit, as the design of new suburban towns evidenced an attempt to conceal the class issue altogether. In contrast to older, more affluent suburbs such as New York's Westchester and Connecticut's Fairfield counties, the models for Cheever country, the design of typical postwar suburban towns emphasized uniform social identity by presenting an image of *classlessness*. Since most subdivisions featured very little variation in lot size or home design, size, or price, the equality of social class among postwar suburbanites seemed literally verifiable by the naked eye. And much as the design of suburbia worked to mask class concerns, other societal forces shaping the image of suburbia did the same. Most notable among these was network television: Angling to make television more than merely a new "appliance" in the suburban home and instead a focal point of family life, network programmers did all they could to encourage identification between new suburbanites and the world of television. As Nina Leibman has argued, the rise of suburban situation comedies (*Father Knows Best, Ozzie and Harriet, Leave It to Beaver, The Donna Reed Show,* et al.) in the late 1950s through early 1960s helped to facilitate the psychic as well as physical mass migration to the suburbs.[18] In the process, such programs created an image of the contented, white, solidly middle-class family that continues to be associated with suburban America.[19] Predominantly set in the suburban home and neighborhood, these sitcoms created an imaginative vision of a landscape devoid of social competition and striving, a place altogether free from any connection to the social and economic concerns of the world "outside." In effect, these programs created what Lynn Spigel has aptly termed a "fantasy of antiseptic electrical space," a simulated sense of community between the viewer and on-screen counterpart based, as was the design of postwar suburbia itself, on the suppression of difference.[20]

Moreover, the intense sociological scrutiny leveled on suburbanites in the postwar years only underscored the sense of this new middle class as a "universal class," in Barbara Ehrenreich's terms, a class "everywhere represented as representing everyone."[21] Ironically, it was the very mystique of suburban classlessness, the pervasive sense that suburbia had spawned a new, uniform, and dominant middle class, that exacerbated concerns regarding social position. Consider the view from the already established middle class: Much of the criticism in the 1950s directed toward the spread of "cookie-cutter" suburbia proceeded from the belief that this new middle-class landscape was threatening both established towns and previously untouched countryside; implicit in such critiques was a sense of imperiled bourgeois class prerogative. For example, Robert Moses, the highly influential parks and highway planner from New York state, railed in a 1950 *Atlantic Monthly* essay at real estate "speculators [who] aim their schemes at the lowest common denominator" and in turn threaten to "wreck most of the countryside before the next big boom arrives"[22] Five "boom" years later, Moses was referring to real estate developers as "jackals" and foreseeing the emergence of "suburban slums as sure as God made little apples."[23] Along similar lines, a 1959 piece in *Commonweal* magazine warned of the suburban developments "which are spreading like so many giant oil stains," concluding that the only antidote to suburban infiltration lay in holding fast to the "conviction that there is a value in order, lucidity, and the passionate pursuit of standards of beauty."[24]

In scholarly journals, the tone of such critique was hardly more sanguine and at times was equally vitriolic. Writing in the *Yale Review,* sociologist William Dobriner lamented the fate befalling residents of established villages that had subsequently been "sacked" by new suburbanites, seeing these villagers as victims under siege by the "pushy, progressive, and plastic world of the newcomers."[25] Another piece in the *Yale Review* saw the process of suburban sprawl as the inevitable encroachment of the urban sphere onto a once-pristine rural landscape, describing the "countless rows of boxlike houses" that had, by the late 1950s, "absorbed towns, hamlets, and rural areas."[26] In a 1957 article on upper-middle-class "exurbia," part of the special series entitled "The New America," *Newsweek* magazine concluded that "the exurban way of life is under thunder clouds" blown up by increasing suburbanization, noting exurban New York—Cheever country—as one area already "being transformed by housing developments."[27] Summing up the haute-bourgeois reaction to "invasion" by suburbanites, Dobriner drew a sharp contrast between the vanishing pastoral paradise of once-rural villages—the disappearing "farmlands," "cove valleys," and "woody ridges"—and the prefabricated suburban environment that had superseded it: "Here among the asbestos shingle or 'hand-split shakes,' the plastic and stainless steel, the thermopane and picture window, the two-car garages and pint-sized dining areas, the weathered wagon wheel and ersatz strawberry barrel, live the suburbanites in their multi-level reconstructions of Colonial America. It is impossible to avoid them."[28]

On one hand, it is difficult to dispute the prognostications of the countless social commentators in the 1950s who saw in the unchecked and unplanned spread of suburbia a future of paved-over countryside and diminished place associations. At the same time, one of the most fascinating aspects of the antisuburban reaction is the degree to which an essentially environmental issue became overlaid with hierarchical class concerns: To many commentators espousing the viewpoint of the already established middle class, both real estate developers and the rows of "ticky-tacky" houses they left in their wake were anathema; the residents who came to occupy those houses were nothing less than the barbarians at the gate. As early as 1948, at the outset of the postwar housing boom, a joint committee of the National Association of Housing Officials and the National Public Housing Conference recognized as much, noting that the "greatest opposition" to the spread of lower-middle-class suburbia in the coming years would come from "those upper-class communities whose primary preoccupation is protecting themselves against 'invasion.'"[29] Indeed, "invasion," "inundation," "devouring," and similar tropes were recycled frequently in critical analyses of the spread of suburbia in the 1950s.[30] And while an *American City* article from 1948 already cites the phenomenon of "suburban blight," some six years later, during a half decade that saw a 28 percent increase in the suburban population of the United States, the verdict was yet more grim, as *Time* magazine reported on "erstwhile country dwellers" who were now experiencing "a second taste of city life with all the familiar problems of heavy traffic, congestion, even slums."[31]

Such dire prognostications as these serve as reminders that postwar suburbia was very much a contested terrain. While commentators like Riesman and Keats bristled at socioeconomic homogeneity in suburbia, others resisted continued suburban development, seeing such "sprawl" as a challenge to the prerogatives of the established middle class. William Whyte, in *The Organization Man,* addressed this paradox, suggesting that the seeming classlessness of the suburbs was less a demographic fact than a welcomed illusion. Whyte saw in the suburbs a good deal of concern over social position; not only did the new suburbanites seek to move up the social ladder by relocating to higher-prestige developments, but also, he argued, they often were consumed by the fear of economic failure, of "going back" to lower-prestige suburbs and the "sub-middle class."[32] Sociologist C. Wright Mills echoed this point, arguing in *White Collar: The American Middle Class* (1956) that postwar middle-class culture was in the grips of a "virtual status panic."[33] Such arguments point toward a central reality of postwar suburban life, one that infuses Cheever's suburban fiction as well: that beneath the seeming placidity of a terrain symbolizing economic success lay a wealth of concerns over class status.

Such social concerns of the postwar middle class informed a growing body of suburban fiction emerging in the 1950s and early 1960s. The source for much writing concerning the middle class and life in the suburbs at this time was the *New Yorker* magazine, which became almost a handbook of sorts for the would-be sophisticated suburbanite. From the postwar years onward, *New Yorker* writers such as Cheever, Mary McCarthy, and John Updike enjoyed popular success with stories characterized by a form of ironic realism noted for its meticulous attention to the details of contemporary bourgeois life. And while critics at times wrote off Cheever and others associated with the *New Yorker* school as purveyors of a form of empty realism, the success of the magazine and of these writers indicates that the readership felt otherwise, perhaps because they saw in the work of Cheever and others glamorized mirror images of their own lives.[34] Although Cheever himself downplayed the significance of the suburban setting in his work, once flatly stating that "it goes without saying that people in my stories and the things that happen to them could take place anywhere," his analysis conveniently overlooks the crucial connections between the cultural cachet of *New Yorker* fiction and the author's own success.[35] Consistently modeling the trappings of suburban affluence, the polished realism of *New Yorker* writers such as Cheever provided an imaginative model of

[handwritten margin notes: "Cheever provided an imaginable model of "elite experience""]

elite experience for a middle-class readership eager to identify with such a landscape and populace.[36] The irony of Cheever's position in this cultural and economic exchange is that his treatment of suburban affluence questioned the very foundations of the prevailing suburban mystique: Countering the image of suburban classlessness, Cheever repeatedly suggested that suburban class concerns manifested themselves in a materialistic landscape and a prohibitive, unforgiving social structure.

Cheever's bleak view of suburban social structure merits consideration, as few writers were better suited than he to chronicle his generation's movement into the suburbs. Like his characters—and, indeed, like many of his readers—Cheever settled in New York City after the war, before eventually moving to the suburbs of Westchester County. Examining the progression of Cheever's tales from the New York City stories of the late 1940s and early 1950s to the suburban stories of the middle 1950s through the 1960s, then, provides an acute angle from which to observe his generation's changing sensibilities in the suburban age. In this sense, it is tempting to consider Cheever a spokesperson for the suburban age. A 1964 *Time* magazine cover story on the author goes further; dubbing him "Ovid in Ossining," the *Time* article suggests Cheever to be nothing less than the poet and mythmaker of the suburbs.[37] And the mythical world Cheever creates in his suburban settings is decidedly dark, a corrective revision of the fantasy image of suburbia promoted by real estate developers and television executives. He positions his characters in a landscape whose commodification leaves them longing for more elemental environments even as they continue to partake in the "culture game" of the suburbs, trying—often desperately—to maintain their "place" in the social landscape. Indeed, as Cheever's characters evolve from the struggling city dwellers of his early stories to the troubled exurbanites he portrayed in his most famous works, they continue to be torn between dreams of a place apart from their society and a compulsion to maintain a tenable position within the social structure.

[handwritten margin notes: ""corrective" of developers & television execs"; ""place apart" versus "maintaining place""]

🏠 🏠 🏠

Such is the case with Jim and Irene Westcott, the central characters in one of the major stories of Cheever's earlier years, "The Enormous Radio." The Westcotts are members of the old East Side New York middle class that Cheever depicted in his short fiction of the late 1940s and early 1950s. Like the characters who appear in the other stories of Cheever's 1953 collection, *The Enormous Radio and Other Stories,* and indeed like Cheever himself in this period, the Westcotts live in an apartment building near New York's tony Sutton Place.[38] As the story unfolds, the seemingly contented and upwardly mobile Westcotts learn—through the powers of their omnipotent new radio—of the financial hardships and consequent familial difficulties ensnaring the other residents of their apartment house. After learning of the plight of their neighbors, the Westcotts come face-to-face with their own precarious financial position, in a heated discussion that reveals a mounting sense of marital discord. The radio, a means of surveillance on the lives of their neighbors, comes to act as a mirror reflecting the Westcotts' own experience: After seizing the ability to look beyond or through the surface contentedness of their neighbors' lives to the turmoil that lies beneath, the Westcotts are inevitably thrown into an examination of their own life. That life has become increasingly characterized by duplicity and rancor, as a result of their attempting to mask or hide from an increasingly vulnerable financial position. The couple finally are forced to confront, as Patrick Meanor succinctly puts it, the "fictiveness of [the] fictions" by which they live their lives, and the results are disastrous.[39]

This story provides an apt introduction to Cheever's subsequent treatments of suburban class dynamics through its interweaving motifs of surveillance, paranoia, and the pursuit of cultural capital. All of these issues stem from the protagonists' class position, as the opening of the story demonstrates. The Westcotts are initially described as "strik[ing] that satisfactory average of income, endeavor, and respectability that is reached by the statistical reports in college alumni bulletins" (33). In other words, the Westcotts—who, we are told, have two young children and go to the theater "on an average of 10.3 times a year" (33)—epitomize the postwar, aspiring young middle-class family, a point underscored by the detached, statistical voice adopted by the narrator in the opening of the tale. If their proximity to Sutton Place suggests an old money, upper-middle-class existence, markers of the couple's financial concerns—such as Irene Westcott's winter wear, "a coat of fitch skins dyed to resemble mink" (33)—indicate that they are not nearly as well off as they would like to be. But as the Westcotts and the reader are soon to learn, this condition of economic uncertainty is only another point of resemblance between the protagonists and their neighbors in the apartment house.

What sets the Westcotts apart from their neighbors is the strength of their social aspirations. In his exposition, Cheever deftly conflates their dreams of upward mobility—presented in the form of their hope to relocate to the elite suburbs of Westchester—and their cultivation of refined social habits. In addition to their love of the theater, the Westcotts avidly pursue a taste in classical music. This musical preference reflects a desire to exhibit the discriminating taste of the upper class, through a process Bourdieu describes as "cultivating a pleasure which 'cultivates.'"[40] Ironically, the purchase of the enormous radio, a state-of-the-art device meant to enhance the pleasure of their musical experience, signals the end of the Westcotts' dreams of social advancement. Denying them the pursuit of a "cultivating" pleasure, the radio instead subjects the couple to what Irene describes as the "sordid" details of her neighbors' lives. Even in its physical properties, the radio disrupts the Westcotts' carefully cultivated sense of decorum: Standing out like "an aggressive intruder" amid Irene's furnishings, it plays at such a high volume when Irene first turns it on that "it knock[s] a china ornament from a table to the floor" (34). Cheever's symbolic scheme here foreshadows the disruption of his protagonists' visions of acquiring proprietary, affluent tastes: Disturbing, even destroying, Irene's "carefully chosen" furnishings, the radio also eventually shatters their dreams of social advancement.

Thus it is that the enormous radio—a major investment that pushes Jim Westcott to the edge of financial collapse—serves both as a symbol of the couple's dreams of upward social mobility and a constant reminder of the threat of economic ruin. It fulfills the latter function by allowing the Westcotts—and particularly Irene—to eavesdrop on the conversations of neighbors, which increasingly revolve around money and reveal their financial desperation. Both fascinated and repulsed by what she hears, Irene finds it difficult to tear herself away from the radio. She learns of her neighbors' overdrawn bank accounts, unaffordable school tuitions, and dubious social practices. In particular, she hears one hostess advise her maid, "Don't give the best Scotch to anyone who hasn't white hair" (38), and another couple deciding to pocket and sell a diamond they have found in their apartment following a party, concluding, "We could use a couple of hundred bucks" (38). Realizing that her neighbors are "all worried about money" (39), Irene begins to wonder if her own prospects are as limited as theirs are. Devastated by all she has heard, Irene confronts Jim, in the hope of hearing something different: "We are happy, aren't we?" she asks Jim, "And we're not hypercritical or worried about money or dishonest, are we?" (40). The haranguing she receives in return reveals that she and Jim are, in fact, all of the above—and it is on this tragic note that the story ends.

This much-anthologized story remains memorable for the power of its central symbol, which serves a number of thematic functions. Beyond invoking a fear of technology and its increasingly powerful role in human lives and interactions, the radio—in its relentless dredging up of the "sordid" details of the lives of various apartment dwellers—suggests the increasing power of surveillance in postwar America and the impact such surveillance may have on community dynamics. Concerns about the increasing visibility of private lives were to become part of the critique of suburbia in the cold war era, as the "picture window," a standard feature of the postwar suburban house, symbolically eliminated the distinction between the public and private sectors. Tawdry behavior viewed through the picture window was to become a staple image in critiques of the suburban lifestyle, and most works of fiction and film set in the suburbs play on the heightened sense of visibility fostered by the suburban environment.[41] Cheever's own suburban works are filled with such visual "gazes" into the private worlds of his characters, who are often viewed through living room windows or from the windows of the passing commuter train.

Jim Westcott senses that his wife's behavior is crossing this boundary between public and private lives and cautions her that her use of the radio is "indecent. . . . It's like looking in windows" (39). Irene's behavior—indecent or not—reflects her desire to distance herself from the troubled position of her neighbors. In this regard, the enormous radio reminds one of a latter-day incarnation of Bentham's panopticon. Much as the panopticon operator maintains dominance through what Michel Foucault calls a "machinery of a furtive power," Irene initially is reassured of her own superior position by her ability to listen in on the troubles of her neighbors.[42] Soon enough, however, she becomes entangled in this web of surveillance and begins to believe that others can listen in on her. Interrupting Jim as he is lecturing her on spending beyond their means, Irene reveals a growing dread of the machinery of surveillance: She begs Jim to be quiet, claiming that the radio will overhear them and broadcast their misfortunes.

Irene's eventual subordination to—if not victimization by —the eavesdropping machine reveals her double bind: Afraid to speak, and unable to stop listening, Irene may be the perfect emblem of the alienated individual in a paranoid new society. As Foucault argues, panoptic vision in its various guises serves to induct individuals into society's matrix of power relations: "Our society is one . . . of surveillance," writes Foucault, "We are . . . in the panoptic machine, invested by its effects of power, which we bring to ourselves since we are part of its mechanism."[43] In the case of the Westcotts, we might consider the nature of Foucauldian internalized discipline in terms of its relationship to class position; although Jim scoffs at Irene's fear of being heard by the radio, he too has internalized a pervasive form of self-discipline, as he reveals near the end of the story in a heated argument with his wife over their financial future:

"We've got to start cutting down," Jim said. "We've got to think of the children. To be perfectly frank with you, I worry about money a great deal. I'm not at all sure of the future. No one is. . . . I've worked awfully hard to give you and the children a comfortable life," he said bitterly. "I don't like to see all of my energies, all of my youth, wasted in fur coats and radios and slipcovers and—"

"Please, Jim," she said. "Please. They'll hear us."

"Who'll hear us? Emma can't hear us."

"The radio."

"Oh, I'm sick!" he shouted. "I'm sick to death of your apprehensiveness. The radio can't hear us. Nobody can hear us. And what if they can hear us? Who cares?" (41)

Seeing his life and labors amounting to little more than a collection of unwanted material goods—overpriced slipcovers, faux mink coats, monstrous radios—Jim seems to realize the futility of his efforts to maintain the appearances of an upper-middle-class lifestyle.[44] Put another way, Jim realizes that what he and Irene have considered to be their "cultural capital" in fact retains little, if any, value. And yet, despite the cavalier attitude he expresses toward his neighbors' opinions, Jim's advice to Irene suggests that he will continue to adhere to a strict code of self-negation, in the hopes of future social advancement. The irony of Jim's position is that if he were successful, he and Irene would one day find themselves in a place like Johnny Hake's Shady Hill or Neddy Merrill's Bullet Park, suburban terrains where the "culture game" is played by more complex rules, where a rigidly defined and defended social stratification breeds yet more persistent paranoia and alienation.

🏠 🏠 🏠

With its dark vision of surveillance and paranoia undercutting hopes for class advancement, "The Enormous Radio" anticipates the central concerns in much of Cheever's suburban fiction. The most extended treatment of these themes can be found in the 1958 short story collection *The Housebreaker of Shady Hill and Other Stories,* a work Cheever's biographer, Scott Donaldson, appropriately identifies as the author's "Suburban Sequence."[45] In this collection of eight stories, seven of which had appeared in the *New Yorker* between 1953 and 1958, Cheever most fully maps out the suburban New York terrain that he would revisit on occasion in his subsequent short story collections of the 1960s, *Some People, Places, and Things That Will Not Appear in My Next Novel* (1961) and *The Brigadier and the Golf Widow* (1964), and again in his suburban novel of 1969, *Bullet Park.* In contrast to his later short story collections, *The Housebreaker of Shady Hill* is set entirely in one specific landscape, the fictional New York suburb of Shady Hill.[46] By creating a single, unified fictional milieu, what Meanor calls a "mythopoeic cosmos," Cheever offers in this sequence his cartography of the suburban experience, mapping the lives of his characters against the backdrop of an affluent suburban landscape of the 1950s.[47]

More coherent and restrained than the later *Bullet Park,* this sequence creates through its intertwined stories a composite vision of a society compromised by its social dynamics. Exploiting the polyvocal potential of the story sequence form, Cheever depicts a parade of liminal figures—a thief, an aging and doomed former athlete, a self-absorbed alcoholic, and others—who occupy various positions on the periphery of Shady Hill's social landscape. But rather than contributing to a vision of the wealthy suburb as a dynamic, heterogeneous terrain, these marginal players are silenced: The thief magically reforms himself, the athlete is killed off, the drunk remains mired in his solipsistic delusions. Indeed, the fates of such characters suggests a desire on the part of the author to reveal Shady Hill's dogged persistence in keeping up "appearances," a trait that is nowhere more apparent than in the treatment Cheever affords issues of class distinction. Although *The Housebreaker of Shady Hill* does feature a number of economically marginal figures, even their destinies demonstrate Shady Hill society's compulsive need to maintain class prerogative.

In approaching economic and class issues in Cheever's suburban fiction, it is important to note the socioeconomic contrast between the inhabitants of "Cheever Country" and those of "cookie-cutter" suburban developments like Levittown. In contrast to the homogeneous, petit-bourgeois subdivision towns, the northern Westchester County exurbs that provide the model for Shady Hill were wealthy areas, signifying the affluence of homeowners through expansive lots and individualized archi-tectural styles.[48] Indeed, the inhabitants of Cheever's suburban world resist and fear nothing more than the specter of Levittown-like develop-ments popping up on their horizon, as for them the terms "development" and "subdivision" foretell an incursion of economic and social inferiors into their high-status landscape.[49] As one resident of Shady Hill imagines it, lying constantly in wait is "a stranger at the gates—unwashed, tirelessly scheming, foreign, the father of disorderly children who would ruin their rose gardens and depreciate their real-estate investment."[50] Observations such as this suggest the extent to which Cheever's environmental concerns intertwine with matters of class consciousness; in Shady Hill the landscape itself becomes the primary marker of social distinction.

If landscape provides the means into examining class dynamics in Cheever's suburbia, the author treats the physical environment itself only indirectly and sporadically. In contrast to the well-defined topography characteristic of the short story sequence from its origins in nineteenth-century regionalist writing onward, *The Housebreaker of Shady Hill* cre-ates an elusive sense of physical place. Lynne Waldeland is quite right when she suggests that "one immediately notices how few trees, ponds, winding roads and gently sloping hills contribute to one's sense that one knows Shady Hill."[51] Cheever relegates to the margins his depictions of the natural environment; typically nature appears in spectral form, as the dream vision of a character longing for a more elemental connection to landscape and place. Itself a tacit comment on the commodification of the suburban environment, Cheever's tendency to omit natural details in his depiction of setting leaves characterization and descriptions of architectural and decorative tastes to carry the weight of establishing a sense of place. As Waldeland concludes, for Cheever "setting is more a matter of artifacts and is created heavily by accounts of manners."[52]

And yet matters of landscape are by no means ignored in the collection; instead, Cheever situates the Shady Hill terrain through the sustained use of contrasting visions of landscape. It is no coincidence that the city, when it appears in this collection, is associated with violence, promiscuity, and unsavory financial practices, for the author uses the urban terrain as both a contrast to the seemingly placid, contented life in Shady Hill and a reminder of the very nearness of such social woes. In contrast to the threatening urban environment, Cheever does offer several lyrical descriptions of the natural beauty of the Shady Hill environs, although they are often undercut by the reminder of the fragility of this exurban paradise, as is the case in this passage from "O Youth and Beauty!":

> Then it is a summer night, a wonderful summer night. The passengers on the eight-fifteen see Shady Hill—if they notice it at all—in a bath of placid golden light. . . . On Alewives Lane sprinklers continue to play after dark. You can smell the water. The air seems as fragrant as it is dark—it is a delicious element to walk through. . . . Mrs. Carver—Harry Farquarson's mother-in-law—glances up at the sky and asks, "*Where* did all the stars come from?" She is old and foolish, and yet she is right: Last night's stars seem to have drawn to themselves a new range of galaxies, and the night sky is not dark at all, except where there is a tear in the membrane of light. In the unsold house lots near the track a hermit thrush is singing. (215)

Seen from the perspective of the passing commuter train, itself both the community's lifeline and a reminder of the constant rush of urban activity, Shady Hill appears an idyllic landscape in this passage.[53] And yet there are incongruities in the description: The contradictory interplay of light and darkness is reconciled only with the mention of an occasional "tear in the membrane of light," an image whose violence disrupts the otherwise pastoral imagery. Even more telling is the closing image of the passage: The hermit thrush, whose warble provides the soundtrack for this lyrical moment, can be found only in the unsold house lots near the track, places that—given the ongoing process of suburban development—cannot remain the last outposts of the natural world indefinitely. Indeed, the thrush's home is even at that moment already compromised and is only masquerading as "nature": Already parceled out into "house lots," the fate of the remaining natural landscape is sealed.

In addition to his counterpoised images of the threatening urban world and the tranquil but doomed natural environment, Cheever offers contrasting visions of the hamlet of Shady Hill itself, creating distinctions between different sections of the town through description of architecture and artifact. For example, Francis Weed, the neglected and troubled protagonist of "The Country Husband," resides in the Blenhollow neighborhood, an area whose wealthy expansiveness is suggested by a description of the opulence of the Weed family home: "The Weeds' Dutch Colonial house was larger than it appeared to be from the driveway. The living room was spacious and divided like Gaul into three parts. . . . The room was polished and tranquil, and from the windows that opened to the west there was some late-summer sunlight, brilliant and clear as water. Nothing here was neglected; nothing had not been burnished" (326).

In contrast to the shimmering magnificence of the Blenhollow home, a place where a brilliant sheen connotes not only wealth but also tranquility—or, better put, the seeming tranquility that can be purchased with sufficient wealth—other neighborhoods are not nearly so well heeled. Maple Dell, for example, offers a stark contrast to Blenhollow's opulence; as the reader learns in the story "The Trouble of Marcie Flint," Maple Dell "was more like a development than anything else in Shady Hill. It was the kind of place where the houses stand cheek by jowl, all of them white frame, all of them built twenty years ago, and parked beside each was a car that seemed more substantial than the house itself" (291).

Maple Dell's relative shabbiness is symbolically central to "The Trouble of Marcie Flint," a story that most directly demonstrates Shady Hill's exclusionary sense of class prerogative. The narrative chronicles the Shady Hill Village Council's resistance to building a public library in the town, for fear that it might make the town more appealing to "developments." The Town Council's uneasiness over the potential incursion of lower-class development dwellers is voiced by Mrs. Selfredge, an elitist spokesperson who fears that, should the library be constructed, all of Shady Hill might begin to resemble Maple Dell or—worse yet—the neighboring village of Carsen Park. In a passage that demonstrates her fear of encroaching "suburbia," Mrs. Selfredge reacts to the continued lobbying efforts on behalf of the library by a Maple Dell resident: "So it wasn't over and done with, Mrs. Selfredge thought indignantly. They wouldn't rest until Shady Hill was nothing but developments from one end to the other. The colorless, hard-pressed people of the Carsen Park project, with their flocks of children, and their monthly interest payments, and their picture windows, and their view of identical houses and treeless, muddy, unpaved streets seemed to threaten her most cherished concepts—her lawns, her pleasures, her property rights, even her self-esteem" (296).

In confronting the specter of large-scale suburban development, the councilwoman invokes and decries the very image of "suburbia" that was celebrated in the popular media as the promised land of the new middle class. And in this sense, the voice of Mrs. Selfredge helps to clarify and illuminate the sense of suburban place Cheever constructs throughout the collection: As a social landscape characterized by "possessive individualism," Shady Hill defines itself in opposition to the petit-bourgeois terrain of suburbia. One's "sense of place" in this affluent environment has as much to do with "property rights" and other verifiable evidence of exclusive financial and social standing as it does with any connection to the lived, natural environment itself.

Indeed, this story suggests that the class prerogative of Shady Hill residents relies on their continued ability to define themselves in opposition to the growing physical and social landscape of suburbia. They do so by controlling access to the very cultural capital they possess, as the debate over the proposed public library demonstrates. A heated conversation between the mayor of Shady Hill and Noel Mackham, a proponent of the library and resident of Maple Dell, illustrates the centrality of cultural distinction in maintaining the social landscape of the town:

> "I just want to say a few words in favor of a public library," [Mackham] rasped. "When I was a kid we were poor. There wasn't much good about the way we lived, but there was this Carnegie Library. I started going there when I was about eight. I guess I went there regularly for ten years. I read everything—philosophy, novels, technical books, poetry, ships' logs. . . . For me, the library amounted to the difference between success and failure. . . . I just hate to think of bringing my kids up in a place where there isn't any library."
>
> "Well, of course, we know what you mean," Mayor Simmons said. "But I don't think that's quite the question. The question is not one of denying books to our children. Most of us in Shady Hill have libraries of our own." (292)

The mayor's proprietary response to Mackham indicates what is at stake in the library debate, which turns on the issue of controlling cultural capital. If, as Bourdieu argues, the possession and consumption of cultural goods serve to "fulfill a social function of legitimating social differences," then the Town Council's resistance to a public library represents in microcosmic form the drive toward maintaining social "place" in Shady Hill.[54] Denying access to cultural capital as a means of separating themselves from the lower classes, the residents of Shady Hill wield cultural distinction as their primary method of controlling the environment. As a result, their landscape becomes heavily invested with markers of cultural distinction, a symbolic field signifying the elite status of its inhabitants.

The symbolic resonance of landscape itself is a central factor in the title story, which begins the collection by foregrounding the relationship between environmental concerns and class status that recurs throughout. Here we learn in first-person narration the story of Johnny Hake, a member of the old New York upper middle class who, as a result of running into dire financial straits after losing his job, turns briefly to a life of crime, breaking into and burglarizing his neighbors' homes in Shady Hill to support himself. Although he actually commits just one successful robbery, Hake's mounting sense of mental and even spiritual anguish over his thievery is only finally assuaged when he has an epiphany while on the way to burgle another of his neighbors' homes: Caught in a sudden evening rain shower, Hake is cleansed and rejuvenated. Declaring that "the rain on my head . . . showed me the extent of my freedom" (268), Hake decides on the spot to give up his short-lived career as a housebreaker and thief. The next day he gets his old job back, and on the following evening, after securing an advance on his paycheck, he secretly returns the money he had stolen from his neighbor, Warburton. No one ever catches on to Hake's experiment in crime, and in the end all is right in his world. In fact, things work out so well for Johnny Hake—Cheever closes the story with the image of Hake "whistling merrily in the dark" on his walk home after returning the stolen money—that one might be tempted to conclude that the story is no more than a tale of tremendous good fortune. Nevertheless, through the eyes of this marginal figure in Shady Hill society, Cheever illustrates both the visibility of markers of class status and the extent to which such commodification of the landscape serves to create a superficial, alienating environment.

As narrator, Johnny Hake begins the tale—and the collection—by drawing attention to both his old East Side New York upbringing and the nature of his current existence in Shady Hill. Explaining that he was "conceived in the Hotel St. Regis, born in the Presbyterian Hospital, raised on Sutton Place, christened and confirmed in St. Bartholomew's," and later met his wife, Christina, "at one of those big cotillions at the Waldorf," Hake then goes on to offer his vision of his current life: "I served four years in the Navy, have four kids now, and live in a *banlieue* called Shady Hill. We have a nice house with a garden and a place outside for cooking meat, and on summer nights, sitting there with the kids and looking into the front of Christina's dress as she bends over to salt the steaks, or just gazing at the lights of Heaven, I am as thrilled as I am thrilled by more hardy and dangerous pursuits, and I guess this is what is meant by the pain and sweetness of life" (253).

Hake's exposition is significant in that it suggests the insular and tepid nature of the suburban experience—shown through the contrast of the pinnacle of his current life, the recurring backyard barbeque, with the dramatic recitation of his early history, a compendium of sacramental events enacted against a monumental New York backdrop. Moreover, Hake's autobiographical recountings—which remind us that he is a member of the old New York middle class, an old-money East Sider—along with his faintly disappointed, if not anesthetized, tone when recounting his existence today ("*I guess* this is what is meant by the pain and sweetness of life")—suggest that his current position in the suburbs is less the culmination of his life's plans than a *retreat,* both physically and psychologically speaking, from the metropolitan milieu that forms the basis of his identity.[55]

In this sense, Hake embodies the spirit of the Shady Hill populace, exurbanites whose varying measures of affluence dictate both their level of comfort in this highly stratified society and their ability to disconnect themselves from the concerns of the workaday world. And while most of the male residents are, like Hake, commuters who daily ride the train to and from the city, their most readily apparent connections to the urban landscape are symbolic; such is the case with the Warburtons, who have—in a gesture underscoring their urbanity—imported to their own home the marble floor of the old Ritz Hotel in New York. If, as Bourdieu argues, the power of cultural capital such as this "can only be acquired by means of a sort of withdrawal from economic necessity," then the investment of the Shady Hill landscape with such markers of social distinction signifies a successful "withdrawal" from financial striving and need.[56] Nevertheless, this commodification of landscape also works toward rendering Shady Hill an artificial and ostentatious environment, a place where the persistent display of class prerogative creates a materialistic, but ultimately unfulfilling, sense of place. Hake reveals as much as he reacts to his burglary of the Warburtons. Dismayed by his actions, Hake sits alone in his kitchen and rhapsodizes about his lost connections to the natural landscape of his youth: "Oh, I never knew that a man could be so miserable and that the mind could open up so many chambers and fill them with self-reproach! Where were the trout streams of my youth, and other innocent pleasures? The wet-leather smell of the loud waters and the keen woods after a smashing rain; or at opening day the summer breezes smelling like the grassy breath of Holsteins—your head would swim—and all the brooks full then (or so I imagined, in the dark kitchen) of trout, our sunken treasure. I was crying" (258).

Pastoral reveries such as this are common in Cheever's fiction, and they consistently suggest a sense of alienation from the natural world occasioned by the commodification of the suburban landscape. Cheever, like Fitzgerald in *The Great Gatsby*, characteristically uses nostalgia for lost natural landscapes as a means of critiquing the materialistic environment of the affluent suburb. He presents the suburban environment as a pale imitation of the "real thing," a place where nature itself is subsumed under "zoning" considerations and becomes merely another element of maintaining visual evidence of dominant class status.

Cheever examines this primacy of appearances through his portrayal of Hake, whose position on the fringes of Shady Hill's social structure makes him a keen observer of his society's materialistic practices. Indeed, Hake sees his own financial predicament in terms of surface appearances. Himself little more than an "organization man," an underlying recently fired from his post at a cling-wrap manufacturer, Hake dreams of his former job in a manner that parodies Shady Hill's obsession with superficial concerns: "I had been dreaming about wrapping bread in colored parablendeum Filmex. I had dreamed a full-page spread in a national magazine: BRING SOME COLOR INTO YOUR BREADBOX! The page was covered with jewel-toned loaves of bread—turquoise bread, ruby bread, and bread the color of emeralds. In my sleep the idea seemed to me like a good one" (256). The image of "jewel-toned" loaves of bread dramatically underscores Hake's problem: Living in a culture driven by commodity fetishism, a world that values evidence of conspicuous wealth beyond concerns of mere sustenance—the prize in his dreamed breadbox is after all the dazzling, jewellike Filmex, not the bread itself—Hake must at all costs "maintain appearances" in the midst of his financial crisis.

That Hake's predicament is indeed a matter of appearances is made clear in his one actual burglary. At home after the Warburtons' party, Hake thinks about his position relative to these ostentatious neighbors and concludes that "I had never yearned for anyone the way I yearned that night for money" (257). Decided on his plan, he dons what will become his official thieving outfit—"some old blue sneakers and a pair of pants and a dark pullover" (257)—and heads back to the Warburtons'. Cheever's subsequent image of Hake, in his commoner's garb, quietly stealing across the living room of the Warburton home, crossing the floor of "black and white marble from the old Ritz" (255), perfectly captures the link among appearances, taste, and class status at the heart of this story and much of the collection. Intentionally or not, Hake masquerades as the lower-class "other," the "stranger at the gates" so feared by Shady Hill residents, to effect his crimes. That he is able, at the end of the tale, to "reform" himself and sneak back into the Warburton home to return the money renders the spectral image of the lower-class intruder just that: Reinstating Shady Hill's logic of proprietary appearances, Hake's reformation also reinforces the illusion of the elite suburb as a placid, untroubled landscape.

Still, Hake struggles in the wake of his burglary with the incongruity between the nature of his crime and the prosperous charm of his suburban world: "Had I looked, the next morning, from my bathroom window into the evil-smelling ruin of some great city, the shock of recalling what I had done might not have been so violent, but the moral bottom had dropped out of my world without changing a mote of sunlight" (258). Resisting the sense that he has somehow corrupted Shady Hill, Hake instead projects his newfound criminal sensibility onto the urban landscape. The workday following his burglary finds him in the city, surrounded by evidence of all sorts of financial treachery; after reading on the inbound train of robberies in the Bronx and Brooklyn, Hake sees a customer steal a tip in a midtown restaurant, and later he is propositioned by a business partner to join in a deal the partner describes as a "steal" and a "burglary." Physically sickened by the offer, Hake retreats to Shady Hill, only to be driven by financial necessity to other attempted burglaries before his eventual moment of realization and reform.

Considering Hake's increasing desperation, the ecstatically happy ending to the tale appears difficult to fathom. Waldeland suggests as much when she argues that Cheever's happy ending "would be irritating if it weren't clear that the point of the story is finally the importance of being in phase with the moral order of one's world."[57] And yet it seems that the "point" of the story, to say nothing of the "moral order" of Shady Hill, is more of a mystery than Waldeland would have it. For although Hake eventually retrieves his "old life," his experience as the housebreaker of Shady Hill temporarily positions him as a figure on the periphery of his suburban society, one whose magical reformation replaces the specter of economic struggle with the illusion of affluent self-satisfaction. That the reinstated social order of Shady Hill is predicated on a degree of such willful ignorance is driven home by Hake's position at the end of the story, after he returns Warburton's money:

> As I was walking away from the house, a police car drew up beside me, and a patrolman I know cranked down the window and asked, "What are you doing out at this time of night, Mr. Hake?"

"I'm walking the dog," I said cheerfully. There was no dog in sight, but they didn't look. "Here, Toby! Here, Toby! *Good* dog!" I called, and off I went, whistling merrily in the dark. (269)

Cheerily waving off questioning policeman while walking an imaginary dog in the dark of night, Hake hardly reflects a sense of "moral order" in Shady Hill at all; instead, he remains something of an outsider, a "child of darkness"—as he had earlier described himself—who exits the story, and inaugurates the collection, as an emblem of the self-delusion among Cheever's affluent suburbanites.[58]

Cheever explores the theme of self-delusion further in "O Youth and Beauty!"—a story that recounts the tragic downfall of another peripheral character, one whose social misfortunes are tied to the loss of youth and a consequent falling stature within the Shady Hill community. Cash Bentley, the ironically named protagonist, relies on his still-youthful appearance as his ticket to acceptance in class-conscious world of the Shady Hill country club set: "Cash and his wife, Louise, had two children, and they lived in a medium-cost ranchhouse on Alewives Lane. They belonged to the country club, although they could not afford it, but in the case of the Bentleys nobody ever pointed this out, and Cash was one of the best-liked men in Shady Hill. He was still slender—he was careful about his weight—and he walked to the train in the morning with a light and vigorous step that marked him as an athlete. His hair was thin, and there were mornings when his eyes looked bloodshot, but this did not detract much from a charming quality of stubborn youthfulness" (210-11). A former track star, Cash trades on his fading youthful glory in an effort to retain his otherwise imperiled position in the community; at the end of nearly every "long, large, Saturday-night party" in Shady Hill, Cash—in response to being chided by his friend Trace Bearden "about his age and thinning hair"— arranges the living-room furniture in the shape of a track and ritualistically runs a hurdle race, to the cheers of the onlookers. Meant as an affirmation of his "stubborn youthfulness," his sole remaining piece of cultural capital,

Cash's bizarre race retains symbolic overtones: Hurdling his neighbors' furniture, Cash—if only for a moment—symbolically transcends his meager lot in life.

After finally failing in one of his hurdle races—"it was a piece of carving on a chest that brought him down, and down he came like a ton of bricks" (213)—Cash is confined to his home to recuperate, and he becomes embittered. One evening during his convalescence, he overhears the playful sounds of a "young people's party" next door; eavesdropping on the party guests, Cash reflects bitterly on his own loss of youth and social stature, on his fall from the garden:

> There is nothing on their minds but the passing summer nights. Taxes and the elastic in underpants—all the unbeautiful facts of life that threaten to crush the breath out of Cash—have not touched a single figure in this garden. Then jealousy seizes him—such savage and bitter jealousy that he feels ill.
>
> He does not understand what separates him from these children in the garden next door. He has been a young man. He has been a hero. He has been adored and happy and full of animal spirits, and now he stands in a dark kitchen, deprived of his athletic prowess, his impetuousness, his good looks—of everything that means anything to him. He feels as if the figures in the next yard are the specters from some party in that past where all his tastes and desires lie, and from which he has been cruelly removed. He feels like a ghost of the summer evening. (216)

Recalling Johnny Hake's pastoral reverie, Cash's longing for the garden suggests estrangement from his physical and social landscape. Like Hake, who also refers to himself as a "ghost," Cash senses the loss of his social position in Shady Hill. Eventually shunned by the community for his increasingly distant behavior, he makes a last bid to regain his "youth and beauty," compulsively arranging his own furniture for another race. He instructs his wife, Louise, to fire the starter's pistol, which she does as

Cash hurdles over the sofa: "The pistol went off and Louise got him in midair. She shot him dead" (218). The ambiguity of Louise's final action is left unresolved with this abrupt ending; nevertheless, Cash's ultimate downfall underscores the superficiality of the suburban dream, one that sees the promise of life revealed in material success, youth, and beauty. As Meanor notes, "Cash's essential emptiness points to only one cause: the materialistic, narcissistic American dream that proposes suburbia as its Edenic reward of eternal youth."[59] And in this regard, Cash Bentley serves as a precursor to Neddy Merrill, the protagonist of "The Swimmer," a story that renders most forcefully Cheever's increasingly bleak vision of suburban alienation.

Published in Cheever's 1964 collection *The Brigadier and the Golf Widow*, "The Swimmer" chronicles the downfall and expulsion of one member of a suburban community. In a sense, this story continues the examination of class concerns put forth in "The Enormous Radio" and the *Shady Hill* stories; if Irene Westcott learns of her own economic vulnerability by witnessing the plight of others, and the stories of Johnny Hake and Cash Bentley emphasize exurban class consciousness, Neddy Merrill's fate reveals the unwillingness of the upper middle class to tolerate financial weakness. Over the course of Neddy's swim down the Lucinda River we learn of his financial setbacks, and in the closing image of the story we see the price he must pay for them: Alone in the twilight, locked out of his own empty house, Neddy Merrill has been ousted from the very society of which he had once been the perfect symbol. Despite the thematic similarities to previous works, in "The Swimmer" Cheever approaches the theme of class hierarchy in a decidedly bleaker fashion. His increasingly dire treatment of the class issue in this and other of his later suburban works is part of what Richard Rupp has observed to be a more generalized "darkening of vision" in Cheever's suburban fiction of the 1960s.[60]

The quasi-mythical journey Cheever presents in "The Swimmer" may be the most fully realized of the author's ruminations on the unforgiving social structure of the suburban upper middle class. Perhaps more than any other story in Cheever's suburban story cycles, "The Swimmer" reveals the rigid social hierarchy that lies beneath the seeming ease and contentment of his Westchester. Indeed, as Waldeland notes, the "real point" of "The Swimmer," notwithstanding the general air of mystery surrounding the goings-on in the story, lies in "the juxtaposition of the celebratory motive of Neddy's act with the social realities that emerge as the story progresses, realities that have to do with the role wealth and social status play in this world which Neddy wishes to invest with legendary beauty and meaning."[61] Waldeland's point is well taken: More than the story of one man's economic woes, "The Swimmer" is most provocative as a study of the class-bound identity of an affluent suburban community. Over the course of Neddy's swim we learn as much about his friends and neighbors as we do about Neddy. Eventually Neddy's downward economic spiral renders him an outcast, rejected by his neighbors in Bullet Park, a society that perfectly exemplifies Benedict Anderson's notion of the "imagined community."

As Anderson notes, all communities are "imaginary," in the sense that they posit a fictive "horizontal comradeship" as their very foundation.[62] Such a definition would seem to fit Cheever's Westchester—a place characterized by, more than anything else, its familiar cocktail parties and shared commuter trains—quite nicely. Indeed, the panoramic sweep of the county offered by the narrator at the opening of this story reinforces just such a sense of "horizontal comradeship": "It was one of those midsummer Sundays when everyone sits around saying, 'I *drank* too much last night.' You might have heard it whispered by the parishioners leaving church, heard it from the lips of the priest himself, struggling with his cassock in the *vestiarium,* heard it from the golf links and the tennis courts, heard it from the wildlife preserve where the leader of the Audubon group was suffering from a terrible hangover. 'I *drank* too much,' said Donald Westerhazy. 'We all *drank* too much,' said Lucinda Merrill" (603).

United by their suffering from the previous night's festivities, the denizens of Bullet Park seem to feel and speak as one as the story opens. Moreover, Neddy Merrill appears as the perfect embodiment of the Bullet Park spirit: As we first meet Neddy, a man who "might have been compared to a summer's day, particularly the last hours of one" (603), he is sitting by the green water of the Westerhazys' pool, "one hand in it, one around a glass of gin" (602). Neddy's posture, at once narcissistic and hedonistic, reflects the ease and self-satisfaction of the Bullet Park community. And his plan to traverse the eight miles from the Westerhazys' to his own home in Bullet Park by swimming through the backyard pools of all his neighbors would seem to be an act meant to underscore the communal connections, or the "horizontal comradeship," of the community. In envisioning himself as an "explorer" who will bring together this disparate assemblage of private pools into a single body of water—which he names, after his wife, the Lucinda River—Neddy attempts to position himself at the center of his "imagined community."

As much as Neddy's swim reflects his desire to underscore community connections, the pastoral impulse also behind the act is unmistakable: By undertaking this journey, Neddy hopes symbolically to transform a materialistic landscape—as exemplified by what may be the most loaded signifier on the suburban landscape, the swimming pool—into a natural environment once again. But at the outset of Neddy's journey, Cheever offers a vision of the horizon that foretells the eventual dissolution of the protagonist's pastoral dream: "In the west there was a massive stand of cumulus cloud so like a city seen from a distance . . . that it might have had a name. Lisbon. Hackensack" (603). The juxtaposition of exotic and mundane locales here suggests the incongruity of Neddy's dream-vision, a fact that becomes more apparent as he gets halfway through his journey and the skies darken: "It would storm. The stand of cumulus cloud—that city—had risen and darkened, and while he sat there he heard the percussiveness of thunder again. . . . A train whistle blew and he wondered what time it had gotten to be. Four? Five?" (606). Neddy's disorientation suggests his misreading of the landscape; like Fitzgerald, Cheever pairs booming peals of thunder with the roar of a passing commuter train to emphasize the elusiveness of pastoral dreams in the suburban context. Moreover, through the recurring image of a dark, looming city on the horizon, Cheever undercuts Neddy's desire to transcend the material trappings of his environment.

Nevertheless, as he prepares for his swim, Neddy surveys the terrain ahead with a "cartographer's eye" (603), attempting to map both the physical and the symbolic landscapes he hopes to traverse. For Neddy, who considers himself a "pilgrim," a "legendary figure," and "a man with a destiny" (604), sees his swim in symbolic terms. Robert Slabey is quite right in arguing that "Neddy's westward swim is into the eternal country of the imagination"; more than just an effort to imaginatively reinvent a lost landscape, Neddy's swim—and his creation of the Lucinda River—also amount to an effort to reenvision the Bullet Park landscape and community in his own image.[63] He underscores this notion of his journey as a symbolic reimagining of community in his final thought before leaving the Westerhazys' home and beginning his journey: "He knew that he would find friends all along the way; friends would line the banks of the Lucinda River" (604). And, for a time, Neddy does find friends; however, he eventually falls from grace within his own imagined community, as the revelation of his financial setbacks is played out against evidence of the increasingly mercenary and fractious social fabric of Bullet Park society.

The first turning point in Neddy's journey comes when he finds a dry pool and a deserted house at the Welchers; the name is significant, as Meanor notes, in its phonetic similarity to *welshers,* or those who have failed to meet financial obligations.[64] And that may indeed be the case: The Welchers—whose dinner invitations, we learn, had rated only regrets from the Merrills in the past—have put their house up for sale, suggesting their inability to meet the financial obligations of life in Bullet Park. This discovery leaves Neddy "disappointed and mystified" (606), and with good reason: The disappearance of the Welchers causes a break in the

[handwritten margin note: He "knows" he would find friends]

Lucinda River and also foreshadows Neddy's own eventual demise. On leaving the Welchers', Neddy must cross Route 424 to enter the village of Lancaster. A symbolic as well as literal crossing, this "most difficult portage" (607) finds Neddy humiliated, standing amid the roadside debris, jeered at by the passing motorists, even pelted with a beer can hurled from one of the passing cars. In contrast to Johnny Hake, who briefly masquerades as the lower-class "other" before his eventual reform, Neddy's debased position on the side of Route 424 foretells his irrevocable fall from social standing. As subsequent events reveal, the highway serves as a marker of this community's rigid social stratification; Neddy is moving downward through the social ranks, and he realizes as he prepares to cross the road that "he could not go back" (607) if he wanted to.

Neddy encounters a vision of the future as he enters the Lancaster public pool, a commoners' spot teeming with swimmers. The dominant image of this scene comes in a description of the lifeguards. Cheever's rigid, abrupt rendering of these authority figures and their actions—they are described as "A pair of lifeguards in a pair of towers" who "blew police whistles at what seemed to be regular intervals and abused the swimmers through a public address system" (608)—underscores the notion that Neddy has entered another world, one characterized by its strict disciplinary superstructure. After initially fearing that he "might contaminate himself—damage his own prosperousness and charm" (608) by swimming in the "murk" of this public pool, Neddy eventually dives in, only to be accosted by the lifeguards. He is thrown out of the pool, for failing to wear an "identification disk." This is a telling moment for Neddy: Captured by the penetrating, panoptic gaze of the lifeguards, he is ousted from the public pool for being a "nobody." In much the same manner, he is finally outcast from his own community, a nonentity in the eyes of his peers.

The decisive moment comes at one of his final stops, the Biswangers', where a party is taking place. After referring to Neddy as a "gate crasher," Grace Biswanger is overheard telling her guests that Neddy "went for broke overnight" (611). Neddy's reaction to these words reveals the measure of his alienation: He thinks to himself that Grace "was always talking about money. It was worse than eating your peas off a knife" (611). Still clinging to codes of conduct and taste that once distinguished him as a member of the elite set, Neddy does not yet realize that the "vulgar" Biswangers now epitomize Bullet Park society. Only after learning at his penultimate stop that his former mistress, Shirley Adams, has replaced him with another, younger man does Neddy seem to understand his plight. Leaving Shirley Adams's property, he begins to cry. It is in this fallen condition that he approaches his own deserted house; alone, and utterly rejected by his community, Neddy at the close of the story stands as a symbol of the tenuousness and treacherousness of upper-middle-class, suburban affluence.

🏠 🏠 🏠

Cheever's focus in "The Swimmer" on the acute class consciousness of affluent exurbanites provides as well the focal point for the 1968 Columbia Pictures film version of the story. Directed by Frank Perry and starring Burt Lancaster as Neddy Merrill, *The Swimmer* continually draws attention to Neddy's economic setbacks—more so than does the story—and expands on the theme of Neddy's rejection by the other members of Bullet Park society.[65] Screenwriter Eleanor Perry, in adapting Cheever's story, faced a difficult dilemma: how to convey on the screen a story that resides so much in the realm of imagination and mystery. And while Perry's script does retain the general air of mystery that pervades Cheever's story, her ample foreshadowing of Neddy's eventual ruin, along with sustained use of dramatic irony, offers the viewer a more privileged interpretive position than does Cheever's story. In viewing *The Swimmer,* one is aware almost throughout of the incongruity between Neddy's vision of his privileged life and the reality of his economic circumstances. Beyond this amplification of the economic theme of the story, Perry's screenplay also emphasizes Neddy's imperiled masculinity. The film draws parallels between Neddy's economic ruin and his now-failing sexual potency—the twilight of his career as a "suburban stud," as his former mistress calls him—as well as his inability to "control" his wild daughters and spendthrift wife, women who have compromised his position as respected father and provider. In effect, then, Perry's take on the story links Neddy's economic and social demise to his failing "manhood" in a more general sense, marking the film version of *The Swimmer* as a study—on many fronts—of the insecurity of the upper-middle-class suburban male.

The connections between Neddy's economic troubles and his deteriorating sense of manhood are set up in the second scene of the film, in which Neddy stops at the Bunkers' pool. Here Neddy's confession of his onetime love for Mrs. Bunker—"I was crazy about you!"—falls on deaf ears, in an exchange that otherwise focuses on the material success of the latter's husband, Howard. After Mrs. Bunker claims that their new pool and filter "cost a bundle, but Howie's had a wonderful year," Howard himself appears on another of his new toys, a riding lawnmower, and proceeds to brag to Neddy about his material acquisitions. As is the case with the Biswangers, Howard's vulgar materialism signals a change in Bullet Park's social manners, part of the shift in prevailing class structure that also brings about Neddy's ouster from the community. The couple appear mystified at Neddy's subsequent discussion about "swimming home," an early indication that his idealistic dream of a return "home" is nothing but that: Bested as both a love interest and as an economic force, Neddy's position at the Bunkers' pool foreshadows his larger fate as the film progresses.

Tied to this scene's conflation of romantic and economic potency is an extended sequence chronicling Neddy's quasi-romantic experience with his former baby-sitter, the twenty-one-year-old Julianne Hooper. This relationship, a curious wholesale addition to the film version, seems based on the story of another of Cheever's characters, Francis Weed of "The Country Husband." Like Neddy in the film version, Francis falls in love with his young baby-sitter; what Francis and the film's version of Neddy share is a desire to recapture their youth through romantic union. Neddy's chivalric vision of his relationship to Julianne, however (at one point he tells her that he will be her "guardian angel," protecting her from the evils of the outside world), is one-sided. Shortly after injuring himself in attempting to leap, stallionlike, over the hurdles in a deserted horse pen (this strange scene itself another borrowing from Cheever, this time from the story of Cash Bentley in "O Youth and Beauty!"), Neddy is rejected by Julianne, who flees, frightened by his advances. As a result of this downfall, it is a visibly debilitated, limping Neddy who is finally rejected for the last time in the scene at the home of his former mistress (renamed Shirley Abbot in the film version). The exchange between Neddy and Shirley in this scene, by far the longest of the film, underscores the sense that Neddy's economic failure and his emasculation are to be considered related phenomena, perhaps even reciprocal processes. In writing off their affair by telling Neddy that "I lied about loving it anywhere with you. . . . You bored me to tears" and in rejecting his advances, Shirley reinforces Neddy's impotence, laying the groundwork for his humiliation at the hands of the working class in the subsequent scene at the public pool in Lancaster.

The public pool scene—expanded and repositioned near the end of the narrative in the film version—is a curious sequence, in that it most clearly demonstrates the depths to which Neddy has fallen while at the same time offering the most excuses for his downfall, effectively pinning his failure on the aberrant behavior of his wife and daughters. Upon entering the pool, Neddy is in an utterly fallen position: After unsuccessfully begging the attendant to waive the 50 cent admission fee and subsequently borrowing the money from an acquaintance, Neddy must endure the humiliation of the public pool staff, twice being sent to the showers to wash himself off before being admitted to the overcrowded, overchlorinated pool. After completing his swim and managing to drag himself out of the pool, Neddy is accosted by Howie, the man who had lent him the entrance fee, and Hank, the Merrills' former grocer. Sensing Neddy's vulnerability, an irate Hank sarcastically asks, "What's the matter, Mr. Merrill, your friends' pools run out of water? How do you like our water, Mr. Merrill?" Hank's weighty question reinforces the distinction Perry builds between the tranquil pools that dot the suburban landscape and the public pool of lower-class Lancaster, which is so ludicrously crowded as to render Neddy's attempts to swim across nearly impossible. In contrast to the scenes shot at the homes of Neddy's acquaintances, whose private swimming pools are framed by opulent, manicured natural surroundings, the desultory setting of the public pool emphasizes the sense that Neddy's fall from stature has also left him ousted from the suburban landscape and now merely a commoner, simply one of the crowd.

Indeed, in the conversation that ensues between Neddy and Hank, it becomes apparent that Neddy has sunk not only *to* the level of the working class, but actually *below* it. We learn that Neddy had failed to pay his bills at the bar where Howie used to serve him and at Hank's grocery. And while Howie's wife attacks Neddy, referring to him as "the first deadbeat we ever got in our place," Hank suggests that the Merrills most likely went broke because of Lucinda's outrageous spending habits: "You oughta see the orders I had to send up to their place: French strawberry jam his wife made me stock for her. American strawberries aren't good enough for her. . . . Hearts of palm, hearts of artichoke, hearts of this, hearts of that. That's some rich diet you have up there." The language here is ironic, in that the loss of Neddy's "rich" lifestyle is in effect pinned on matters of the "heart." That is, here near the end of the film we get the distinct impression that Neddy's adoration of his careless wife is what has led him astray. Moreover, as Hank, Howie, and their wives begin to discuss the reckless behavior of Neddy's daughters, who had "wrecked cars" and engaged in other aberrant behavior that forced Neddy to pay off reporters to "keep their names out of the papers," Neddy emerges ever more clearly as a tragic hero. This scene suggests that Neddy's financial security, as well as his sense of manhood itself, has been undercut by the wrongdoings of the women in his life. In specifically gendering Neddy's problems in this manner at the close, *The Swimmer* positions the suburban male as a doubly imperiled figure, one whose need to maintain class status is undercut by his inability to maintain control over his domestic affairs.[66] The film's implicit demonization of the women in Neddy's life sets them up as the root cause of all of his problems, offering—in contrast to the story—something of an "answer" to the riddle of his life and his downfall. In this sense, the film version of "The Swimmer" anticipates what would become a recurring theme in suburban film, as Hollywood would continue over the ensuing decades to depict the suburbs as a threatening terrain for the male head of household.

If such attention to matters of gender identity—and more specifically to the vulnerability of the male and the treachery of the female—sets the film version apart from the story, ultimately both versions stand as indictments of the intolerance of Neddy's suburban community. Like the story, the film version emphasizes the irony of the class disparity apparent in Neddy's appearance at the Biswangers' party. Perry sets this scene up to emphasize the change in social manners the Biswangers represent. In contrast to the urbane sense of decorum that prevails at Neddy's other visits in the neighborhood, the Biswangers' party is a raucous affair, complete with loud rock music in the background, poorly attired guests, and a man doing a "cannonball" leap into the pool. A measure of the shift in social standards in this affluent suburb, Perry's take on the Biswangers' party suggests that what Cheever's suburban residents most fear has come to pass: The "stranger at the gate" has taken over, destroying their carefully constructed veneer of social propriety in the process. But if the behavior of the vulgar Biswangers represents a sea-change in suburban manners, they have learned to maintain the unforgiving standards of the land: Shouting "You crashed in, now crash the hell out," the vulgar, nouveau riche Biswanger physically throws Neddy out of their party and off their grounds.

Even more telling than this scene in terms of landscape concerns is the one that transpires at the Hallorans' pool. The Hallorans are faithfully transcribed from the story, appearing as Cheever had described them: an "elderly couple of enormous wealth" (608) with a penchant for reform and also for nude bathing. But while in the story the Hallorans' plans for "reform" are never specified, in the film we hear the specifics of "The Halloran Proposal": The couple had proposed breaking an old estate into two-acre parcels, rather than the usual five-acre lots. As Mrs. Halloran reads from the local paper, we learn that the plan had met with sharp resistance from local citizens, who felt that it would lead to "overcrowding of the public schools." Daring to take on the prohibitive zoning laws of Bullet Park, the Hallorans indeed emerge as reformers who would challenge the restrictive class structure of their affluent suburban society. Given this information, all the more revealing is the couple's—and particularly Mrs. Halloran's—attitude toward Neddy. Disgusted by Neddy's appearance at their home, Mrs. Halloran insists that her husband not lend him any more money. As Neddy swims their pool and leaves the grounds, Mrs. Halloran mocks his fallen class position, an indication that even the most "reform-minded" of Bullet Park's citizens are unwilling to tolerate evidence of financial failure in their community. The disparity between the Hallorans' token gestures toward the reform of Bullet Park class structure and their rejection of Neddy helps to make apparent the most vital connection between the film and the story: In both narratives, the sense of "community" in Bullet Park remains an imaginary construction, a vulnerable illusion that is broken apart by the specter of a financial downfall.

🏠 🏠 🏠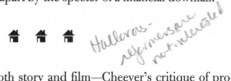

Hallorans—reformers not interested

With "The Swimmer"—both story and film—Cheever's critique of prohibitive social standards in the postwar suburbs reached its peak. In contrast to the utopian myth of suburban "classlessness" promulgated by the popular media in the postwar years, Cheever, throughout much of his suburban fiction, imagined an existence driven by the desire to maintain class prerogative and "place." His affluent suburbanites live their lives against a numbingly materialistic backdrop, and even as they yearn for stronger connections to both landscape and community, they engage in a near-constant struggle to maintain the appearances of class distinction. The effects of such an ongoing battle for class stature form the subject matter of a satirical story from the *Housebreaker of Shady Hill* collection entitled "The Worm in the Apple." This story centers on the Crutchmans, a family of means who seem to live a life of perfect contentment. Driven by his envy of the Crutchmans' inherited wealth, Cheever's unnamed narrator struggles to find the fatal flaw that will one day bring the family down. Consistently thwarted in his attempts to find the "worm" in the Crutchmans' "apple," the narrator eventually must concede the family's true happiness. He closes the story by observing that the Crutchmans "got richer and richer and richer and lived happily, happily, happily, happily" (288). This ecstatically happy ending—like the image of Johnny Hake "whistling merrily in the dark" that concludes "The Housebreaker of Shady Hill"—satirically reinforces the persistence of a continuing class hierarchy in Shady Hill. In putting his wealthy neighbors under the microscope, looking for faults that perhaps resemble his own, the narrator reveals the real "worm in the apple" of Cheever's world, after all: It is the paranoid fear of losing one's place in society—of falling through the cracks. Itself evidence of an unforgiving social structure, this dynamic suffuses the middle-class "communities" of Cheever's fiction, while at the same time always working to break them apart.

Babbit Redux

The Perils of Suburban Masculinity

The final freeze frame of Frank Perry's *The Swimmer* offers a disturbing suburban tableau, highlighting the vulnerability of the suburban male. After tracking Neddy's trek across the ruined grounds of his home, Perry's camera frames the protagonist against the backdrop of the deserted house and shows him pounding on the outside of the locked door, crying, sinking to the ground, and growing increasingly weak until the camera finally freezes on this scene of utter despair. At the completion of his suburban "odyssey," Neddy Merrill bears little resemblance to Homer's Odysseus, and his return "home" brings the devastating realization that there is no home to return *to*. This closing reinforces the notion, alluded to throughout the film, that for men (and particularly male heads of household), the suburban milieu is fraught with peril.

The ending of Perry's film offers a corrective vision to the images of stable patriarchal domesticity so carefully and forcefully promulgated on television in the era of that medium's—and suburbia's—youth. Most television viewers can easily conjure up the classic image of the secure, preternaturally bland suburban "dad" who was such a ubiquitous figure on the sitcoms of the 1950s: [Walking in the front door, briefcase in hand, hailing his wife and the household at large with a hearty "Honey, I'm home," Ward Cleaver or any of his various counterparts became staples not only of television's but indeed of our culture's vision of suburbia] Needless to say, this image of the suburban patriarch was overly simplistic, and as the golden age of the suburban sitcom waned, even the TV industry itself began to offer alternative visions of the suburban family. As Dana Heller has argued, the 1960s' vogue of "monstrous" family sitcoms such as *The Munsters, The Addams Family,* and *Bewitched* offered "allegories of difference," antidotes to the [hypernormal TV families of the 1950s, which had been characterized by highly restrictive gender roles and codes of conduct.]

In eventually recasting the suburban sitcom family, the TV industry was finally catching on to what social critics and commentators had been sensing for the past decade: that something was never quite right with the image of suburban domesticity presented on television in the 1950s.] Indeed, as early as the mid-1950s, the image of the secure suburban patriarch was already being called into question. Particularly vociferous on this point was novelist John Keats, who argued that there was something in the very uniformity of the new suburbs that contributed to the [erosion of masculine power and self-determination:] "the familiar box on the slab contributes toward the father's becoming a woman-bossed, inadequate, money-terrified neuter, instead of helping him to accomplish the American dream of the male: rich, handsome, famous, masterful, and the dispenser of even-handed justice."[2] If Keats's hyperbolic phrasing now sounds distinctly dated, if not downright laughable, his splenetic intensity suggests that the subject of masculinity in the suburban age was [not merely a topic of debate, but one that inspired passionate opinions.][3] Other critics of the suburbs concurred with Keats, and many were nearly as vitriolic as he: Social critics Richard E. Gordon, Katherine K. Gordon, and Max Gunther, for example, lamented the fact that by the end of the 1950s, the suburban man had become "the great sad joke of our time."[4] More notable figures, including Lewis Mumford, put a different spin on the dilemma of the suburban male. Mumford argued that the persistent focus on child rearing in the suburbs was a factor that eroded the quality of adult life. Claiming that the postwar suburb was "not merely a child-centered environment" but instead was itself "based on a childish view of the world," Mumford saw the suburban patriarch not as an emasculated figure, as Keats would have it, but instead as little more than a boy, an overgrown child himself.[5] Suggesting that this psychological return to childhood manifested itself in suburban males' fascination with the sporting life[6] and weekend social events, Mumford concluded that, from the outset in postwar suburbia, "compulsive play fast became the acceptable alternative to compulsive work," as a state of suspended or perpetual boyhood replaced more traditional masculine ambitions.[7]

Taken together, these various social critics' views of the suburban male—as, alternately, a regressed figure trapped in a childlike state, the pathetic target of scornful humor, or an ineffectual, symbolically castrated victim dominated by an all-powerful matriarch—have a decidedly Freudian ring. And while decades of perspective may allow us now to see the exaggerated intensity of the "alarm" being sounded in the early days of suburbia over the future of masculinity, looking back at such observations affords a sense of the breadth and depth of cultural concern over the issue of masculinity in the age of suburbia. Ironically, less than a decade after the publication of this series of works lamenting the fate of the suburban male, Betty Friedan would publish *The Feminine Mystique,* a work that chronicled the dispiriting plight of suburban housewives and labeled the suburbs a "comfortable concentration camp" for women. Friedan argued that the removal to the isolated terrain of suburbia and a consequent confinement to the domestic sphere led to the social and psychological imprisonment of women in the postwar years. In contrast to this argument, the connections male social critics were attempting to establish between the new suburban landscape and a heightened cultural sense of imperiled masculinity remained less fully defined.

Perhaps the most plausible catalyst for this overlap between landscape and gender psychology can be found in the homogeneous design of the new suburbs themselves: At once instantly recognizable and unavoidably disorienting for their very sameness, the postwar suburbs eliminated any visual evidence of difference between residents, thus positioning new suburbanites as interchangeable elements of a planned environment, rather than as individuals active in the shaping of their own space and identities.[8] Indeed, the notion of suburban homogeneity as an alienating and even emasculating reality was not new to the postwar years but was evident as early as Sinclair Lewis's 1922 novel, *Babbitt*. While *Babbitt* is remembered primarily for Lewis's satiric take on the provinciality of middle-class Americans of the 1920s, the central drama of the novel turns on George Babbitt's embattled sense of himself as a man. To be sure, such thematic territory—in Nina Baym's words, the "melodrama of beset manhood"—is familiar enough in American literature; like Rip Van Winkle and Huck Finn, and like such protagonists as Kerouac's Sal Paradise and Updike's Harry "Rabbit" Angstrom in the postwar years, Lewis's George F. Babbitt feels trapped in a feminized domestic sphere and longs to escape and prove himself as a man.[9] What distinguishes Lewis's take on imperiled masculinity is his specific attention to the physical and social landscape of the suburbs as emasculating factors; in this regard he influenced generations of suburban chroniclers to come.

Early in the novel, George F. Babbitt is a vocal, even frenetic supporter of the middle-class suburban lifestyle. As a real estate salesman, Babbitt has a vested interest in promoting the spread of suburbia; and in a speech to a Realtors group, the highlight of his professional life, Babbitt offers his vision of America as a suburban utopia, arguing that "it's the fellow with four to ten thousand a year, say, and an automobile and a nice little family in a bungalow on the edge of town, that makes the wheels of progress go round!" (181). As this speech progresses and Babbitt further develops his suburban vision, he takes care to emphasize the manliness of the suburban experience:

"Our Ideal Citizen—I picture him . . . putting the zip into some store or profession or art. At night he lights up a good cigar, and climbs into the little old 'bus, and maybe cusses the carburetor, and shoots out home. He mows the lawn, or sneaks in some practice putting, and then he's ready for dinner. After dinner . . . maybe the folks next-door drop in and they sit and visit. . . . Then he goes happily to bed, his conscience clear, having contributed his mite to the prosperity of the city and to his own bank-account. . . . Here's the specifications of the Standardized American Citizen! Here's the new generation of Americans: fellows with hair on their chests and smiles in their eyes and adding-machines in their offices. . . . So! In my clumsy way I have tried to sketch the Real He-man, the fellow with Zip and Bang." (181-183)

The prospect of increasing homogenization of landscapes and lifestyles does not bother Babbitt; in fact, he heralds suburban standardization as the key to a "new type of civilization" and thus a cause for celebration: "There are many resemblances between Zenith and . . . other burgs, and I'm darn glad of it! The extraordinary, growing, and sane standardization of stores, offices, streets, hotels, clothes, and newspapers throughout the United States shows how strong and enduring a type is ours" (184). Eventually, however, it is the numbing routine of his suburban life— "Mechanical business . . . selling badly built houses. . . . Mechanical golf and dinner parties and bridge and conversation" (234)—as well as the small-mindedness of his colleagues and neighbors that drives Babbitt to a despair he vainly attempts to counter through an extramarital affair, as well as trips to the Maine wilderness where he longs to live "a life primitive and heroic" (294). Babbitt is driven to Maine

Babbitt neither succeeds nor fails completely in his desire to live of a "Real He-man"; while he eventually gives up his sexual and behavioral transgressions and reluctantly joins the "Good Citizens League," he sees hope for the future in his son, who has defied community standards by secretly marrying and dropping out of college in favor of a factory job. Nonetheless, when Babbitt concludes to his son at the novel's close, "I've never done a single thing I've wanted to in my whole life!" (401), he utters a lament that would characterize the suburban male in both fiction and films of coming decades. Like George F. Babbitt, male suburbanites of postwar novels and films would continue to be characterized by ambivalence, restlessness, and failure. And like Babbitt, characters ranging from Cheever's Neddy Merrill or Johnny Hake all the way to such recent antihero protagonists as Lester Burnham, the beleaguered, randy paterfamilias from Sam Mendes's *American Beauty* (1999), are shown to suffer because of their environment. Reluctant suburbanites, these characters represent what Stephen Birmingham has referred to as "that curious anomie, that sense of disorientation, that indefinable 'feeling of separation,' which living in suburbia so often seems to convey."[10]

If there is any way to explain this consistent portrayal of suburbia as an alienating terrain, it would seem to lie in the fear of a soulless landscape producing a soulless populace—a point perfectly captured by songwriter Malvina Reynolds in her 1962 antisuburbia folk song, "Little Boxes":

> Little boxes on the hillside,
> Little boxes made of ticky tacky,
> Little boxes on the hillside,
> Little boxes all the same.
> There's a green one and a pink one
> And a blue one and a yellow one,
> And they're all made out of ticky tacky,
> And they all look just the same.
>
> And the people in the houses
> All went to the university,
> Where they were put in boxes
> And they came out all the same,
> And there's doctors and lawyers,
> And business executives,

And they're all made out of ticky tacky,
And they all look just the same.

And they all play on the golf course
And drink their martinis dry,
And they all have pretty children
And the children go to school,
And the children go to summer camp,
And then to the university
Where they are put in boxes
And they come out all the same.

And the boys go into business
And marry and raise a family
In boxes made of ticky tacky
And they all look just the same.
There's a green one and a pink one
And a blue one and a yellow one,
And they're all made out of ticky tacky
And they all look just the same.

The deadening environmental relationship Reynolds depicts reflected the dilemma of the suburban professional class who, in the postwar years, often found themselves shuttling between the corporate work world and what amounted to a strangely "corporate" home environment. Postwar depictions of the suburban male, from Keats's protagonist John Drone to William Whyte's "organization man," suggested as much as well, emphasizing the alienating effects of life in a landscape whose precise sense of order mirrored the business world's organizational structure.[11] In this regard, the two images of suburban masculinity—a spiffy, smiling Ward Cleaver walking in his front door, briefcase in hand, and a bewildered, desperate Neddy Merrill howling and banging from the outside—may not be as diametrically opposed as they first seemed. For if, as postwar commentators argued, suburbia presented a dislocating landscape that reduced men to little more than functional roles in a faceless, corporate environment, then both men can be thought of as similarly alienated from place. Indeed, as images of the alienated suburban male, Ward and Neddy differ only by degree of *exposure,* with the shivering, near-naked Neddy serving as a howling emblem of the very anxieties repressed by the buttoned-down Ward Cleavers of postwar suburbia.

Another factor that separates these two images is time itself: Frank Perry's Neddy Merrill appeared on screen in 1968, some twenty years after the onset of mass suburbanization and ten years beyond the heyday of the suburban family sitcom.[12] And while certainly the historical perspective afforded by such a passage of time might have been a helpful factor in examining the alienation and isolation that impacted men in the suburban age, it is worth noting that alienation itself had already been a dominant theme in post–World War II fiction.[13] Nevertheless, the late 1960s and early 1970s were to see a renewed exploration of this theme of masculine alienation in fiction and film, as various unsettling social factors such as the Vietnam War, the increasingly volatile civil rights movement, and the rise of a rebellious youth culture spearheaded by the first-generation children of the age of suburbia worked to undercut traditional sources of authority.

Two texts from this era that specifically situate the crisis of masculinity in the suburban sphere are John Updike's *Rabbit Redux* (1971), the second book in what would become his Rabbit Angstrom tetralogy, and Mike Nichols's *The Graduate* (1967), a film that chronicles the coming of age of a "son of suburbia," Benjamin Braddock. Considering these two works together might help to shed light on the issue of masculinity in suburbia, as both *Rabbit Redux* and *The Graduate* present protagonists who are acutely aware of their embattled place within a confining, alienating suburban milieu. In their self-reflexive awareness of their own spatial and psychological confinement, both Harry "Rabbit" Angstrom and Ben Braddock illustrate Peter Schwenger's notion that "self consciousness . . .

in regard to masculinity . . . has a particularly disconcerting effect. To be self-conscious is to stand off from the self, to be alienated enough from it to observe its arbitrariness and artifice."[14] These characters' sense of alienation within the suburban world is manifested in similar ways: Both transgress social and sexual taboos, expressing their desire for self-definition and difference through regressive and oedipal sexual relationships. Moreover, each finds himself eventually separated, even barred, from his hostile and confining suburban milieu—though the stories of both Rabbit and Benjamin end on an ambivalent note, suggesting that the entrapment they have felt within the social confines of suburbia may indeed still be a central factor in their lives. Although they are of different generations and have in many ways contrasting relationships to place, as they understand their respective suburban environments in different terms, Rabbit and Ben stand as equally vulnerable suburban males, telling figures in American culture's struggle to understand and resolve the dynamics of masculinity in the age of suburbia.

🏠 🏠 🏠

Rabbit Redux is the second novel in what would become John Updike's four-volume sequence chronicling the life of Harry "Rabbit" Angstrom, a former high school basketball star originally from Mt. Judge, a small town on the outskirts of Brewer, Pennsylvania.[15] The four novels, *Rabbit, Run* (1960), *Rabbit Redux* (1971), *Rabbit Is Rich* (1981), and *Rabbit at Rest* (1990), trace Harry's life from his midtwenties, when he was an already over-the-hill former athlete, through his struggles and eventual business success in Brewer, Pennsylvania, to his retirement in Florida and finally his death from a heart attack.[16] The Rabbit tetralogy has been hailed by critics as a monumental achievement, an American epic of sorts that posits a twentieth-century middle-American "Everyman" whose fate parallels that of the nation. As Donald J. Greiner has argued, in Harry Angstrom, Updike has created a figure that conforms to R. W. B. Lewis's notion of the

"American Adam," in that Harry "seems to have sprung from nowhere and thus stands outside the accepted norms of the culture." But while Harry struggles to remain at all costs outside these norms, the very landscapes he traverses in his life—from his small-town roots to his uneasy stint in the cookie-cutter suburbs, to his eventual return to a more genteel small-town landscape before his final move to a Florida retirement village—suggest his utterly typical status; hence, for Greiner, "Updike's essential paradox in the *Rabbit* tetralogy is that Harry is distanced from yet wholly exemplifies his culture."[17] It is precisely Harry's position as both an "insider" and an "outsider" that makes him an apt focal point for a series of novels that, as Paula Buck notes, offer "a poignant image of twentieth-century manhood in search of itself."[18]

Other critics concur with Buck's suggestion that the *Rabbit* novels offer something of a case study in the travails of later twentieth-century American manhood; indeed, Mary O'Connell goes so far as to refer to the *Rabbit* tetralogy as "the longest and most comprehensive representation of masculinity in American literature."[19] Such a characterization seems only fitting, for Harry, as both American Everyman and idiosyncratic, self-conscious outsider, maintains an acute angle of vision on the experience of the twentieth-century American male. In that regard, he shares a crucial trait with many of the protagonists already discussed in this study, as Jay Gatsby, George Bailey, Johnny Hake, and Neddy Merrill are all "outsiders" who nonetheless find themselves positioned in the midst of a troubled, alienating society.[20] Updike foregrounds the conflict between the individual and society in the first and best known of the novels, *Rabbit, Run.* Picking up on the fictional ethos of the period, Updike offers a vision of what Sidney Finkelstein has called an "all-encompassing alienation."[21] In this novel, Rabbit, disgusted with his job as a salesman of kitchen gadgets and frustrated by his increasingly strained marriage to an alcoholic wife, flees his small apartment and his hometown in search of freedom. While his quest for self-realization is played out mainly in terms of sexual experimentation, Rabbit's larger dilemma centers on a spiritual longing, a void that is left unfulfilled by his mundane life in a banal culture. As Howard Harper has argued, *Rabbit, Run* works to "define the boundaries of the modern wasteland, the trap in which man must run, but from which there is no exit. Rabbit . . . cannot break out of the trap of existence into the certainty of essence."[22] Rabbit's running hardly results in a Kerouacian celebration of reckless freedom; instead, his fleeing eventually contributes to the drowning death of his infant daughter, an event that temporarily brings him back into the family before he finally takes off running again at the novel's close.[23]

Rabbit Redux picks up on Rabbit's life ten years later. Now thirty-six, Harry Angstrom (who is no longer referred to as Rabbit, except by his author) remains the angst-ridden, outsider/Everyman. At the opening of the novel Harry, marginally employed at a struggling, near-defunct printing press, is back with his wife, Janice; along with their son, Nelson, they live in a small, "apple-green" house in the suburban village of Penn Villas on the outskirts of Brewer. The marriage remains unhappy, however, and Janice begins an affair with a colleague, Charlie Stavros, that culminates in her moving out of the Penn Villas house. On his own, Harry makes lifestyle changes that not only alarm his family but also incite the ire of his suburban neighbors. After taking in and beginning a sexual relationship with Jill, an eighteen-year-old runaway hippie from a rich family in Connecticut, Harry eventually brings into the household Skeeter, a young black dope dealer, revolutionary, and self-proclaimed "messiah." Harry's neighbors on Vista Crescent, after warning him of the dangers of maintaining what one man calls a "menagerie" in his home, eventually burn the house down while Harry is out, causing Jill's death and Skeeter's flight.

Despite a good deal of action in this narrative, one gets the sense that Harry as protagonist is rarely in control of, or even having much of an effect on, the turbulent events that are going on around him. This in itself is a distinct departure from Harry's character in *Rabbit, Run;* in that novel, despite the tragic consequences that result from his own penchant for flight, Harry at least for a time retains some measure of self-determination.

This trait seems to be lost in *Rabbit Redux,* as Harry's befuddlement in his home and work relationships, along with an increasing sense of alienation within his new, confining suburban landscape, manifests itself in utter avoidance of conflict. As Gordon Slethaug argues, "Although Rabbit has himself made a bid for freedom in *Rabbit, Run,* in *Rabbit Redux* he is acted on, [and] for the most part . . . passive."[24] No longer running, in *Rabbit Redux,* Updike's most political and socially involved novel to that point, Rabbit seems buffeted by forces outside his control that cause him to retreat into a reactionary caricature of conservative white masculinity. As Mary O'Connell has argued, this evolution in Harry—from the reckless seeker of existential bliss in *Run* to the sedentary windbag he seems to become in *Redux*—has everything to do with the dynamics of a culture that has been working toward displacement of the white male worker as the totemic emblem of its citizenry: "Rabbit's passivity is socially induced, the consequence of sweeping changes in a society that has abandoned old institutions, values, traditions, and rituals. These . . . changes devalue Rabbit as an American, a white, a male, a husband, and a worker."[25] And yet despite his increasingly reactionary stance—he quickly emerges and remains throughout the novel a vocal bigot, a jingoistic defender of America's involvement in the Vietnam War, and a cantankerous figure utterly disdainful of the concerns of the younger generation—this novel also finds Harry engaging in increasingly transgressive social and sexual behavior, as his need for self-expression takes the form of resistance to the restrictive codes of conduct of his uniform and socially conservative community.

That Harry's aberrant behavior is linked to a confused and unfulfilling connection to his landscape becomes apparent from the very opening of the novel. Updike establishes the thematic importance of milieu with his opening image, one that parallels the decay of the city (Brewer), brought on by suburbanization, with a sense of alienation among its male workers. As Harry and his father emerge from the printing press at the opening of the novel, the blinding brightness that surrounds them highlights the utter barrenness of downtown Brewer, while at the same time rendering the men nearly "ghostly," translucent figures whose lack of substance is linked to the deserted quality of the landscape that once sustained them: "Men emerge from the little printing plant at four sharp, ghosts for an instant, blinking, until the outdoor light overcomes the look of constant indoor light clinging to them. . . . [T]he granite curbs starred with mica and the row houses differentiated by speckled bastard sidings and the hopeful small porches with their jigsaw brackets and gray milk-bottle boxes and the sooty ginkgo trees and the baking curbside cars wince beneath a brilliance like a frozen explosion. The city, attempting to revive its dying downtown, has torn away blocks of buildings to create parking lots, so that a desolate openness, weedy and rubbled, spills through the once-packed streets."[26]

In contrast to this cityscape, which despite its fallen and now nearly spectral condition offers at least the reminder of a bygone era of vibrance, difference, and "hopeful" domesticity, Harry's new suburban neighborhood of Penn Villas is first described, rather flatly, as a "ranch-house village of muddy lawns and potholed macadam and sub-code sewers" (15) left behind by hasty, uncaring developers. And after Harry takes the bus home from Brewer and walks from the bus stop toward his house, Updike's description of Harry's housing development underscores the collapse of the pastoral dream of the suburbs into an unsettling space of homogeneous facelessness: "Rabbit gets off at a stop in Penn Park and walks down a street of mock Tudor, Emberly Avenue, to where the road surface changes at the township line, and becomes Emberly Drive in Penn Villas. He lives on Vista Crescent, third house from the end. Once there may have been here a vista, a softly sloped valley of red barns and fieldstone farmhouses, but more Penn Villas had been added and now the view from any window is as into a fragmented mirror, of houses like this, telephone wires and television aerials showing where the glass cracked" (15). " houseolrlleπis" noUrslo

If the contrast between the landscapes of Brewer and Penn Villas emphasizes the unsettling sense of dislocation inherent in the suburban endeavor, the phenomenon is further highlighted in the even more distinct contrasts between Penn Villas and Harry's boyhood home in Mt. Judge, an older, established small town on the other side of Brewer. Harry ruminates on this difference early in the novel as he stands in his Penn Villa yard beside his lone tree, a "spindly maple" whose vulnerability is evident in the fact that it remains "tethered to the earth," itself a revealing contrast to the stately maples that anchor his parents' yard in Mt. Judge. In a telling passage, Harry compares the two yards, noting the loss of a generational sense of rootedness in the oddly sterile suburban outdoors, the preplanned pastoral appeal of which has fallen flat, leaving instead an uninviting, desolate landscape: "[I]t is true, Park Villas [*sic*] with its vaunted quarter-acre lots and compulsory barbecue chimneys does not tempt its residents outdoors, even the children in summer: in the snug brick neighborhood of Rabbit's childhood you were always outdoors, hiding in hollowed-out bushes, scuffing in the gravel alleys, secure in the closeness of windows from at least one of which an adult was always watching. Here, there is a prairie sadness, a barren sky raked by slender aerials. A sky poisoned by radio waves. A desolate smell from underground" (60).

The focus on childhood memories in this passage reveals a nostalgic mode, a characteristic gesture in suburban fiction. Updike, like Fitzgerald, Cheever, Beattie, and Naylor, invokes the resonance of "eulogized spaces" from the past to suggest the flatness of experience in the contemporary suburban landscape. And while this passage exhibits the more general tendency that Robert Detweiler has seen in Updike of a "longing for the security of a romanticized past," still there is more at work in this passage than simply a desire to regain lost memories.[27] Instead, Updike's contrast of the groundedness of Harry's childhood home with the focus on the sky itself in the description of the Penn Villas environment presents diverging views of the stability of landscape. As opposed to the view we are given of the Mt. Judge outdoors, where the parental gaze from windows above provided a comforting sense of security, the angle of vision outdoors in

the "spindly maple" (margin note)

"eulogized spaces" of the past (margin note)

Penn Villas seems inevitably drawn to the sky itself. Rather than offering a reassuring vision of stable authority, this suburban "vista" is composed simply of the bewildering infinity of space itself, broken only by the network of crosshatched television antennae that symbolize the utter disconnectedness of the suburban community. Alone in his yard without a neighbor in sight, positioned between an imposing, "poisoned" sky and the stench of befouled earth, Harry stands as an emblem of the isolated, imprisoned suburbanite.

The attention paid to the sky in the above passage also serves to extend what emerges early on as the controlling metaphor of *Rabbit Redux:* space exploration and, more specifically, the *Apollo XI* moon landing as symbolic renderings of the increasing alienation of life in this turbulent era. Updike foregrounds this theme with his epigraphs to each of the novel's four sections, which recount bits of dialogue among American astronauts and, alternately, Soviet cosmonauts. Beyond the epigraphs themselves, the action of the novel plays out against the drama of the first Apollo moon landing, with the event appearing periodically in background television reports and in conversation among characters. Moreover, Updike's sustained use of visual imagery drawn from the language of space exploration—the cityscape of Brewer, for example, is more than once likened to the surface of the moon, while the house in Penn Villas is repeatedly described as resembling a lonely spacecraft—in addition to pointed, intertextual references to the film *2001: A Space Odyssey* make the idea of space exploration itself an ever-present motif. More than merely a historical referent to situate the action of the novel, these sustained references to space exploration and moon landing act work to literalize Updike's metaphoric treatment of Harry's "alienation."[28] As the moon landings themselves were perhaps most notable as emblems of America's frantic search for a new frontier, the recurring references to the Apollo mission underscore Harry's own spatial dilemma. Like Gatsby, George Bailey, and Neddy Merrill, Harry seeks a new "frontier," a place apart from the enclosed, entrapping terrain of suburbia. And if, as Greiner suggests, in *Redux* Updike posits "a relationship between the loss of space in the United States and the dilution of heroism," then the recurring references to the astronauts also throw into relief the predicament of the now-static Harry, who is relegated to the status of antihero merely because he is trapped in what Greiner aptly calls the "cul-de-sac" of late-twentieth-century American culture.[29]

Above all else, the sustained space exploration metaphor serves to mirror the placelessness of contemporary existence, a phenomenon brought home persistently to Harry, who sees in the careless design of his suburban surroundings something inhuman and repugnant. And while his complete disconnection from his family and neighbors marks Harry as a rather solitary character, in his spatial dilemma he emerges as a representative figure for the late twentieth century. As J. Gerald Kennedy has argued, the "space age" has indeed been an era character-ized by the search, often futile, for a still-livable landscape: "The epoch of global exploration . . . has perhaps, in the wake of the Apollo moon landings, reached an apocalyptic final phase, marked by the frantic search for that great good dwelling place not already depleted, poisoned, bombed out, or overpopulated."[30] As Updike's narration so forcefully emphasizes, such a dwelling place is not to be found in Brewer and its environs, as the "poisoned" suburban space of Penn Villas stands in counterpoint to depleted, dying Brewer even as it facilitates the decay of that city. Perhaps the one possibility for an abiding relationship to place lies in the future of Penn Villas, the hope that one day the postwar dream of suburban community will flourish in this troubled place; at one point, standing in his front yard, Harry considers this notion: "And he looks, and sees that his neighbors have trees, saplings like his, but some already as tall as the housetops. Someday Nelson may come back to this, his childhood neighborhood, and find it strangely dark, buried in shade, the lawns opulent, the homes venerable. . . . This isn't a bad neighborhood, he thinks, this could be a nice place if you gave it a chance. And around the other houses men with rakes and mowers mirror him" (302).

The irony of this thought, however, lies not only in the fact that it occurs shortly before Harry's neighbors team up to burn down his house in reaction to his transgressive lifestyle, but also in that it directly echoes a previous passage, one in which he reads in his neighbors' anonymous, mechanical lifestyles the antithesis of the suburban dream of community. In this earlier passage, Updike again employs the spatial metaphor, in the form of a mirroring sky, to emphasize the alien feel of the environment and the utter sense of disconnection in the community: "He goes outside to finish the yard work he began last night. All around him, in the backyards of Vista Crescent, to the horizons of Penn Villas with their barbecue chimneys and aluminum wash trees, other men are out in their yards; the sound of his mower is echoed from house to house, his motions of bending and pushing are carried outwards as if in fragments of mirror suspended from the hot blank sky. These his neighbors, they come with their furniture in vans and leave with the vans. They get together to sign futile petitions for better sewers and quicker fire protection but otherwise do not connect" (76). Here Updike offers his most telling vision of the dislocation fostered by the suburban environment: In depicting the inhabitants' lack of common purpose and values—indeed, the lack of a "community" altogether—he suggests that these men do not connect with each other because they lack connection to their place. Little more than transients, interchangeable "husbands" of a manufactured environment, the men of Penn Villas remain isolated from one another, each tending to his own identical plot. And while Harry's self-consciousness may set him apart from the others, it does so only insofar as it allows him to see more clearly the manner in which the surrounding landscape emphasizes his own insignificance and ineffectuality.

This sense of interchangeability, which is brought home to Harry through the fragmented, endlessly "mirrored" nature of his suburban landscape and its male residents, is precisely what threatens his masculinity and his larger sense of identity. Harry's front yard ruminations on his own environmental replaceability are only part of what becomes a sustained reflection on his insignificance or even obsolescence. The most telling reminder of Harry's fading stature is Janice's affair with Stavros; in a dream he has shortly after learning of the affair, Harry unconsciously links his sexual and environmental replaceability. With imagery that is (to borrow a phrase from Ralph Wood's analysis of Updike) "more Freudian than Freud,"[31] Updike tracks Rabbit's unconscious fixation on his status as a cuckolded suburbanite, as he dreams of a city named "The Rise": "He dreams of driving north with Charlie Stavros, in a little scarlet Toyota. The gear shift is very thin, a mere pencil, and he is afraid of breaking it as he shifts. . . . Stavros sits in the driver's seat . . . masterfully gesturing. . . . [A] strange white city materializes beside the highway; hill after hill of tall row houses white as bedsheets, crowding to the horizon, an enormous city, strange it seems to have no name. They part in a suburban region beside a drugstore and Stavros hands him a map; with difficulty Rabbit locates on it where they are. The metropolis, marked with a bull's-eye, is named, simply, The Rise" (71). It is little surprise that Harry is dropped off by the "masterful" Stavros in a nondescript suburban outpost of this most phallic of cities: As is true for Harry's waking condition, his dream world counterpart finds himself disassociated from the masculine power associated with the massive metropolis. Fragile, breakable, and relegated to the sidelines of this phallic landscape, Harry, through his dream image, imagines himself an ineffectual, neutered suburbanite. Awaking from the dream with an erection that feels "glassily thin," Harry discusses the Stavros affair with Janice, deflecting her vow to break it off with the advice "see him if you want to" (78). Later that day Harry returns to find that Janice has left him and that his dream image of himself—superseded, symbolically castrated, abandoned in the suburbs—has become reality.

Indeed, Janice's departure serves as a driving factor in the novel, as her abandonment of Harry and Nelson in the "little apple-green" suburban house leads indirectly to the appearance of Jill and Skeeter and the creation of a new, inverted and surrogate, suburban "family." Updike has received a good deal of criticism for his stereotyped portrayal of the "rich hippie" runaway Jill and the "angry black revolutionary" Skeeter, and with good reason: The voices of these two characters never ring true—the tendency in their speech is for platitudes to replace dialogue, as if Jill and Skeeter are more quasi-sociological *types* than fully realized characters. Indeed, the artificiality of Jill and Skeeter may be most revealing of Updike's own insecurities as a white male author broaching for the first time the turbulence of the era; nevertheless, the caricatured "radical" identities of these two characters function to highlight, by pointed contrast, aspects of Harry's embattled status as a white male head of household. And if such a use of stereotyped identities, conscious or otherwise, to an extent compromises the political relevance of the novel, critics such as Greiner have suggested that painting an accurate portrait of contemporary political upheaval was never Updike's primary aim in the first place. Arguing that Updike was no more than "passingly concerned with his characters' brush with historical forces" such as the war and race relations, Greiner asserts that domestic instability is the paramount issue in the novel, as such instability "reflects a larger center that seems less than secure."[32] Greiner's point is worth considering: Reading *Rabbit Redux* as primarily a novel about the breakup of the family, something urban planning historian Robert Fishman has aptly identified as "the great suburban theme in serious American fiction," one gains a fuller understanding of the novel's more subtle "political" insights.[33] That is, in counterpoising the dissolved Angstrom family with its radical, inverted replacement, Updike suggests the instability of the patriarchal family unit long considered not only the cornerstone of the suburban landscape, but indeed the foundation of middle-class American culture.

What is accomplished, then, with the appearance of Jill and Skeeter, is a kind of defamiliarization—however stilted it may be—of the suburban family group itself. More than mere stereotyped caricatures of an angry and alienated youth culture, Jill and Skeeter also serve as projections or manifestations of Harry's own otherness, of the sense that he does not belong in his conservative, homogeneous physical and social landscape.

The two characters present Harry with an untenable situation: Even as he plays the social conservative in reaction to their radical views—Jill's idealistic pacifism and Skeeter's vision of a coming black revolution—Harry's very maintenance of this unconventional household positions him as a transgressive outlaw in Penn Villas. As Matthew Wilson puts it, "the very existence of this intergenerational community in Harry's white suburb . . . emphasizes how marginalized he has become . . . but as a marginalized defender of the status quo, he is compromised by Jill and Skeeter."[34] As the patriarchal head of this radical suburban household, Harry finds himself playing at the roles of both the conservative Everyman and the radical freethinker; in this regard, he is exercising what Dana Nelson has identified as "white manhood's privilege, the liberal franchise of individual exceptionality" through which white American males have, historically, claimed both membership within the "imagined fraternity of white men" and independence from it.[35] The problem for Harry is that he cannot have it both ways; a transgressor in a relentlessly corporate environment, Harry quickly becomes ostracized from the community and increasingly alienated from his suburban world as the relationship with his new "family" develops.

Hence the caricatured "otherness" of Jill and Skeeter emerges as an important factor in the novel, for it is through Harry's increasing identification with these two outsiders in the midst of homogeneous suburbia that Updike measures his protagonist's evolution. Eventually internalizing the otherness represented by Jill and Skeeter, Harry becomes something of a divided man, both a de facto suburban patriarch and the antithesis of the kind of staid conformity epitomized by his house and his bland suburban development. Updike captures the extent of Harry's isolation while suggesting the environmental concerns that foster it, through Harry's repeated vision of his suburban home as a "lonely spacecraft"; with this metaphor Updike suggests that Harry's suburban surroundings offer not the comfort of neighborly community, but instead vast stretches of threatening, vacant space. Recognizing himself as increasingly a stranger in his suburban landscape, Harry faces a predicament that resonates with what Julia Kristeva identifies as the logical end of Freud's theory of the unconscious, the auto-alienation that became increasingly prevalent in late-twentieth-century societies. As Kristeva notes, "with the Freudian notion of the unconscious, the involution of the strange in the psyche loses its pathological aspect. . . . [F]oreignness is within us: we are our own foreigners, we are divided."[36] Thus a foreigner even to himself, a curious amalgam of Ward Cleaver's benevolent patriarch and Neddy Merrill's howling outcast, Harry Angstrom emerges as a fitting emblem of the contradictions of suburban masculinity.

Updike renders Harry's exploration of his own masculinity in specifically Freudian terms, staging his regressive sexual relationship with the childlike Jill alternately with his ruminations on and visits to his dying mother.[37] Evincing the kind of struggle between Eros and Thanatos that Freud describes in *Beyond the Pleasure Principle,* Harry seems never fully comfortable with his sexual relationships, tending instead to be more at home in the presence of his mother, who, despite her increasingly frail condition, maintains a powerful hold over his imagination.[38] Indeed, critic Paula R. Buck, who sees in the Rabbit novels as a whole a "case study of the oedipal conflict in the small-town American hero," notes that the mother's presence is all-pervasive, arguing that Harry, "marked by fierce, neurotic clinging . . . hauls memories of Mom into every new situation."[39] Buck's observation has wider ramifications than the mere diagnosis of Harry as a "neurotic"; Harry's regression to a childlike identity—he even reflects that he is "still too much a son himself" (91)—also serves to undercut his own efficacy as a father, a role he ironically tends to neglect almost completely on his unwanted promotion to the status of sole caregiver for Nelson. Resisting identification with his own father, whom he sees as "one of the hundreds of skinny whining codgers in and around [Brewer], men who have sucked this same brick tit for sixty years and have dried up with it" (5), Harry nonetheless unwittingly occupies the same position himself. Indeed, Harry's status as patriarch seems yet more embattled than those of the older generation he disdains; for Harry, left alone to care for Nelson and their home—effectively positioned, as Slethaug notes, as both father and "mother"/caregiver—seems utterly mystified as to his duties and his identity.[40]

The clearest manifestation of Harry's embattled self-identity in this period comes in the shifting erotic and power dynamics of his relationships with Jill and Skeeter. Harry is increasingly cruel in his treatment of Jill, who eventually becomes little more than a conduit for the homoerotic, antagonistic relationship between Harry and Skeeter.[41] And if, as Freud asserts in his "Three Essays on Sexuality," the "impulse for cruelty arises from the instinct for mastery,"[42] then Jill's debasement at the hands of both Harry and Skeeter is indicative of the power struggle between the two men, a struggle that explicitly assumes the dynamics of a master/slave relationship.[43] The climactic moment of this relationship comes during one of the nightly "consciousness-raising" role-playing sessions Skeeter conducts for Harry's benefit in the darkened living room. One night after asking Harry to take on the role of Frederick Douglass and read from Douglass's autobiography, Skeeter revisits the topic of slavery, positioning Harry as a witness—a "big black man . . . chained to that chair"—as he and Jill role-play a white slave owner's rape of a female slave. Aroused by the scene, Harry turns on the lamp beside him, in time for he and Jill to see a face peering in at them from outside the living room window. And while the actions of the unknown spy outside mirror Harry's position inside, Harry's reaction to the sight of this voyeur reveals his utter disconnection from the world outside his living room window: "In the corner of his vision, he saw it too: a face. At the window. Eyes like two cigarette burns. The lamp is out, the face is vanished. . . . Rabbit runs to the front door and opens it. The night air bites. October. The lawn looks artificial, lifeless, dry, no-color: a snapshot of grass. Vista Crescent stretches empty but for parked cars. . . . Rabbit decides not to look, not to give chase; he feels that there is no space for him to step into, that the vista before him is a flat, stiff, cold photograph" (298).

[margin handwriting: Jill becomes a conduit for the homoerotic, antagonistic rel. between R & Skeeter]

Updike's play with visual perspective in this passage evokes fears of both the heightened visibility of private lives in suburbia and the disorienting "placelessness" of the suburban environment. First positioning Harry as the object of voyeuristic observation, Updike uses an anonymous gaze through the picture window to underscore the broken distinction between public and private places, recalling the specter of surveillance common to suburban fiction and film. When Harry attempts to return the gaze, he can see only a landscape both unmarked and unremarkable, a "photographic" image of a "flat," two-dimensional landscape. This "artificial" rendering of landscape is only fitting, given Harry's by now complete divorce from his surroundings and community. As a result of the voyeur's vision, members of the community band together on a subsequent night to burn down Harry's house, removing from the landscape the offending home and homeowner. Hence Harry's final sexual transgression, itself a product of his effort for mastery over his crisis in masculinity, leads to the destruction of his home and his ouster from the community altogether.

Although specific blame for the act is never placed in the novel, the burning down of the Angstrom home seems the culmination of a process of surveillance and threats of vigilantism levied by Harry's neighbors in response to the incorporation of Jill and Skeeter into the household. This is something Harry's father had warned him specifically about, cautioning that by allowing Skeeter into the household he was "playing with fire" (237). Harry seems to understand as much, realizing that Skeeter's presence, given the otherwise complete racial homogeneity of Penn Villas, cannot go unnoticed for long. And even before he receives specific threats from his neighbors, Harry fears that Skeeter will somehow contribute to the destruction of his house, an anxiety that he expresses at one point while rushing back to check on his home: "Hurry, hurry. The bus takes forever to come, the walk down Emberly is endless. Yet his house, third from the end of Vista Crescent, low and new and a sullen apple-green on the quarter-acre of lawn scraggly with plantain, is intact, and all around it the unpopulated stretches of similar houses hold unbroken the intensity of duplication. That the blot of black inside his house is unmirrored fools him into hoping it isn't there" (223). Rendered as a stain on an otherwise pristine landscape, a "blot of black" tainting the colorless uniformity of the surroundings, Skeeter is, even in Rabbit's mind, an all-too-visible addition to the environment, one that will soon be "erased." In this sense, of course, Skeeter mirrors Harry: Both transgressive and highly visible figures, Harry and Skeeter through their very difference incite the drive for their expulsion from the suburban landscape. Indeed, the architecture of the Penn Villas development establishes their identities as transgressors, for it is through the picture window of the living room—which Harry himself had rightly described as a "two-way mirror," something that permits "outdoors to come indoors, other houses to enter yours" (306)—that the behavior of Harry, Skeeter, and Jill is made a public, lurid entertainment for neighborhood voyeurs and fodder for the vigilantes who unite to remove the blight that Harry, Skeeter, and even the Angstrom house represent in the neighborhood.

That the neighborhood has in some sense united in opposition to him is made clear to Harry when he is accosted by two of his neighbors, Showalter and Brumbach. Claiming to speak for others in the neighborhood, the two warn Harry about his standing in the community. And while Showalter, the diplomat, speaks to Harry in general terms about the need to maintain decorum in the neighborhood, Brumbach, a scarred Vietnam veteran who is the "muscle" of the pair, is more direct. Telling Harry that "this is a decent white neighborhood," he makes his demands clear: "The black goes" (290). But Harry so infuriates Brumbach that the latter eventually transfers his outrage from Skeeter to Harry himself, finally warning Harry that he had "better fucking barricade the whole place" (289) because "no wiseass is crowding me in my own neighborhood" (291). Finding himself thus positioned alongside Skeeter outside the bounds of this suddenly united community, Harry reflects on the corporate nature of the hostility being directed toward him by these representative antagonists: "Rabbit sees the structure: one man is the negotiations, the other is the muscle. An age of specialization and collusion" (289). And once the neighbors do act, dramatically torching his house in the middle of the night, Harry's position at the scene of the crime emphasizes his marginality. Although he expects as he races toward his house to encounter a monumental blaze and a rush of activity in which he would stand as the central embattled figure, what he experiences instead is a scene that underscores not only the artificiality and anonymity of the environment, but also his utter lack of consequence to the scene, his near invisibility: "Indeed, the house burns spitefully, spitting, stinkingly: the ersatz and synthetic materials grudge combustion its triumph. Once in boyhood Rabbit saw a barn burn in the valley beyond Mt. Judge; it was a torch, an explosion of hay outstarring the sky with embers. Here there is no such display. There is space around him. The spectators, the neighbors, in honor of his role, have backed off. . . . [N]ow he is at the center . . . and still feels peripheral, removed, nostalgic, numb. He scans the firelit faces and does not see Showalter or Brumbach. He sees no one he knows" (319).

Central and yet peripheral, Harry in this passage is rendered merely an actor playing a "role," a positioning that emphasizes his alienation. It is little wonder, then, that following the burning of his house, he feels liberated; departing the scene the next morning, he reflects on his new situation: "His house slips from him. He is free" (332). As the resolution of his dilemma of alienation, Harry's escape from the suburbs seems to represent nothing less than the dream vision of the entrapped males who recur throughout suburban fiction. Nonetheless, this break from the suburbs fails to resolve his crisis in masculinity. Despite—or perhaps because of—his newfound freedom, on his return to his parents' house in Mt. Judge, Harry begins something of a second childhood, competing with Nelson for his parents' attention and retreating to his boyhood bedroom for long stretches of time, masturbating as he did when he was an adolescent. This regression has everything to do with the loss of his house; despite the sense of liberation it brings, the destruction of Harry's house is a symbolic castration of sorts that leaves him feeling "less of a man."[44] Viewing Harry's Penn Villas experience from the larger perspective of his life to this point, the disastrous effect of this suburban tenure on his masculinity becomes apparent: Reduced from the reckless, hypersexual wanderer of *Rabbit, Run* to a twice-cuckolded, impotent, childlike figure who now nightly struggles to reach masturbatory climax in his boyhood bedroom, Harry has seen over the course of his suburban experience the utter erosion of his manhood. Through his protagonist's struggles, Updike underscores the impression of suburbia as an emasculating environment.

Harry's diminished sense of manhood and his suburban alienation figure prominently in the penultimate scene of the novel, as Harry and Janice return to the site of their ruined home for a reconciliatory meeting. Harry's regression to a childlike state is suggested by his attire, as he arrives at the scene wearing his old, ill-fitting letterman jacket from high school; Janice, too, is "wearing something too young for her, with a hairdo reverting to adolescence" (393). Approaching the house, Harry notices that it "sticks out from way down Vista Crescent: black coal in a row of candies" (392). But as the couple approach one another and look at the house, they discover that it has evolved into something more than merely an offensive stain on the "candied" landscape of the suburban development: "Janice turns and they look together at where they lived. . . . Some person has taken the trouble to bring a spray can of yellow paint and has hugely written NIGGER on the side. Also the word KILL. . . . Also there is a peace sign and a swastika, apparently from the same can. And other people, borrowing charred sticks from the rubble, have come along and tried to edit and add to these slogans and symbols. . . . It all adds up to no better than the cluster of commercials TV stations squeeze into the chinks between programs. A clown with a red spray can has scrawled between two windows TRICK OR TREAT" (395). Here Updike presents the ruins of the Angstrom home as a text chronicling suburban anger and intolerance. Most evident is the racial bigotry behind the drive to preserve suburbia as a white enclave. More generally, this collection of "slogans and symbols" suggests both an almost primitive sense of communal action (after uniting to torch the house and to watch it burn, members of the community come to scrawl symbolic messages on its walls with "charred sticks") and a sense of postmodern dislocation: The sum total of their symbolic messages carries no more sense than a "cluster of commercials" on TV.

Not insignificantly, the couple have nothing to say in response to this tangle of violent signifiers. Themselves isolated victims of an utter breakdown in communication, Harry and Janice hardly seem capable of interpreting the curious text of their former home. Nevertheless, this primal scene, chronicling the return of the broken family to the place that saw—even fostered—their dissolution, does offer avenues toward an interpretation of the landscape that has figured so prominently in the novel. Most telling is the final bit of text they see scrawled on the walls, the "TRICK OR TREAT" message posted by an unknown "clown." The carnivalesque nature of this missive seems most appropriate, given the manner in which their home has inverted the faceless, conservative life of the suburban subdivision. Loosed from the constraints of subdivision homogeneity, the once apple-green house now stands witness—in its charred, defaced, inside-out state—to the violent, transgressive impulses of Penn Villas, its ruins symbolizing the collective unconscious of a troubled suburban society. In that sense, it is an appropriate closing image for a novel that explores the underside of life in a landscape portrayed as threateningly corporate, alienating, and emasculating. *transgressive*

🏠 🏠 🏠

In chronicling the alienation of a suburban Everyman, Updike used the recurring image of the Apollo astronauts to suggest both Harry's disconnection from his society and his dreams of a place apart from that society. This symbolic rendering of the suburban male's fantasies of exploration and escape reminds one of Cheever's Neddy Merrill: Considering himself an "explorer," Neddy sought to transcend the materialistic landscape of suburbia and resurrect pastoral landscapes of memory—and in that sense he, in turn, recalls the dream of Fitzgerald's Jay Gatsby. In his 1968 film adaptation of Charles Webb's 1963 novel *The Graduate,* Mike Nichols adds another figure to this group of suburban would-be explorers. Setting the coming-of-age drama of his hero, Benjamin Braddock (Dustin Hoffman), in the materialistic and confining milieu of the upper-middle-class suburbs of Southern California, Nichols aligns the attainment of manhood with the escape from suburbia. Like Fitzgerald and Cheever, Nichols uses the swimming pool as a symbol of the materialistic sensibilities of suburbanites; like Updike, he offers an image that captures his protagonist's alienation and dreams of exploration/escape: In a symbolically crucial scene, Benjamin is shown standing alone, isolated at the bottom of his pool in full scuba gear. Looking much like an astronaut himself in the full-body diving suit and mask, Ben in this sustained shot stands as a fallen explorer in his own right, a young man "drowning" in the sea of suburban mediocrity and conformity.

Another similarity between Nichols's and Updike's works can be found in their ambiguous endings. In *Rabbit Redux,* the drama of Harry's embattled masculinity is left unresolved with the ambivalent atmosphere of his ultimate reunion with Janice: They seem to come together again, yet their final moment in a roadside hotel is curiously sterile, a tentative and ineffectual coupling that is described in prose thick with the "space" imagery that had served throughout the work to connote a strong sense of alienation. Likewise in *The Graduate,* Ben and Elaine Robinson's triumphant escape on the bus at the end of the film can be read as both a victory and the ultimate defeat for its protagonists. As the final shot of the two lovers on the back of the bus perfectly captures the evolution in their facial expressions from excitement and laughter to sheer bewilderment and worry, one wonders whether Ben and Elaine have escaped the confines of their artificial suburban world or whether they are being "driven" further into that world, merely quasi-radicals who have now, through their commitment to each other, taken the first step on what will be an inevitable road toward the "American dream" of marriage, family, a good job, and a house in the suburbs. And while readers of the *Rabbit* tetralogy had the benefit of two more novels in which to trace Harry's evolution—eventually finding that he remained, to his death, both an emblem of American middle-class masculinity and an alienated "outsider" existing on the fringes of that middle-class world—viewers of *The Graduate* were left with a far more vexing question concerning the future of Ben and Elaine. Some critics viewed the end of the film, with its forceful negation of the institution of marriage, as a truly radical move, while others were apt to concur with the reading of Robert Kolker, who saw the film as ultimately co-opted by the very societal forces it attempted to critique, referring to it as a "hymn to the paradoxically passive rebellion of the sixties . . . a gentle massage."[45] For his part, Mike Nichols tended to side with the latter view, asserting to *New York Times* critic Leslie Aldrige that the romantic plot of Ben and Elaine served to set a "trap" for Ben and that ultimately, in his opinion, Benjamin would "end up like his parents."[46]

All of which serves to highlight a crucial difference between these two works that portray the imperiled status of the suburban male in the late 1960s—their generational perspectives. Unlike Harry, a former small-town athletic hero who finds himself, in midlife, trying to come to terms with what for him is a new and confounding environment, Benjamin is, presumably, a "son of the suburbs," a young man who is not only coming of age in the suburban milieu but would seem, by virtue of that fact, to represent the very promise of suburbia. If, as commentators such as Mumford have asserted, the postwar suburban landscape emerged as a "child-centered environment," a breeding ground for the baby boom that itself illustrated the optimism of the newly established and growing middle class, then the generation that came of age in the late 1960s would seem to hold a unique symbolic significance as keepers of the suburban dream. But by the time *The Graduate* appeared, signs were already everywhere in American popular culture that this was not to be the case: From the general disdain for suburban conformity and propriety expressed in the dress and appearance of hippies to such pop culture artifacts as Pete Seeger's hit version of Malvina Reynolds's "Little Boxes," or the Monkees' 1967 hit song "Pleasant Valley Sunday," a wry commentary by songwriters Gerry Goffin and Carole King on the materialistic and anesthetized sensibilities of the adult generation in suburbia, it was clear that the suburban dream was under attack from the younger generation. And as film critic Ivone Margulies points out, it was precisely this "shaky status" of the suburban dream in the late 1960s that informed *The Graduate* and other like-minded films she describes as "mild leftist critiques of the golden promise of capitalist society."[47] Clearly, Ben Braddock's predicament transcended the personal: If Rabbit Angstrom symbolized the embattled middle-class patriarch buffeted by the turbulence of the 1960s, Ben Braddock also stood as an emblem of his generation, his dissatisfaction with materialist conformity fueling a fear of impending adulthood and hence his transgressive behavior.

Ben's story, then, highlights one of the essential paradoxes of postwar suburban experience that was just beginning to surface as the children of suburbia came into adulthood: that the same material success that was reflected in the symbology of suburbia—in its swimming pools, its spacious yards and "compulsory barbecues"—and that had all along provided the impetus for ongoing suburban development began to be perceived as evidence of the *failure* of the suburban dream. That is, capitalism's victory was seen as spelling the death of a sense of community in the suburbs, as the utopian vision of inclusion and togetherness that informed the postwar suburban migration had given way—at least in the popular imagination—to disjointed development neighborhoods characterized by a form of crass materialism readily observable on the very landscape itself. Perceived as being united only by their shared interest in material acquisition and the display of "status symbols," late 1960s' suburbanites became the target of critique by their children, as the first generation born in suburbia saw in their own landscape a symbol of their parents' commitment to a suffocat-

ing, oppressive materialism. One thinks in this regard of The Monkees'
"Pleasant Valley," a place whose interchangeable residents remain mired in
their self-induced banality, unable to see the trap they have made for
themselves in the suburbs:

> Another Pleasant Valley Sunday
> Charcoal burnin' everywhere
> Rows of houses that are all the same
> And no one seems to care
>
> See Mrs. Gray she's proud today because her roses are in bloom
> Mr. Green he's so serene, He's got a TV in every room
>
> Another Pleasant Valley Sunday
> Here in status symbol land
> Mothers complain about how hard life is
> And the kids just don't understand

Above all else, "Pleasant Valley Sunday" trumpets the need to break out of
the confines of suburbia, a sentiment expressed in the song's bridge:

> Creature comfort goals
> They only numb my soul and make it hard for me to see
> My thoughts all seem to stray, to places far away
> I need a change of scenery

The similarities between Pleasant Valley and Benjamin Braddock's Southern California suburban home are all too apparent; in both places, the
"creature comfort goals" of the older generation are not enough to sustain
the younger. Indeed, material success itself becomes odious in both
worlds, evidence of capitulation to an unreflective consumer society. In
Ben's case, this sense of estrangement from his parents' world is the central

factor motivating his actions throughout the film. As Leonard Quart and Albert Auster aptly note, "The reasons for Ben's alienation are projected into the sterility of a middle-class affluence . . . precisely at the moment when the American dream seemed at its peak of material fulfillment."[48]

And if Nichols's aim was to create in *The Graduate* a generational critique on soulless materialism, an updated and debased *Gatsby,* then the suburban milieu—which was already being hailed as the symbol of the vacuousness of the American dream—was the perfect setting for the film. And yet the argument could be made that the suburbs are not particularly a focal point in the film; Ben's time at his parents' suburban home, after all, comprises only the first half of the movie, while the rest of the film offers a restless travelogue, with Ben's relentless shuttling between Southern California and Berkeley serving as a reminder of both the wanderlust and the aimlessness of the younger generation. Nevertheless, to discount the suburban milieu entirely would be to overlook the entrapment theme that is so central to the film, for the other cause of Ben Braddock's persistent motion is the fact that he is, as Glenn Man notes, "trapped in a mercantile middle-class environment."[49] Ben, who tells his father at one point that he dreams only for his life to be "different," sees in his parents' suburban world a suffocating environment whose challenges to his own sense of masculinity seem almost insurmountable. This point is only reinforced by the film's conclusion, as Ben's frenetic flight is not so much halted as co-opted: With his racy, masculine red sports car out of gas, abandoned by the roadside, Ben finds himself alongside his new "bride" in the backseat of a bus filled with older people, being shuttled down the shady, tree-lined streets of a residential district of Santa Barbara, traversing a landscape that resembles nothing more than a typical American suburban nowhere.

Hence, the crushing irony here, as in *It's a Wonderful Life,* is that the joyous, romantic conclusion directly anticipates the failure and entrapment of the male protagonist. In essence, Ben is dumbfounded at the conclusion of the film because he is at last coming face to face with his future as a suburban husband and perhaps father. In its final frames, then,

The Graduate returns to the suburban entrapment theme with which it had begun. As a rumination on the imperiled nature of masculinity in the suburban milieu, *The Graduate* finds much company. From postwar films, ranging from broad comedies such as *Mr. Blandings Builds His Dreamhouse* to melodramas like Nunnally Johnson's *The Man in the Gray Flannel Suit* (1956), to later films belonging to such subgenres as the suburban youth-rebellion drama—perhaps most memorably realized in Jonathan Kaplan's 1979 thriller *Over the Edge*—to more recent, big-budget Hollywood fare such as Joe Dante's 1989 suburban comedy of manners *The 'Burbs,* as well as Peter Weir's *The Truman Show* (1998) and Sam Mendes's *American Beauty* (1999), suburban movies tend to be predicated on the ineffectuality of the male head of household. Indeed, considered as a group, the major films chronicling the suburban experience present an environment whose culturally overdetermined middle-class, family-centered identity tends—for often mysterious, unidentified reasons—to foster the development of overbearing wife/mothers, obnoxious children, and husband/fathers entrapped by social, familial, financial, and work woes.

Nichols and screenwriters Calder Willingham and Buck Henry set up the entrapment theme in *The Graduate* even as the opening credits are rolling: An initial close-up of Ben's face pulls back to show him aboard a passenger jet descending into Los Angeles International, and this is closely followed by a medium shot of Ben first walking, then being carried by a conveyor belt through the airport. As Simon and Garfunkel's anthem of isolation, "The Sounds of Silence," plays, the canned voice of airport security drones repeatedly in the background, exhorting conveyor belt riders over and over, "Please hold handrail and stand to the right. If you wish to pass, please do so on the left." Ben, framed against the bare white wall behind him, stares straight ahead and is otherwise motionless as he is carried, cattlelike, along. Hence even before the narrative proper begins, we have the sense that Ben, returning to suburban Southern California after his graduation from a university in the East, is being led against his will back to a confining existence. The subsequent scene helps to clarify Ben's predicament: At a graduation party thrown by his parents, Ben is accosted by a series of older well-wishers, friends of his parents who all want to know about his future plans. He tries to escape, feigning the need to go to his room, or outside to "check on the car," but these escape plans are thwarted as he continues to be buffeted about by a series of garrulous older guests. The entire scene is captured in a series of close-ups in which the camera in a sense "crowds" Ben much as the partygoers do, creating an effect that, as Man notes, highlights Ben's "feelings of suffocation."[50] The root causes of this sense of suffocation are summed up most succinctly by one of the partygoers, Mr. Maguire, who corners Ben by the backyard pool to advise him on future career plans. Suggesting that Ben think in this regard of "just one word. . . . *Plastics*," Maguire unwittingly offers up the very metaphor used by the young to characterize his generation, whose lifestyle is seen as materialistic and contrived, a plastic existence reflected most clearly in their choice of landscape.[51]

Nor is it insignificant that Maguire's weighty if brief pronouncement is delivered poolside, for the shimmering backyard pool is used here, as it is in so much of the fiction and film of suburbia, to symbolize not only the materialism, but also the superficial, self-destructive narcissism of the suburban dream. Indeed, one can almost sense the textual echoes of Jay Gatsby and Neddy Merrill as Ben Braddock's uneasy relationship with the backyard pool is developed throughout the first half of the film. If Gatsby's long-neglected swimming pool eventually claims him, in death positioning him within the centerpiece of his vacuous exurban palazzo, and if Neddy Merrill is finally cleansed—at whatever painful cost—of his illusions about suburban community by the waters of the many pools he swims, then Ben Braddock also is characterized in terms of his relationship to this jewel of the suburban backyard. Much of the first half of the film is shot poolside, with Nichols in effect using the pool as a metonymic reminder of the significance of the suburban milieu. Nichols carefully manipulates the abundant water imagery to set up a kind of dialectical relationship between

Ben and the water in which he is so often immersed: On one hand, a series of shots of Ben lounging on a raft in the pool—particularly those that appear in a five-minute musical montage that chronicles the course of his sexual relationship with Mrs. Robinson—suggests his emerging sexual identity; however, this symbolic use of water is undercut by the recurrent drowning imagery, which paints Ben as a victim, isolated and submerged beneath the shimmering waters of suburban mediocrity. In the contraposition of these two symbolic uses of water, we get the sense that Ben's relationship with Mrs. Robinson is a reaction against the suffocating influence of his parents, an oedipal response to their challenge to his manhood.

This focus on water imagery begins with the first shot of the film proper; after the opening credit sequence fades out, we get a shot of Ben staring into his fish tank, a recurring symbol that emphasizes Ben's feelings of entrapment and aloneness. In the midst of the circling fish, at the bottom of the tank, stands a miniature plastic man in scuba gear, a thematic counterpart to Ben and a foreshadowing of the very role he will play at the bottom of his pool in one of the central scenes. This opening frame goes a long way toward establishing the predicament that Ben faces at his parents' suburban home—the glass fishbowl symbolizes not only entrapment and futility, but also the same heightened sense of visibility that characterizes the suburban world of picture windows Ben finds himself in once again.[52] The connections between this water imagery and his sexual affair with Mrs. Robinson are cemented later in the same scene when Ben escapes his graduation party to return to his room and his position before the fishbowl; it is here that Mrs. Robinson insists that Ben drive her home, throwing his keys into the tank. His retrieval of the keys marks the beginning of their relationship, which is established through the water imagery as an escape from the suffocating world of his parents' existence.

That this affair also stands as an oedipal reaction to his parents' denial of his own manhood is made clear in a subsequent party scene, the thematically central sequence that chronicles Ben's twenty-first birthday party. Another telling poolside moment, this scene features an assemblage of family friends and relatives awaiting the arrival of the guest of honor. Ben's father controls the action, proudly proclaiming to the guests that Ben is about to thrill them with a "practical demonstration" of his birthday present—a set of scuba gear that the crassly materialistic Mr. Braddock blithely informs his guests "set me back over 200 bucks." As Ben, embarrassed, attempts to delay or avoid appearing on the scene, Mr. Braddock kills time by ad-libbing a mock-grandiose introduction for his son. Mentioning (yet again) Ben's collegiate accomplishments, the father seems undecided as to whether his son is still a schoolboy or now a "man." In his rambling introduction, he first expresses his desire "to bring this boy out here," before correcting himself: "No, wait a minute. Oh let me amend that. To bring this *young man* out here . . ." His vacillations between the designation of "boy" and "man" continue throughout the introduction, and he twice more refers to Ben as a boy before the latter finally emerges in his scuba gear, to the delight of the cheering crowd. Playing to perfection the role of the castrating father, Mr. Braddock seems to delight in assailing Ben's manhood while orchestrating the party—and Ben's appearance in it—as a celebration of his own paternalistic munificence.

The remainder of this scene is shot from Ben's perspective, an innovative shift in narrative focalization that serves to highlight his sense of total isolation while also underscoring the parental cruelty that reinforces his sense of being less than a man. As Ben makes his way to the pool, past the crowds of cheering well-wishers and his father, who is gesticulating excitedly and offering unheard instructions, the only sound is that of Ben's breathing through the scuba apparatus. After he plunges into the pool— already a thematically weighty moment, given the careful setting up of the preceding water imagery—Ben quickly attempts to emerge again, only to be thwarted by his father. As Ben makes his way to the surface, he is greeted—in a shot that seems to resemble an odd reimagining of the birthing process—by the smiling faces of both of his parents, who are kneeling by poolside. The father reaches out and grabs Ben's mask, in what seems like a playful fashion, but then aggressively uses his grip to forcefully push Ben back underwater. Ben again attempts escape from the water, only to meet the same fate—once again forced back underwater by the hand of the father. After this second rebuke from his father, he retreats to the bottom of the pool, and the perspective shifts to a shot of Ben, standing alone at the bottom of the pool, in full scuba gear and staff in hand, in an image that portrays him as a fallen explorer, having discovered little more than his own futility and alienation.[53] Recalling the fates of Jay Gatsby and Neddy Merrill, Nichols's image of Benjamin here employs the swimming pool as a trope for suburban purgatory.

It seems only fitting that this scene is followed immediately by the sequence chronicling Ben and Mrs. Robinson's first sexual encounter; indeed, the phone call that initiates this meeting is first played, in voice-over form, while the camera maintains its long shot of Ben alone at the bottom of the pool. The narrative link here is unmistakable, and with it Nichols suggests the correlation between Ben's submerged, emasculated position—one engineered and enforced by the father—and his desire to initiate a sexual relationship that will reaffirm his masculinity. The oedipal connections do not end there; if the phrase "Mrs. Robinson" has entered the cultural lexicon as a signifier for the older, motherly object of postadolescent male desire, it is due in large part to the repeated emphasis the film makes on the close connections between the Braddocks and the Robinsons. While Mr. Robinson and Mr. Braddock are partners together in a law firm, a fact that suggests their interchangeability, Mr. Robinson goes further, telling Ben at one point that "In many ways I feel as though you were my own son." Nichols draws parallels as well between Mrs. Robinson and Mrs. Braddock; H. Wayne Schuth, for example, notes Ben's conflation of the two in a scene when he peers out the window and spies his mother dressed in a zebra-striped outfit, a pattern that resembles Mrs. Robinson's consistently "animal-like" clothing.[54] And the connections between the two women are not limited to this one instance of Ben's

scopophilic gaze; in the only scene that features simply Ben and his
mother, he is in the bathroom shaving when she enters, dressed in a black
negligee, and asks him what it is he does when he "goes off" at night. The
question makes Ben freeze, and the camera captures in close-up the razor
poised at his throat. On his mother's further prodding, Ben cuts his thumb
with the blade, a symbolic castration that further underscores the oedipal
connections among Ben, his mother, and Mrs. Robinson.[55] The abrupt
ending of this scene and beginning of the next, which features Ben and
Mrs. Robinson in bed together, underscores the connection between the
two women, fixing Ben's emerging sexuality within the oedipal sphere.[56]

Hence Ben's sexual affair with Mrs. Robinson, the thematic focal
point of the film, arises from his desire to prove his manhood in opposition
to the emasculating power of his parents. As Schuth argues, "Ben . . .
live[s] out his rage against his parents by 'screwing' the Robinsons, who
stand for his parents in his mind."[57] And yet Mrs. Robinson, as much as
she becomes a symbolic replacement for Ben's mother, also serves as a
kind of mirror to Ben himself. Both face the same predicament; like Ben,
Mrs. Robinson finds herself imprisoned within the confines of her suburban world. When she reveals to Ben that she was once an art major at
college but now knows "nothing" about art, Mrs. Robinson hints at the
larger sense that her life has lost direction as she has come to find herself
trapped in the stultifying role of upper-middle-class suburban housewife.
As Ethan Mordden aptly notes, Mrs. Robinson's essential problem is that
she has "grown old and beyond happiness in a suburban Californian
nowhere," a fact that makes her represent, for Ben, the futility and self-
destructiveness of suburban adulthood.[58] The antagonistic nature of their
relationship, then—Ben at one point bitterly refers to Mrs. Robinson as a
"broken-down alcoholic," while she informs Ben that he is not "good
enough" to date her daughter, Elaine—has much to do with their equally
troubled relationships to their shared landscape. While Mrs. Robinson
attempts to prolong the relationship with Ben to sustain the one outlet
(however self-defeating) to her deadening life as a suburban housewife,

Ben, despite his ambivalence, eventually breaks off the affair and so his connection—now all too intimate—to the suburban world of his parents and the Robinsons.

Although it begins as a kind of contorted, de facto incest taboo, Mrs. Robinson's refusal to allow Ben to date Elaine becomes a matter tied to landscape concerns; once Ben rejects Mrs. Robinson in favor of her daughter, he escapes what Mrs. Robinson cannot—the psychological as well as physical confines of suburban existence. The cinematography of the second half of the film underscores the enormity of this change, as Nichols's sumptuous rendering of such landmarks as the San Francisco Bay Bridge, the UC Berkeley campus, and Berkeley's student thorough-fare, Telegraph Avenue—not to mention the focus on wide-open high-ways and the sheer prevalence of driving footage—positions the second half of the film in marked contrast to the first, which, with its unyielding emphasis on the generic backyard and swimming pool, paints the suburb as a most confining milieu. Indeed, the sheer immensity of the contrast between Ben's suburban imprisonment and his subsequent awakening in the Berkeley section of the film would seem to provide justification enough—since little other is given—for his relentless pursuit of Elaine. To invoke again the psychological framework Freud offers in "Beyond the Pleasure Principle," it seems not unreasonable to read Ben's desire for Elaine as an unconscious drive to postpone, as long as possible, his eventual return to the "death" in life that is the suburban existence he has known and tried to flee.

But as Freud argues, irrespective of the pleasurable dilatory space provided by the erotic drive, the death drive reigns supreme, and that it is the case in this film as well. Ben's dogged pursuit of Elaine, and Elaine's eventual capitulation, finds them both, at film's end, in precisely the position they were trying to avoid: that of the conventional, suburban couple. And this is the irony of the film's closing sequence: After Ben completes his final, frantic pursuit of Elaine, abandoning the car (which from the beginning of the film had continually been associated with his sexual potency) at the roadside, out of gas, he rescues Elaine from the horrors of her conventional wedding only (presumably) to embark on the same road of life themselves. After they board the Santa Barbara municipal bus and collapse into laughter, and then deeper contemplation, in the backseat, the camera pans back to a long shot showing the bus driving down an unremarkable, tree-lined suburban street. A direct echo of the opening-credit sequence, this final shot emphasizes Ben's powerlessness: Despite his conscious rejection of suburbia and his unconscious transgressions against it, the close of the film finds him in the same position he was in at the beginning—being carried along into the confining, emasculating landscape of the suburb. Perhaps the only difference at the end is that he by then seems less aware of the direction in which he is heading. Whether such ignorance is a blessing or a curse is a matter left unresolved, but given *The Graduate*'s thoroughgoing indictment of the suburban landscape— which over the course of the film is associated with the imprisonment of the female, the unmanning of the male, and in a more general sense the spiritual bankruptcy of its adult inhabitants—one can only imagine that it is a little bit of both.

🏠 🏠 🏠

Considering Nichols's and Updike's texts alongside one another affords a glimpse into ongoing concerns over the relationship between masculinity and the suburban environment. From the onset of mass suburbanization in the postwar years, social critics decried the emasculating potential of a landscape whose uniformity deemphasized masculine agency and ambition. While *Rabbit Redux* and *The Graduate* offer evidence that concerns over suburban masculinity persisted throughout the 1960s, the historically specific social dynamics of these narratives suggest the ways in which the question of suburban masculinity evolved over time. For Updike, suburban homogeneity reflects a politically charged response to the emergent cultural pluralism that threatened white masculinity; for Nichols, the vacuousness of the materialistic suburban dream marks the suburbs as an entrapping, emasculating terrain for the first-generation "sons of suburbia" then coming of age. While both texts focus on the gender dynamics of suburban life, each offers only a glimpse into the tradition of female disempowerment in the suburbs, a topic of debate in the 1960s that would surface in fiction and film of the coming decade.

At the Crossroads: *It's a Wonderful Life*'s George Bailey (James Stewart) stands at the crossroads of his town and his life. Just as George's actions will preserve the small-town identity of Bedford Falls, so too will the town's evolution establish the direction—and confines—of George's life.

A Dangerous Woman: The independence and overt sexuality of Violet Bick (Gloria Grahame) align her with the threatening urban environment. A central figure in the nightmarish Pottersville sequence, Violet possesses an energy that is eventually suppressed as Bedford Falls reestablishes its small-town identity for the postwar, suburban years.

he Lady of the House: In contrast to Violet, Mary Hatch/Bailey (Donna Reed) represents a more traditional vision of feminine
smesticity. Mary's independence is contained throughout the film, and her position here, surrounded by the Bailey brood, is
pical of her association with the domestic sphere.

Sea Change: In Frank Perry's *The Swimmer*, protagonist Neddy Merrill (Burt Lancaster) suffers a devastating loss of social standing and is ostracized by his acutely class-conscious exurban community. Here, he has fallen so far as to be bounced from the raucous pool party being thrown by his onetime social underlings, the Biswangers.

The Fallen Explorer: The scuba gear worn by *The Graduate*'s protagonist Benjamin Braddock (Dustin Hoffman) is emblematic of both his futile longing to escape and his submersion in the waters of his parents' materialistic suburban experience.

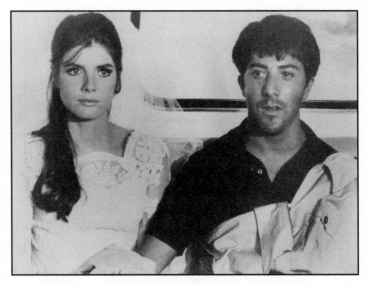

We're On the Road to Nowhere: Perhaps beginning to sense defeat in the very moment of their triumph, Ben Braddock and Elaine Robinson (Katharine Ross) become pensive as the film's close finds them being driven down the tree-lined streets of suburban Santa Barbara.

cture Perfect: For Joanna Eberhart (Katharine Ross), protagonist of *The Stepford Wives*, the seeming comforts of her new home and rroundings cannot hide the horrors that await her in exurban Stepford. Here, she gazes at a drawing of her face made by a member Stepford's "Men's Association," unable to decipher the significance of the image.

Everything New is Old Again: Filmed on location in the New Urbanist town of Seaside, Florida, *The Truman Show* seems to question the neotraditionalist values driving some of the latest waves of American suburbanization.

Time Out of Joint: Truman Burbank (Jim Carrey), protagonist of *The Truman Show*, struggles to understand his anachronistic existence. His life seems eerily like an old-fashioned suburban sitcom, and eventually he (along with the viewer) discovers that it is.

Approaching Stepford

Suburbia and the Limits of Domesticity

Perhaps the most telling scene in Bryan Forbes's 1975 film adaptation of Ira Levin's 1972 novel *The Stepford Wives,* a horror/fantasy about the psychological and emotional imprisonment of suburban women, comes when the protagonists, Joanna (Katherine Ross) and Bobbie (Paula Prentiss), arrange a "consciousness-raising session" for what they perceive to be the curiously anesthetized wives of the town of Stepford. While the scene begins seriously enough, with Joanna and her neighbor Charmaine (Tina Louise) sharing stories of the emotional estrangement they feel from their husbands, the focus of the conversation quickly shifts as another of the assembled women begins to relay her fears that she is falling behind in her housework, particularly her ironing. She is counseled by another of the group of women to try using "Easy-On Spray Starch," a product that will, apparently, greatly improve her success in ironing endeavors. Before long the group as a whole—with the exception of the bewildered protagonists—is extolling the virtues of Easy-On. When one of the assembled wives makes an impassioned speech about the starch, concluding that she would happily do a TV commercial for the product, even claiming she would do it "for free," the scene comes to a close—but not before a shocked Bobbie mumbles "Holy cow" to herself. This humorous scene goes a long way toward establishing not only the dominant theme of *The Stepford Wives,* but indeed a pointed concern, evident from the earliest days of the suburban age, regarding the peculiar relationship between gender and the suburban dream: that somehow the women of suburbia had become so enveloped within a stifling domestic sphere as to have lost perspective on or access to the world beyond the walls of the home.

The comic value of this scene, which stems from its exaggeration of the overly domesticated sensibilities of suburban housewives, does not entirely occlude the serious commentary it and the film as a whole make about the confinements the domestic sphere levied on the women of suburbia. And while *The Stepford Wives* emerged as a particularly memorable cinematic treatment of suburbia's disorienting effects on women's lives, it was hardly the first such commentary on the subject in American cultural discourse. As Lynn Spigel argues, "By the time of *The Stepford Wives,* popular culture had fully pronounced its own social critique of suburbia, presenting it as a decidedly inauthentic space where the social conventions of gender roles turned humans into artifacts."[1] The numbing nature of the suburban housewife's existence—famously dubbed "the problem that has no name" by Betty Friedan in her groundbreaking feminist study of 1963, *The Feminine Mystique*—had, by the late 1970s, become a familiar issue, as evidenced not only by the popular success of *The Stepford Wives* but also by the representation of the suburban housewife in such fictional works as Ann Beattie's 1980 novel *Falling in Place,* a portrait of family dysfunction in late 1970s' suburbia. Both Beattie's novel and Forbes's film—works set in an era when the American women's liberation movement was at its height of power and influence—react to the naturalization of the role of the domestic homemaker, a phenomenon that coincided with the mass migration to the suburbs in the postwar period.

As numerous social critics have argued, the suburban migration in the years following the end of World War II, along with the postwar baby boom, effected a profound shift in social and economic gender roles. These concurrent phenomena contributed to a totalizing celebration of domesticity and family life at the expense of the social freedoms and economic responsibilities women possessed during the war years.[2] This period is often considered significant for marking the return of "traditional" family structure and gender identities; nevertheless, a consideration of the various cultural practices involved in defining postwar gender roles suggests that the shifting social dynamics of this time bespoke less a return to the "traditional" than a socially constructed revolution in gender identity. As Christopher Lasch argues, the "traditional family" as we know it in the United States is in fact largely a "mid-twentieth-century innovation," a phenomenon tied to the suburban migration and fueled by the boom in postwar housing and the rebirth of the pastoral imaginary that it facilitated.[3] And if, as Kaja Silverman has suggested, the experience of World War II threw into relief the displacement of masculine presence on a national level, then the emergence of new, purportedly "traditional" gender roles in the years following the war also reflected a desire in mainstream national culture to reinforce the sense of masculine agency temporarily lost during the war years.[4] The suburban migration, then, both fueled and was driven by the new domesticity that characterized postwar, middle-class culture, a formula that marked the new suburbs as a prescriptive environment for women. As architectural critic Annmarie Adams notes, "There is no doubt that the mass movement of young American families to the suburbs in the 1950s and early 1960s had devastating implications for women's status. . . . The suburbs isolated them from political, social, and financial power and segregated them from opportunities for employment, education, and cooperative parenting."[5]

The movement toward the suburbs and the baby boom overlapped to create an entrapping space for women of the postwar years; relocating to isolated and, in Lewis Mumford's terms, "child-centered" environments, suburban women often suffered from a sense of dislocation and purposelessness, even as the culture at large was celebrating them as the central symbols in a new cult of domesticity. As Brett Harvey argues, this "all-out embrace of domesticity" in the 1950s "elevated family life into a kind of national obsession," ushering in "decade-long celebration of maternity."[6] Ironically, the suburban housewife and mother was of central importance as the symbol of the new domesticity, even as she found herself increasingly estranged from society at large. Although the effects of suburban migration and heightened attention to domesticity in the 1950s onward were often totalizing for women, "traditionalist" rhetoric served to naturalize these phenomena. Nevertheless, the "new domesticity" of the suburban age—and the prescriptive, limiting gender roles on which it was founded—did not emerge fully formed from some sort of national consensus; rather, it was the product of manifold cultural practices and discourses. Indeed, the celebration of the domesticated housewife in this era is a classic case study of the reification of gender roles that Judith Butler has discussed; and, as Butler notes, "even when gender seems to congeal into the most reified forms, the 'congealing' is itself an insistent and insidious practice, sustained and regulated by various social means."[7] In the early days of suburbia, the social means employed toward the solidification of reactionary and limiting gender roles were ubiquitous, as popular magazines, television sitcoms, and even the discourses of popular psychology and sociology were filled with admonitions—ranging from the subtle to the absurd—designed to persuade new suburban housewives to accept a domesticated role.

Perhaps the most obvious model for the role of the new housewife promulgated in popular culture during the years of the baby boom was to be found on television, as characters such as June Cleaver, Donna Stone (*The Donna Reed Show*), and other wife/mother characters from popular suburban sitcoms reflected what came to be the socially acceptable role of the suburban housewife. Contained within the space of the suburban home, these characters were presented in ways that worked to naturalize the distinction between the male, who served as breadwinner and familial authority figure, and the female, whose primary duty was presented as the

maintenance of a clean home and a contented family unit.[8] As Nina
Leibman has argued, in programs such as *Leave it to Beaver* and *The
Adventures of Ozzie and Harriet,* the complete absence of aspirations on
the part of the matriarch to venture beyond the suburban hearth was itself
a prescriptive statement concerning gender identity: In these shows,
"woman is treated as synonymous with housewife, her behavior effort-
lessly naturalized by the serene June and Harriet."[9] Of course, the spon-
sors of suburban sitcoms profited from the vision of the new domesticity
being presented in these sitcoms; and as Mary Beth Haralovich points out,
the suburban housewife, even as her small-screen "role model" found
herself marginalized often to the point of near disappearance, was at the
same time "being targeted, measured, and analyzed for the marketing and
design of consumer products."[10] Hence the double bind of the suburban
housewife in the 1950s: Positioned amid the interlocking discourses of
entertainment and consumer-product marketing, the married woman of
suburbia was at once a highly visible, even "targeted" social phenomenon,
while at the same time being conditioned to accept a role characterized by
confinement and estrangement from the world outside the home.[11]

As much as television helped to facilitate America's psychic migration
to suburbia, shaping gendered identities for decades to come, worth
considering is the fact that the socialization of American women in the
direction of this "new traditionalism" occurred in other discourses as well,
in a process that had been ongoing since the war years. Numerous
contemporary feminist theorists have pointed, for example, to the socializ-
ing effects wrought by a trio of psychosociological studies of womanhood
in America that emerged during and immediately following World War II:
Philip J. Wylie's *Generation of Vipers* (1942), Ferdinand Lundberg and
Marynia F. Farnham's *Modern Woman: The Lost Sex* (1947), and Margaret
Mead's *Male and Female: A Study of the Sexes in a Changing World* (1949).
Conspicuous for their appearance in rapid succession after the end of the
war (Wylie's book was published in a second, expanded edition in 1946),
these three works all sought—by various means and wildly divergent

approaches—to position the "modern woman" within a containable sphere of action and influence. Wylie's work, the most vitriolic of the three, exhibits a seemingly uncontrollable male paranoia as the author reads the escalation of wartime work by women as evidence of females "taking over the male functions and interpreting those functions in female terms," a process that Wylie felt would fuel the onward march of "Momism" and eventually reduce the working man to the status of a "feminine tool."[12] Lundberg and Farnham also lament the "masculinization of women," particularly since they read this phenomenon as potentially damaging to "the children," as well as to the ability of both men and women to "obtain sexual gratification." Arguing that this masculinization was the result of women encroaching on "traditionally" male spheres of action, the authors, looking forward to the great suburban migration, suggested simpler goals for women—namely, a "home, a husband's love, and children."[13] Mead's study, while by far the least reactionary of these three works, does make, despite its relatively reasoned tone, a bold case for the return of the woman to the domestic sphere; in fact, the subtlety of Mead's argument makes it, in some ways, the most pernicious of these three influential attacks on women's freedom.[14]

It did not take long for the rhetoric of female domesticity to reach mainstream outlets. A perfect example of this phenomenon can be found in a special year-end double issue of *Life* magazine from 1956 entitled "The American Woman: Her Achievements and Troubles." Something of a primer on appropriate female behavior for the suburban age, the issue juxtaposes glamorous photo pictorials—the direction is set with the opening piece, a ten-page photo spread entitled "The American Girl at Her Beautiful Best"—with essays concerning what are rendered as the praiseworthy and misguided traits of the "modern woman." Typical of the material throughout is this thought expressed by Catherine Marshall in her introduction to the special issue: "Ask any thoughtful, honest woman what the most satisfying moments of her life have been, and she will never mention the day she got her first job or the day she outwitted her boss on his ground. But she will always speak of . . . her first formal. . . . Or the night the man she loved took her in his arms, bringing a special look to her face. Then there was the moment when she held her first baby in her arms." Marshall also captures the tone of the issue as a whole when she goes on to speculate that "many of woman's current troubles began with the period of her preoccupation with her 'rights.'"[15] Other contributors also work toward squelching female voices that were, already by the mid-1950s, calling out for a release from the isolation of suburban living: Cornelia Otis Skinner, for example, in her essay entitled "Women Are Misguided," laments the fact that women of the age were "still waging a shrill, ridiculous war over the dead issue of feminism."[16] The antidote to the "troubles" plaguing the confused modern woman, offered again and again throughout the issue, is acceptance of the role of suburban house-wife. While one contributor argues that the modern woman is best served directing her energies toward maintaining a "well-ordered home, a secure and reasonably happy household, a contented and proud husband," another concludes that "truly feminine women, with truly feminine atti-tudes . . . will accept their wifely functions with good humor and pleasure. They will not think of themselves as 'just a housewife.'"[17]

Needless to say, the sheer weight of the popular discourse working to position her was a lot for the suburban woman to live up to, let alone for her to live down. It was not until the early 1960s that Betty Friedan, in *The Feminine Mystique,* systematically analyzed the varied social practices and discourses that had, since the end of the war, constructed a carefully delineated, restricting space for suburban women. A feminist counterpoint to the popular sociological studies of suburban life that emerged in the 1950s—including White's *The Organization Man* and Riesman's *The Lonely Crowd—The Feminine Mystique* shared the concerns of these works regarding the alienating impact of the suburban milieu, with the difference being that Friedan focused squarely on restrictive gender codes in the new landscape, something that her male predecessors had been either unable or unwilling to see. From her opening paragraph, Friedan adopts a historicizing stance toward the problems facing suburban women, locating "the problem that has no name" as a by-product of the midcentury migration to the suburbs: "The problem lay buried, unspoken, for many years in the minds of American women. It was a strange stirring, a sense of dissatisfaction, a yearning that women suffered in the middle of the twentieth century in the United States. Each suburban wife struggled with it alone. As she made the beds, shopped for groceries, matched slipcover material, ate peanut butter sandwiches with her children, chauffeured Cub Scouts and Brownies, lay beside her husband at night—she was afraid to ask even of herself the silent question—'Is this all?'"[18] Arguing that popular media had developed and espoused a "mystique" regarding femininity, a culturally inflected, essentializing vision of woman as a passive, nurturing figure, Friedan concludes that mass relocation to the suburbs functioned to position women within what she called a "comfortable concentration camp." Reduced solely to the status of caregivers for children within a patriarchal household, suburban women were, in turn, "infantilized" themselves, according to Friedan.[19] As Lasch notes, Friedan's work originated as a "direct response . . . to the suburbanization of the American soul" and, as such, paved the way for the oppositional renderings of suburban gender dynamics offered in fiction and film of the late 1960s, 1970s, and beyond.[20]

It might, in fact, be argued that such an oppositional sensibility was bubbling under the surface of works by female authors purportedly singing the praises of postwar suburban family life. Nancy Walker has suggested that such midcentury suburban humorists as Jean Kerr, Shirley Jackson, and Phyllis McGinley, each of whom penned whimsical chronicles of suburban family life, expressed through their work (even if not consciously) a form of subversive satire. Jackson's *Life Among the Savages* (1953) and Kerr's *Please Don't Eat the Daisies* (1957), both popular accounts of life as a suburban housewife, and McGinley's suburban light verse, collected in *A Short Walk from the Station* (1951), celebrate the foibles of the suburban family while also, at times, betraying undercurrents of dissatisfaction and isolation. Walker astutely notes the ambivalence running through these works, suggesting they reflect an ironic attitude toward entrenched gender roles.[21] McGinley's *A Short Walk from the Station*, in particular, exemplifies this doubled, contradictory perspective with regard to women's life in suburbia. McGinley opens this collection of verse with an essay, "Suburbia, of Thee I Sing!" in which she adamantly defends the suburbs against recurring charges that they are places of conformism, conventionality, and compromise (especially for female residents). Rightly pointing out that "to condemn suburbia has long been a literary cliché," McGinley instead celebrates the varied pleasures of her environment, concluding simply, "for the best eleven years of my life I have lived in Suburbia and I like it." Nonetheless, several of the poems contained in the volume tell a different story of the suburban woman's experience, none more pointedly than "Executive's Wife":

> Her health is good. She owns to forty-one,
> Keeps her hair bright by vegetable rinses,
> Has two well-nourished children—daughter and son—
> Just now away at school. Her house, with chintzes
> Expensively curtained, animates the caller.
> And she is fond of Early American glass
> Stacked in an English breakfront somewhat taller
> Than her best friend's. Last year she took a class
>
> In modern drama at the County Center.
> Twice, on Good Friday, she's heard *Parsifal* sung.
> She often says she might have been a painter,
> Or maybe writer; but she married young.
> She diets. And with Contract she delays
> The encroaching desolation of her days.[22]

The ennui, even helplessness McGinley conveys here anticipates Friedan's indictment of suburbia as a "comfortable concentration camp" in the coming decade. Subsequent portrayals of female protagonists in major suburban works—from *The Graduate* to Joyce Carol Oates's *Expensive People* (1968), a novel of family dysfunction and terror, to Marilyn French's *The Women's Room* (1977), a feminist critique of patriarchal culture, to Ann Beattie's novel of suburban family dysfunction, *Falling in Place*—have similarly depicted these characters as feeling isolated and trapped in suburbia.

Still, one wonders about the relationship between models of suburban living imaged in the baby boom era and critiques of suburban gender roles that appeared in subsequent decades. While Friedan's assessment resonated with women's lived experience in 1963, applying her analysis to fictional and cinematic depictions of suburban women's lives appearing some fifteen years later risks both oversimplification and historical inaccuracy. On one hand, both *The Stepford Wives* and *Falling in Place* echo Friedan's reading of the limiting nature of women's suburban existence. And yet, at the same time, these works also reflect historically specific challenges to patriarchal culture that set them apart from the terms of Friedan's critique. Both texts feature characters and themes associated with the women's liberation movement of the 1970s, invoking the very challenges to patriarchal hegemony that Friedan's influential work had helped to facilitate. In both works, the dynamism of the women's movement—a movement composed largely, as historian Margaret Marsh reminds us, of "suburban women and their daughters"—fails in the end to liberate female protagonists from a masculinist social landscape.[23] In this sense, Forbes's film and Beattie's novel anticipate what Susan Faludi has termed the antifeminist "backlash" of the 1980s.[24] Positioned historically between the postwar embrace of suburban domesticity and the neotraditionalist antifeminism of the 1980s, these texts depict the suburbs of the 1970s as a place torn by conflicting notions of women's social "place."

Indeed, as the activities of the women's movement and the representations of women in the works I will discuss suggests, the 1970s marked a turning point in women's relationship to the suburban landscape. In a decade that saw, for the first time, more Americans living in the suburbs than in either urban or rural areas, the change in suburban women's status, activities, and representations reflected broader changes in our cultural relationship to the suburbs.[25] Evidence that the age of the "comfortable concentration camp" was on the wane can be found as early as 1971, when Linda Greenhouse proclaimed in a *New York Times* article that the "idle, frustrated housewife" of suburbia had, by that time, become little more than a "cliché."[26] Still, as patriarchal—or, at best, gender-blind—perspectives continued to dominate sociological studies of suburbia throughout the 1970s, 1971 may have been too early to declare victory over "the problem that has no name." Consider, for example, this analysis of the fixture of the suburban home, the "family room," offered in 1978 by social critic Stephen Birmingham: "The family room is, as the name implies, a nest—a place where the woman of the house goes to relax and be comfortable, with her children and her husband, her brood, nestled around her."[27] Containing more than a vestige of 1950s' sentiment, Birmingham's vision of the "woman of the house" recalls Friedan's most dire assessments of suburban living and stands as testament to the durability of the "new traditionalist" vision of life in the postwar suburbs, something against which women of the 1970s continued to struggle.

It is precisely this contentious backdrop of gender politics in 1970s' suburbia that fuels the narratives of *Falling in Place* and *The Stepford Wives*. Both Beattie's novel and Forbes's film construct visions of female protagonists imprisoned in the suburban landscape, disconnected not only from work but also largely from social relationships outside of the family and home. Each text does suggest the possibility for escape from this lonely existence, through an empathetic relationship with another like-minded woman. Ultimately, in both the novel and film, these relationships prove insufficient to offset the negating effects of patriarchal structure in suburbia. And while Forbes's dystopian fantasy is the more dramatic and didactic of the two works, Beattie's novel offers a subtly devastating rendering of the isolation of the upper-middle-class suburban housewife, a realistic treatment of suburban despair that emerges from the tradition of Updike and Cheever and implicitly critiques those authors' myopic views of gender issues. Considered alongside one another, these two works compose a revisionary look at the suburban landscape, depicting a place where steps toward female empowerment are offset by the prevailing patriarchal culture and subsumed within a persistent mystique of domesticity.

🏠 🏠 🏠

Set in the late 1970s in suburban Connecticut and New York City, Beattie's *Falling in Place* reflects the author's propensity for chronicling both the minutiae and the larger, underlying tensions of upper-middle-class life. In this regard the novel, like the bulk of Beattie's work, situates her squarely in the tradition of fellow *New Yorker* writers who preceded her, including Cheever and Updike.[28] Like these male authors, Beattie uses attention to the trappings of contemporary life to examine the emptiness often lying beneath the seemingly placid surfaces of suburban affluence. However, in contrast to previous *New Yorker* writers—particularly Cheever—whose precisely detailed portraits of suburban affluence worked toward revealing the dark underside of an apparently sunny existence, Beattie's rendering of the suburban milieu remains curiously difficult to define, featuring self-involved characters acting and interacting often without apparent purpose or direction. Several critics have noted as much about Beattie's fiction in general: While Joseph Epstein detects a sense of "causelessness" in the author's work, John Aldridge claims that both Beattie's hyperrealistic style and the actions of her characters are fueled by "the same acquisitive and materialistic premises," and in that regard serve as reminders of the unreflective consumer culture from which they emerge.[29] Perhaps for these reasons, suburbia of the late 1970s becomes the perfect setting for Beattie's family melodrama; well past the age of the golden dream of postwar suburbia, by the time of Beattie's novel the suburbs were generally recognized for fostering a sense of dislocation and anomie, or what one social critic has referred to as "moral minimalism."[30] Hence, in contrast to her *New Yorker* predecessors, Beattie depicts a suburban world already fallen from grace, less a troubled utopia than a bland testament to the dislocations of a landscape emblematic of the superficiality of late-capitalist consumer culture.

Recurrent intertextual references in *Falling in Place* are made to *Vanity Fair,* and these repeated mentions of Thackeray's satire of upper-middle-class English life resonate with the dynamics of Beattie's novel. Although her novel lacks a figure as mercenary as a Becky Sharp, in her treatment of the affluent Knapp family and those who fall into their circle, Beattie shares Thackeray's concern with exposing the self-centered yearnings among a dissatisfied, comfortably affluent set of characters. Like *Vanity Fair, Falling in Place* features a number of loosely connected plot lines, positing through the juxtaposition of these narratives an aggregate portrait of a disaffected community. If there is a center to the novel, it is to be found in the Knapp family, headed by Louise—who feels lost in her role as a housewife in suburban Connecticut where, she feels, there are not "any intelligent people"[31] —and John, who divides his time commuting between his job in New York, his lover's downtown apartment, his mother's home in the upper-class suburb of Rye, New York, and the family home in Connecticut—where he has taken to spending only the weekends, and that grudgingly. The three Knapp children, fifteen-year-old Mary, enduring uncomfortable adolescence, John Joel, her emotionally unbalanced ten-year-old brother, and Brandt, the youngest, who lives with his grandmother in Rye, complete what quickly emerges as a dysfunctional family unit. While Beattie's widely dispersed narrative is also concerned with John's lover, Nina, and Mary's English teacher, Cynthia Forrest—and those characters' respective locales of New York City and New Haven, Connecticut—the action of the novel both begins and later reaches its climactic moment with a focus on the Knapps and their troubled suburban existence. And if, as both Carolyn Porter and Pico Iyer suggest, Beattie's characters in general tend to lack any significant psychological and emotional attachments to place, instead usually remaining, in Iyer's words, in "a kind of limbo, a no-man's land," then Beattie's consistently flat, surface-level depiction of the Knapps' suburban surroundings mirrors the detached sensibilities of her female protagonists, who are stuck in an unfulfilling landscape that both fosters and mirrors their detached sensibilities.[32]

The physical and psychological entrapment of Mary and Louise is no small matter in a novel that, with its constant, restless shuttling between suburban Connecticut and Manhattan settings, otherwise emphasizes mobility and is in fact structured according to the dynamics of commutation. Indeed, much like Fitzgerald's *The Great Gatsby* and the majority of Cheever's *Shady Hill* stories, *Falling in Place*—featuring countless scenes in parking garages, on commuter trains, and, especially, in the car—is very much a novel *about* commuting, about the bifurcated sense of urban/rural place identification at the heart of the traditional vision of suburban living. But in this regard, too, Beattie's novel is revisionary: In contrast to the vision of suburban life proffered in such cultural vehicles of post–World War II bourgeois sensibility as the *New Yorker* magazine, which has always imagined the life of the suburban commuter as offering the perfect marriage of urban sophistication with the comforts of country living, in Beattie's vision the break between city and outlying suburb becomes a dislocating factor, one that distorts place-bound identifications and understanding. Hence, while Nina, in her cramped apartment on Columbus Avenue, fantasizes about the idyllic existence at John's suburban home—which she imagines must feature a massive, wooded lawn and "stone pillars" at the foot of the driveway— John, going through the motions of suburban fatherhood, taking his family on picnics and barbecues, thinks longingly of Nina's apartment, meticulously reconstructing from memory the various pieces of furniture and decoration that adorn the tiny urban space. For Louise Knapp, the break between city and "country" has had more disastrous implications; having lived so long in the suburbs that she can now no longer "cope" with the city, Louise finds herself consequently relegated to a landscape that she "hates." A suburbanite against her best wishes, Louise faces a predicament reminiscent of those of Rabbit Angstrom and Ben Braddock, with the difference being that she sees no means of escaping the suburbs. In fact, while most of the characters spend the bulk of their time commuting between one place and another throughout the novel, both Louise and her daughter Mary remain fixed in place at their suburban home, enduring an environmental relationship that only worsens as the novel progresses.

This is not to say that a great deal of action transpires at the Knapp family home in Connecticut; indeed, from the opening of the novel, in which an argument between Mary and John Joel is interrupted by an equally rancorous conversation between Mary and her father, the Knapps' inharmonious home life remains something of a constant throughout. Eventually the suburban backyard proves the site of a sudden act of violence when John Joel, increasingly troubled over his father's abandonment of the family and his own sense of isolation, shoots Mary as she returns home from a visit with a friend. The shooting stands as the literalization of a tacit point Beattie makes throughout much of her narrative: that the isolated, upper-middle-class suburb is, in many ways, a threatening landscape for women. For Louise, this environment becomes a "landscape of fear" (to borrow geographer Yi-Fu Tuan's phrase) because it represents her disengagement from the world outside her family, even as it reminds her of her utter lack of control over what transpires *in* her home and family. In this regard, Louise represents what Aldridge has identified as a recurrent character type in Beattie's fiction, the "middle-class woman who is . . . feeling alienated from what is happening around her—or the fact that nothing is happening that she can find real."[33] And in Louise's confounding home and family life we see the paradox of Beattie's vision of suburbia: In contrast to the prevailing cultural vision of suburban family life as the epitome of stable, ordered, even mundane existence, in Beattie's representation suburban family life is characterized by random disorder, as evidenced not only by Louise's aimless sense of malaise but also, in a larger sense, by the fractures and rifts—one of them nearly fatal—in the family structure.

Beattie's bleak vision of suburban family life might strike the reader of today as nothing particularly out of the ordinary, as such sensationalistic treatments of the breakdown of the suburban family have become a staple of popular fiction, film, and reportage in recent years. Often this phenomenon is blamed on the dissolution of the "traditional" two-parent family with a "stay-at-home mom," and hence indirectly on women who seek careers outside the home. In Beattie's narrative the scenario is, if anything, worse for her female character, as Louise's position in a dysfunctional family is only exacerbated by her environmental isolation, her estrangement from the outside world that came with the Knapps' move out of the city. Like Cheever's suburban families before them, Beattie's Knapps are urban émigrés; and if Cheever's typically male-centered narratives evoke both the pleasures enjoyed and insecurities faced by male suburban transplants, Beattie's characterization of Louise suggests that the move to suburbia represented a withdrawal from life as she had previously known it, one that leaves her nearly incapacitated psychologically and emotionally.

Early in the novel, Louise's husband, John, ponders the changes suburban living has wrought on his wife: "In the beginning, he had only thought about making her happy by moving them to the suburbs. Now she hated him for being able to cope with the city when she couldn't. And she hated the suburbs because there weren't any intelligent people. . . . The truth was, she liked *normal* intelligent people, and they were hard to find" (59). When later questioned by her son John Joel concerning her feelings about life in the suburbs, Louise is ambivalent, but ultimately hints at the source of her dissatisfaction: "Sometimes I like it here, I think I'm lucky that we have enough money that I don't have to work," she muses, before tellingly concluding, "I don't know what kind of a job I could get anyway" (137). Lonely, disconnected, and mired in self-doubt, Louise represents the failure of the cult of domesticity, the *feminine mystique,* espoused in the early days of the suburban age; noting the insufficiency of family and homestead alone as defining models of identity, Louise crystallizes her predicament when she exclaims to her friend Tiffy, "It's selling you such a bill of goods to tell you that you should get married and have a family and be *secure*" (150).

If Louise's vaguely defined sense of ennui resembles a latter-day incarnation of Friedan's "problem that has no name," a gradual accumulation of details over the course of the narrative suggests that her problems begin at home, within the family structure. Increasingly estranged from John, an itinerant husband and father who feels like a "house guest" when he comes back to Connecticut for his weekend stays, Louise also has little interaction with her daughter and seldom sees her youngest son, who has been taken to live with his drunken grandmother in Rye. The majority of her interactions are with her emotionally damaged middle child, John Joel, whose bizarre behavior comprises the most pointed facet of Beattie's troubled rendering of suburban motherhood. Along with his friend Parker, John Joel engages in assorted acts of emotional terrorism aimed at the women in their families: While John Joel uses a pair of scissors to tear the seams of his mother's and sister's clothing, Parker pastes photographs of women's faces into scenes he has cut from his hard-core comic books to create troubling composite images. Parker shares with Louise's son one such piece of artwork, in which he has superimposed Louise's face over that of a marine sergeant leading into battle a company of men, one of whom "had stepped on a land mine and was being blown sideways, through smoke and flame" (161). With this startling image, Beattie metaphorizes the perils of suburban motherhood, in a grotesque gesture that foreshadows the eventual explosion of family violence at the Knapp home.

Outside of the troubling realm of the family, Louise's suburban existence offers her little opportunity for growth. Aside from Tiffy, described as a "feminist Professor" at New York University, Louise sees no like-minded counterparts among her housewife acquaintances. While one friend, Marge Pendergast, drinks too much scotch and busies herself perfecting her formidable tennis game, Parker's mother, clearly Stepford material, dedicates herself to baking mastery, and "most of her energy" goes into baking orange cakes that are "perfectly shaped, tall, beautiful" (233). Reflecting on her unsatisfying existence while driving with John Joel down a picturesque tree-lined street in their town, Louise notes that her unhappiness is tied to her landscape: "'I guess you always wonder,' she said, 'if you'd be a different person if you lived somewhere else. It's so beautiful here, and we don't notice it very much, and when we do, it doesn't seem to help us be happy'" (155). Resistant to both the surface-level appeals of suburbia and what she sees as unrewarding relationships with her neighbors and acquaintances, Louise retreats psychologically into the past, conjuring up memories of happier times, specifically through her recurring memories of her now-dead dog, Mister Blue. A measure of the broken connections to those around her, Louise's pathetic fixation on the memory of a dead dog signifies a nostalgia mode that runs not only throughout this novel but indeed, as many critics have noted, throughout the body of Beattie's work.[34] Louise is especially prone to lapsing into reveries of the game of "get the stick" she used to play with her beloved dog; as she explains to Tiffy, the comfort of these memories is tempered by an unwelcome intrusion of self-recognition, as she makes an explicit comparison between her position in life and that of Mister Blue: "No wonder I liked the dog. It was so dogged. It was just like me. It would've played 'get the stick' until it fell over dead, and I'd go on those stupid picnics and trudge through the snow if [John] kept saying we should go there" (143).

In elucidating here a sense of her own subservience in the family structure, Louise engages in one of several attempts to voice the discontent she feels. Typically, her objections fall on dear ears, as both her troubled children and her defensive husband—who at one point bluntly states, "I feel, when I am with my loving family, that everyone is conspiring to beat me down" (81)—fail to comprehend the source of Louise's dissatisfaction. Beattie's narrative approach only exacerbates her female protagonist's predicament; in a novel told from a limited third-person perspective that shifts focalization throughout, Louise Knapp is one of the few major characters whose psychological and emotional states typically come filtered through the perceptions of another character, usually either her husband or son John Joel. Coupled with Beattie's rapid shifts in setting, which tend to marginalize the suburban milieu in favor of the bustle of urban spaces, this peculiarity of Beattie's narrative perspective only reinforces the sense of Louise as a liminal figure in the novel.

Further complicating Louise's "place" in both the family and the narrative structure is her tendency toward living in the past, her continued habit of escaping an emotionally unfulfilling life by revisiting memories from a past both protected and perfected by the distance of time. As Susan McKinstry has argued, this sort of divided temporal consciousness is a staple for Beattie's female protagonists, whom she claims "puzzle readers because they tell two stories at once: the open story of the objective, detailed present . . . juxtaposed with a closed story of the subjective past, a story the speaker tries hard not to tell." While for McKinstry the "point of the story" typically lies in the "space between the two narratives," for Louise getting to the "point" of her story remains a difficult endeavor, for her displacement within the narrative structure—which I believe to be a conscious device of Beattie's, rather than a random flaw in narrative design—mirrors her displacement in her home and community.[35] In light of her unrewarding friendships and unresponsive family, Louise tends to tell her story only to herself, and her solipsistic narrative indeed vacillates, as McKinstry would suggest, between an overly romanticized past and an overdetermined present. Beattie only periodically offers the reader brief glimpses into what one imagines is Louise's ongoing interior monologue, a technique that underscores the sense that Louise is trapped in a kind of suspended animation, a forgotten suburban housewife "falling in place."

So totalizing is Louise's sense of isolation that one would almost mistake her for one of the lonely housewives of a previous generation Friedan describes in *The Feminine Mystique,* were it not for the presence of Louise's one confidante, Tiffy Adamson, a character whose status as a feminist professor and overtly political thinker reminds the reader that the action is taking place in the late 1970s and not the early 1960s. While Beattie's hyperrealistic style includes several precise historical details that do situate the action of the novel in the summer of 1979—Skylab is falling, *hyper-realism* [handwritten margin note]

Blondie's "Heart of Glass" plays endlessly on the radio—time in some sense seems frozen for Louise in her suburban seclusion, a sensation only reinforced by her interactions with the socially involved Tiffy. Indeed, Beattie carefully sets up the two figures as polar opposites: Perhaps taking a cue from *The Stepford Wives,* which constructs a similar relationship between protagonist and friend, she draws Tiffy as a strong-willed, independent Jewish woman active in both the political and cultural scenes of the city, the obverse of Louise as the frustrated, socially disconnected housewife trapped in the numbing culture of WASP suburbia. And despite Louise's sense that she often does not understand Tiffy's analyses of women's place in contemporary culture, Tiffy's unconventionality attracts Louise. At one point Louise confesses to John Joel that "I've always wanted to think that she was nearly perfect, and that she had it all together, and that there was a way I could be like her," concluding that "Tiffy has always been sort of a fantasy" (155). With this passage, Beattie suggests an alternative to the unfulfilling and destructive conventional relationships that fill the narrative, in the form of a closer bond, and perhaps romance, between Louise and Tiffy. Ultimately this relationship does not come to pass—but significantly, in contrast to other romantic relationships in the novel that seem to begin and end haphazardly, the break between Louise and Tiffy is a matter bound up with the same sexual politics that have, from the outset of the novel, isolated Louise in her lonely suburban existence.

Tiffy moves to the city [handwritten margin note]

Indeed, Beattie's decision in the end to separate Louise and Tiffy—the latter leaves behind her friend, her husband, and the suburbs to take an apartment alone in the city—emphasizes the conventionality that entraps Louise. In fact, throughout the course of the narrative, Tiffy's striking difference helps to highlight this conventionality; John, for example, ridicules Tiffy for her stance as a feminist thinker and scholar. His disdain in turn influences his son John Joel, who displays his indoctrination into reactionary gender conventions as he tells his father scornful jokes about feminists. In a broader sense, Tiffy's sensibilities and her nontraditional relationship with her husband have challenged the social conventions of their suburban town; as the reader learns from the diabolical Parker, word has spread that Tiffy is perhaps more "manly" than she should be and that her husband is therefore considered "faggy." John Joel seems threatened by Tiffy's presence as well: As he spends an afternoon with his mother and Tiffy, he wonders if he himself may be "queer." If the reaction Tiffy provokes suggests that she challenges prevailing, restrictive sexual norms, Beattie's eventual withdrawal of Tiffy from the action of the narrative serves to reinforce the sexual status quo. Significantly, Beattie removes Tiffy from the suburb itself; in one of her own final appearances in the novel, Louise informs John that Tiffy has left her husband and moved to the city. Seeing in her friend's action a possible way out of her own position in a ruined, emotionally abusive marriage, Louise threatens to do the same thing and join Tiffy in New York, leaving the children in John's care. But her threat is empty and her vision of a life with Tiffy remains only an unrealized fantasy: After expressing for a final time to her unsympathetic husband her hatred of the Connecticut suburbs, Louise simply disappears from the action, her quiet exit an apt conclusion to her marginal existence throughout.

The sustained contrast between Louise's static, emotionally empty life and her various fantasies of escape strikes an ironic tone when considered in light of her friend's work as a feminist theorist. Tiffy, presumably a literary or cultural critic, questions the social discourses that work to subordinate women like Louise. In particular, she questions the world of fantasy itself, analyzing fairy tales from a gendered perspective; at one point she explains her approach to Louise, in a passage that resonates metatextually with the experiences of the women in Beattie's novel: "'I guess it's obvious to people now that most often it's the women who are monsters or the ones who have to wait for Prince Charming. But I was wondering today what those fairy tales would sound like if . . . women told it from their perspective. . . . I wonder if a lot of them weren't evil just because they were so worn down'" (147). Tiffy's observation aptly describes the situation of Louise—who in her own words was "sold a bill of goods" when she bought into the culturally produced fantasy vision of herself as the matriarch of a "secure" suburban family household; and significantly, for a novel concerned with generational connections and rifts, this passage also resonates with the experience of Louise's daughter Mary, whose thoughts and actions indicate her tacit acceptance of the same mythology of the feminine mystique. Encouraged by her sexually adventurous friend Angela, who ritualistically forces herself to vomit after every meal to avoid gaining weight, Mary attempts to manipulate her physical appearance to make herself more attractive to boys. Following Angela's lead, Mary attempts to pluck her eyebrows and winds up instead with a bruised and swollen face, an incident that evokes in Louise a combination of anger and bewilderment: "What she had done, plucking her eyebrows, hadn't been done as a joke at all. That was pathetic because it wasn't an imitation of a joke . . . it was an imitation of what Mary thought was beauty" (97). Indeed, in her disfigurement in this scene and again, more dramatically, in the shooting that leaves her crumpled in a pool of blood in her backyard, Mary emerges as the literal embodiment in the text of the continuing perils of suburban womanhood; her body becomes the text on which the psychological and emotional struggles of both herself and her mother are manifested.

[margin note: Mary's attempt at beauty prefigure her death]

Beattie's handling of the shooting scene itself is characterized by the same detachment to be found in the rest of the suburban portion of the novel. Indeed, Beattie manipulates the setting carefully to frame the entire incident as a distorted inversion of a typical suburban family scene. As Mary crosses through an adjacent field and enters the backyard, returning from a visit with Angela, Louise and Tiffy sit in the kitchen chatting over iced tea, bumble bees hover in the jetting spray of a sprinkler, and John Joel and Parker are perched in a tree they have just climbed. On the surface, little would distinguish the scene from something transpiring in Beaver Cleaver's Mayfield, until John Joel, posturing with the gun that Parker had told him wasn't loaded, "accidentally" shoots his sister. Immediately thereafter, we learn that Louise and Tiffy had just been discussing the sexual politics of Cinderella; Beattie's careful juxtaposition here reinforces the message sent by John Joel's action, however accidental it may have been: In Beattie's vision, the gender politics of suburbia as the American fantasy landscape have created a space not only restrictive, but in fact dangerous for women.

This point is reinforced by Beattie's subsequent structuring of the narrative; although clearly the climactic scene of the novel, the shooting is then virtually ignored as the narrative follows John's troubled flights to and from the city in the wake of this accident. Ultimately, we revisit the scene of the shooting near the end of the novel, from John's perspective. As he remembers the scene, his son's extreme act of violence was treated as little more than a momentary disturbance of decorum in this upper-middle-class suburb: "The blood on the ground: the cops had blasted it away with the garden hose. They had cleaned up as though someone had made a faux pas. They had taken pictures of the bloody ground, and then they had washed the area with a hose: the polite host, passing no comment, silently mopping up spilled wine" (323). In this passage Beattie, like Cheever, Updike, and Naylor, envisions a suburban landscape whose orderly appearance belies a rigid environmental control, a compulsion to conceal the distasteful. While life goes on in this momentarily disturbed place, and the action of the narrative continues to unfold, Mary, like her mother, essentially disappears after the shooting, her silent departure befitting her troubled position in the family and the dynamics of the narrative.

Unlike Tiffy, whose freedom from the constraints of suburban life is apparent throughout, and who eventually leaves the scene altogether, both Louise and Mary Knapp remain fixed in place throughout the novel, static, marginal characters in a landscape seemingly sealed off from the outside world. Louise sums up the predicament best when she laments the fact that her husband has the freedom to live a life outside of this terrain, what she describes as "another life, a real life, a life she didn't understand anymore" (97). And it is precisely around this tension between motion and stasis, action and immobility, that Beattie shapes her critique of suburban, upper-middle-class life. Indeed, this contrast provides one way of reading the title image of the novel: Although the line "falling in place" comes from Mary's reading of *Vanity Fair,* and her supposition that in the world of that novel things have a way of working out or just "falling in place," in an entirely different sense it is Mary and her mother who eventually "fall in place." While Mary literally falls to the ground in her backyard, victim of her brother turned suburban sniper, Louise in a manner of speaking is "falling" throughout the novel, as she is disengaged from both family and society at large, isolated and forgotten.

What Louise resembles more than anything else in the novel are the sculptures by George Segal that John Joel sees and becomes fascinated by on a trip to the Whitney Museum. Although he hesitates relaying to his mother his fascination with Segal's show, which depicted his famous dehumanized, lifeless forms in typical domestic settings, he tells Tiffy about it; she has seen the show as well, and her analysis, while specifically contrasting Segal's alienated forms with the whimsicality of a Calder exhibit, also reminds us of the emptiness of Louise's existence: "'Maybe I'm just getting old, but when I went through the Segal show, I felt so frustrated. I felt like these things were so still, and when I stopped to look at Calder's Circus again on the way out, I felt like they had little hearts beating, and that their little eyes blinked and their mouths smiled when they were alone. When Segal's people were alone, I thought they'd be just as still. That they couldn't move, under any conditions'" (142). Louise, as we learn over the course of this otherwise bustling narrative, cannot move either; she even remains paralyzed after hearing the gunshot and must rely on Tiffy to rush to her daughter's aid. Her stasis throughout the novel reveals the incapacitating effects of the suburban milieu on the isolated housewife. Even in the age of Skylab, a symbolic effort to put a human face on outer space exploration, Beattie suggests that the most mundane and familiar of spaces, the suburb, remains a dehumanizing environment for women. Indeed, her recurring references in the novel to the impending fall of Skylab serve as an apt metaphor for the world of late 1970s suburbia that Beattie creates: The sky is indeed falling in Beattie country, but it seems that the women are the only ones who notice.

🏠 🏠 🏠

One of the many thematic and symbolic connections between Beattie's *Falling in Place* and Bryan Forbes's 1975 film *The Stepford Wives* can be found in their shared use of the image of lifeless, manufactured female forms to connote the paralysis of the life of the suburban housewife. Beattie uses Segal's exhibit at the Whitney as a means of conveying fractured relationships, emotional paralysis, and a larger sense of the dehumanization of life in the Connecticut suburbs, and Forbes begins *The Stepford Wives* with a similar image. The film opens with the last-minute activities of the Eberhart family, as they clear the remainder of their belongings out of their New York apartment in preparation for their move to the upper-middle-class suburb of Stepford, Connecticut. As the protagonist, Joanna, a wife, mother, and "semi-professional photogra-pher," reluctantly gets in the cab that will take her and the family away from the city for good, she catches a subject of artistic interest: A young man across the street is carrying under his arm a white plastic mannequin of a nude female body. While the young man steals across the street, Joanna emerges from the taxi and photographs him. A crucial moment at the outset of the film, this scene sets up the dynamic interplay among vision, gender identity, and landscape that will comprise the thematic focus of the narrative. As Joanna frames this symbolic tableau of dis-torted and oppressive gender roles in her camera lens, her daughter exclaims from the backseat of the cab, "Daddy, I just saw a man carrying a lady," to which her father replies, "Well, that's why we're moving to Stepford." The unintentional irony of Walter Eberhart's response only becomes apparent as the film progresses; as we are to learn, the move to Stepford becomes not an escape from the "perversions" of urban life but

[handwritten margin notes: the opening scene; the patriarch's have replaced their wives in android form]

instead the removal to a landscape predicated on the very kind of gendered domination Joanna captures in her photograph.

Stepford, as the viewer is soon to find out and the protagonist eventually learns, is a fantasy world of patriarchal control, a place where the men of the town have devised a process of replicating their wives in android form. Perfect physical copies of the eliminated women, the manufactured Stepford wives exist solely to serve the wishes of their husbands, combining sexual subservience with a boundless devotion to and love of housekeeping. Hence, with a process that culminates in the killing of the biological wife and her replacement by the robotic other, the men of Stepford—united under the auspices of their "Men's Association"—ensure their mastery of the domestic sphere while guaranteeing limitless sexual gratification and control. Although this dystopian fantasy has garnered little serious critical attention, it stands as an important testament to America's cultural anxiety over changing gender roles and identities in the 1970s.

That the film is specifically situated in the suburbs is no coincidence; as Betty Friedan had demonstrated over a decade earlier in *The Feminine Mystique,* the growth of the suburbs in the postwar period coincided with a rigorous cultural positioning of females into a domesticated role, an endeavor tied to fears over women's increasing social autonomy and influence during the war years. This drive to reinstitute the social norms of a patriarchal culture—a fixture of both sociological and pop culture commentary from the immediate postwar years throughout the ensuing decades—met in the 1960s and 1970s with resistance from a women's movement populated by, among others, middle-class suburban women dissatisfied with the limitations of the role of housewife. And as we eventually learn in *The Stepford Wives,* it was indeed the rise of the women's movement in suburban Stepford that led to the activities of the Men's Association. In this sense, although the film might seem a timeless horror fantasy about manipulation and takeover, as a commentary on landscape and gender relations it is actually very specifically tied to both

[handwritten margin note: It was the rise of the women's movement that made the men's association]

its terrain and its historical moment. Amid the broad social turmoil of mid-1970s' America, *The Stepford Wives* evidenced an ongoing cultural concern over the connection between suburban living and gender relations.

In his adaptation of Ira Levin's novel, screenwriter William Goldman remained faithful to the author's depiction of Stepford's sinister sexual politics. Although Goldman altered several central points of Levin's text—most notably, in the novel Joanna solves the mystery behind Stepford's bizarre sexual dynamics, but only just before she is killed and replaced—he retained Levin's dark allegorical vision of suburban gender dynamics. Indeed, the screenwriter's decision to leave his protagonist more fully "in the dark" only heightens the film's emphasis on the furtive power of the Men's Association, in turn making the film version a more chilling rendering of patriarchal dominance. Given this thematic focus, Goldman's addition to his script of the early sequence by the taxicab is worth noting. Joanna Eberhart's photo of a man in possession of a lifeless, plastic female form—taken moments before her departure for Stepford—has a metatextual resonance with the course of events to follow in the narrative. Significantly, however, Joanna fails to interpret the text of the photo; a struggling, would-be artist, she does not trust her eye as a photographer and later burns many of her photographs in the fireplace of the Stepford house. Hence, unlike in a film such as Antonioni's *Blow-Up* (1966), the camera eye in *The Stepford Wives* does not serve as a means of gathering crucial evidence toward solving the mystery at hand, but rather as a continual reminder of the protagonist's ineffectual, compromised vision. In this sense, this early scene foreshadows the futility of Joanna's continued efforts later to interpret the bewildering gender dynamics of Stepford society.

That Joanna's difficulty in *seeing* is tied to her change in landscape is made apparent by Forbes's careful sequencing of the film's early scenes. Immediately preceding the incident by the taxicab, in the first shot of the film, Forbes shows Joanna lingering for a final few moments in the now-empty apartment. Tight, eye-level shots emphasize the angular lines and the sense of snug comfort that characterize the small urban space, and it is from Joanna's perspective that the viewer takes in the apartment she is preparing to leave. In contrast, after the scene at the taxicab and the drive north to the suburbs, we eventually see Joanna entering the Stepford house for the first time, alone. Here the camerawork emphasizes the protagonist's insignificance: In a shot from high atop the grand staircase to the second floor, Forbes's camera captures Joanna standing alone in the foyer of what seems an immense house, looking bewildered and, by virtue of the camera angle, small and isolated. The change in perspective here to an outside angle of vision signals Joanna's shift from the subject to the object position. On her removal to the suburban sphere, she enters a world where women quite literally become objectified, and the shift in camera perspective suggests the extent to which she will become the object of increasingly intense observation by the men of Stepford.

Indeed, much of the film emerges as a case study in the psychosexual dynamics of *looking*—of the positioning and pleasurable manipulation of fetishized sexual objects—that has itself been a central concern of film theory at least since the 1977 publication of Laura Mulvey's groundbreaking essay of feminist film theory, "Visual Pleasure and Narrative Cinema." As Mulvey claims, classic Hollywood cinema appeals to the male viewer through its objectification of female characters, as well as through its tendency to feature a narrative point of view tied to a lead male character. Hence in the classic cinematic exchange, the male spectator enjoys a vicarious sense of mastery through his alignment with the male hero, while sharing the hero's scopophilic ability to position women as erotic objects.[36] *The Stepford Wives* does not necessarily conform to Mulvey's analysis of sexual power and the gaze, for ultimately the film indicts the men of Stepford, who are depicted as a patently evil crew. Nevertheless, the film almost seems to anticipate Mulvey's argument with its insistent and self-conscious play with visual perspective and the dynamics of what film theorist Jane Gaines has labeled "looking relations." The men of Stepford predicate their efforts toward re-creation and domination of the females on the power of their gaze. Time and again throughout the course of the narrative, we see the women of Stepford positioned by the male gaze: The "converted" wives are subject to intense surveillance at a neighborhood cocktail party; Joanna joins a Men's Association meeting only to find that this seeming step toward equality only provides a means for their intense scrutiny of her; and, most tellingly, the power of the male gaze affords the men the ability to create visually perfect replicas of all of the "Stepford Wives." In fact, the only element missing from the android recreations is the eyes, so the "replacement" process only becomes complete after the eyes of the victim have been transplanted to her replacement, in the final and ultimate theft of female vision and, by extension, subjectivity.

Through this ongoing play with the power dynamics of the scopophilic gaze, Forbes conveys an image of the suburb as an intensely *visual* landscape, a terrain marked by a compromised subjectivity brought about by the breakdown of distinctions between public and private spaces. In this regard, the film conforms to our ingrained cultural image of the suburbs. Both the architecture and landscape of the suburb— where "picture windows" minimize the distinction between inside and outside, and where separate but contiguous lawns replace urban and rural privacy with the illusion of shared, neighborly space—highlight the visibility of its residents. In Stepford, such visibility is tied to both sexuality and power relations, a point that is emphasized on the Eberharts' arrival in town and throughout the narrative. On her first full day in town, Joanna, out walking in her yard, unwittingly spies her next-door neighbors, the Van Sants, engaged in an amorous embrace in their front yard. Hiding behind a bush, Joanna lingers to take in the scene. The viewer watches the scene from Joanna's perspective, and hence we have a momentary instance of Joanna enjoying ownership of the eroticizing gaze. As we are soon to learn, however, even at this point Joanna's gaze is co-opted by that of the male, for what she is seeing is Stepford's masculine fantasy of female sexual subservience come to its fruition: Joanna's neighbor, Carol Van Sant, has already been "replaced" by her robotic counterpart and thus is occupying the position Joanna will eventually be forced into. In a later scene, Joanna and her friend Bobbie walk into the house of another Stepford couple without knocking, only to overhear the couple making love upstairs. Joanna and Bobbie can barely stifle their laughter as they overhear the woman exclaiming to her husband, "You're the best, Frank . . . You're the king, Frank . . . Oh, you're the champion, Frank, oh, you're the master!" Despite the comic value of the scene, the two protagonists' discovery of Frank's "mastery" also captures in miniature the sexual politics of the town.

In conjunction with the spying and eavesdropping of Joanna and Bobbie, which only serve to reveal the extent of masculine dominance in Stepford, the male gaze assumes an omnipotent capacity, and through the contrast of these visual perspectives Forbes offers his critique of ongoing gender inequities in American suburbia of the 1970s. The most telling aspect of the narrative in this regard centers on Joanna's relationship to the Men's Association, a group that claims all of the adult males of the town as members and is behind the plot to replicate the "Stepford wives" in robotic form. Long before she learns of the association's principal goal, Joanna labels the organization sexist and archaic, and she is opposed from the outset to Walter's joining; however, when asked by Walter to host a meeting of the association's organizational committee she readily accepts, sensing the opportunity to have her voice heard in the affairs of the town. Instead, she finds herself playing hostess to the intensely bland group, fetching drinks and cleaning ashtrays in what amounts to a "tryout" for her eventual role as a full-fledged "Stepford wife." But something more sinister is afoot as well in this scene, and it has everything to do with Joanna's position as the object of an intensely scrutinizing male gaze. Shortly after the members of the Men's Association arrive at the house, Joanna finds herself cornered in the kitchen by Dale "Diz" Coba, leader of the association, whom she finds staring at her while she fixes drinks for the waiting guests. When she questions his presence in the kitchen, Diz unctuously informs her, "I like watching women doing little domestic chores." In her wittiest rejoinder of the film, Joanna answers back, "Well, you've come to the right town." The irony of her response is that Joanna only half-realizes its seriousness: In the discussion that follows among the organizing committee, Joanna becomes the object of intense observation, the point of which is to facilitate the creation of her domesticated, android replacement.

As she joins the men in the living room, participating in their conversation about possible upcoming fundraising events in town, she notices she is again being stared at, this time by a stately older gentleman named Ike Mazzard. A renowned artist, Ike fixes Joanna in his gaze, making her the subject of a number of sketches he produces over the course of the evening. Joanna, unsure of what he is doing, at one point stares back at Ike, and Forbes uses a shot/countershot sequence to shift the perspectives between the two characters as they gaze across the room at each other. With this technique, Forbes explicitly frames the scene as a struggle for ownership of the gaze, highlighting the importance of the moment. Joanna, who as a struggling photographer aspires to possess the artist's capacity to order or create a world through her vision, is—unbeknownst to her at the time—in the process of being painted into oblivion, as it were, being replicated on the sketch pad as she will shortly be replicated in bodily form. At one point the camera pulls back behind Ike to reveal what he has produced on his sketchpad: an array of sketches of Joanna's eyes. The significance of this shot is unmistakable, given Forbes's careful setup of the dynamics of vision in the scene: Although the sketches of Joanna's eyes serve a practical purpose in the process of her replication—contributing to the project of producing a perfect physical copy of her—at the same time they suggest the theft of her vision and, in a larger sense, her identity.

Turning her quest for equality with the men on end, the association, through the power of Ike's vision, in this scene begins the process that will eventually eliminate Joanna altogether as an individual. As the meeting nears a close, Ike hands Joanna a full portrait of her, a seemingly kind gesture that in fact foretells her eventual destruction. Gazing at the image and at last recognizing Ike as a popular artist of a previous generation, a flattered Joanna responds, "You're *the* Ike Mazzard? I used to gawk at all those girls in those magazines. You blighted my adolescence, you know." Here we sense the continuity between Ike's earlier career—involving the production for popular magazines of images of women as objects of beauty—and the activities of the Men's Association: In both cases, the visual objectification of women serves as a means toward masculine control and dominance. Moreover, the dominance of the masculine gaze is only reinforced by Forbes's careful positioning of this sequence: The organizational committee meeting immediately follows—in fact, it inter-rupts—a scene in which Joanna is at work in her darkroom, developing her latest series of photographs; a subsequent sequence shortly after the committee meeting features Joanna seated in the living room before the fireplace, tearing up her photographs and tossing them into the fire.

The intense visual positioning of women evident in this sequence of scenes is only part of a larger network of masculine domination of life in Stepford. Indeed, the town itself becomes a veritable grid of surveillance that serves to entrap the few remaining human women. At the center of masculine control in Stepford is Diz Coba, president of the Men's Associ-ation, who acquired his nickname through association with his former career at Disney World. Apparently Diz has adapted the strategies of his former place of employment and put them to use in Stepford: for, as in the world of Mickey Mouse and Donald Duck, the men's "Magic Kingdom" of Stepford is not only populated by animated puppets and their control-lers, but also is predicated on a close, careful control of all details of the landscape and those who inhabit it.[37] Particularly noteworthy in this regard is the prominent presence of law enforcement in the town; despite Joanna's fears that she would live in complete silence after relocating to Stepford, the film is punctuated regularly by the sound of sirens and the image of police cars and officers in action. A jarring contrast to the tranquility Stepford claims as one of its primary attractions, these signs of ceaseless police activity reinforce a sense of suburban Stepford as a closely monitored, regulatory environment. At one point Joanna herself is accosted by a police officer as she unknowingly nears the center of Diz's operations, walking her dog in the vicinity of the Men's Association headquarters at night. After the police officer pins Joanna in his search-light, he orders her away, explaining that "we can't let people just walk around at night." After Joanna protests that she moved to Stepford so she "could walk around at night," the officer qualifies his objection, suggesting that "this isn't the best place for you to wander around." In many ways the scene is eerily reminiscent of the close of John Cheever's "The House-breaker of Shady Hill," in which the reformed suburban burglar Johnny Hake, caught prowling the neighborhood by night, escapes police ques-tioning by claiming that he is merely out walking his (imaginary) dog. The crucial difference between the two scenes hinges on gender relations and power: Joanna, having inadvertently stumbled into a proscribed environ-ment, is rendered defenseless by the surveillance of a seemingly omnipres-ent male power structure.

A sequence from the middle of the film, chronicling a garden party thrown by Diz, cements the connections between gendered power rela-tions and the suburban landscape. As the scene opens, the camera—positioned behind a large picture window in the rear of the house—pans across Diz's lawn, affording a panoramic view of the guests positioned around the staples of the suburban backyard, the swimming pool and barbecue pit. Next we see a sequence of shots showing Diz prowling the party, presumably working to maintain order as he dispatches whispered instructions to various Stepford husbands. As we soon learn, Diz has good reason to be concerned, for in the midst of the party, one of the "Stepford wives," Carol Van Sant, begins to behave in a mystifying manner. The camera's perspective—here tied to the surveying male gaze—follows Carol as she stumbles about the yard aimless and dazed, quipping to anyone who comes in her path, "I'll just *die* if I don't get this recipe!" Almost as quickly as she "short-circuits," Carol is whisked away by her angry husband and the problem seems resolved; nevertheless, this scene offers one of the few instances in the film where masculine dominance is challenged, even if only through a fault in the programming of the android Carol. In her malfunctioning state, Carol's cyborg replicant could be read as engaging in a sophisticated, ironic critique of her position in Stepford society: By adopting the role of the envious homemaker and repeatedly mouthing this line of inane, fawning praise, the robotic Carol caricatures the very caricature into which she has been made.[38]

The tantalizing interpretive option offered by this scene is that some residue remains of the "original," human Carol Van Sant, a possibility that takes on more significance when the viewer, along with Joanna, learns that Carol was once the head of a "women's group" in Stepford. Joanna is shocked to discover that Stepford was once at the vanguard of a burgeoning women's liberation movement; as she learns from the editor of the town newsletter, Stepford was once considered a "liberal" town and in fact had the "first women's club" of any town in the area. Buoyed by this news, Joanna—who claims she "messed around a little bit with women's lib in New York"—convinces Bobbie to help her restart the women's movement in Stepford. While they are able to coerce a number of women to join their first and only meeting, their utter failure to elicit any kind of meaningful discourse among the group reinforces both the isolation of the individual women and the sense of male dominance in the town. Nevertheless, the pointed reference to past political activity among these suburban women works to evoke a historically specific challenge to male power. What the agenda of the Men's Association reveals, in turn, is the tremendous insecurity of the suburban male in the face of an increasingly strong women's movement. In this regard, *The Stepford Wives* becomes as much a film about the anxieties of the suburban male as it is about the destruction of the suburban woman. In their need to squelch the woman's movement by systematically destroying and replacing every woman who comes to live in town, the men of Stepford work to create what science fiction critic Thomas Byers has described as an "economy of the male and masculine exchange, of the phallocentric 'closed circuit.'" And if, as Byers argues, in science fiction films it is often the "insecurities of male identity and hegemony that at once necessitate and threaten the defensive constructions of patriarchy," then the project of the Men's Association can be read as a combination of equal parts fantasy and phobia, a reactionary positioning that has as much to do with self-definition as it does with domination of the other.[39]

This curious portrayal of oppressive suburban gender relations—in which the destructive omnipotence of the males is rendered as a reactionary, defensive counter to fears of growing female influence—not only situates the film squarely within the tumultuous gender politics of the 1970s, but also opens the text out into larger concerns (characteristic of suburban fiction and film in general) over the erasure of identity and loss of individual agency. In this sense, the film closely resembles other science fiction works centering on the theft of identity, such as Don Siegel's *Invasion of the Body Snatchers* (1956). Like *Body Snatchers*—a film that has been read as a critique of the homogenization of identity in postwar suburbia—*The Stepford Wives* broaches the possibility that something in the suburban experience fosters the erosion of personal autonomy.[40] The crucial difference between these works, however, is that by the time of *The Stepford Wives*, the threat of "takeover" is no longer imagined as alien, but rather comes from within a community fractured by a legacy of gendered inequality and insecurity.[41] After discovering the replacement of Charmaine and, finally, Bobbie by inane, domesticated androids, Joanna— sensing that she is the only "real" woman left in town—realizes that her only choice is to flee Stepford. Her instincts are confirmed by a female psychiatrist she visits for counseling; conceding that for women, the city-to-suburb move is often like a "jaunt to Siberia," the doctor counsels Joanna to leave town immediately. In the midst of a mounting tension that threatens to efface the political commentary of the film entirely in favor of sensationalistic thrills, the doctor's comment reminds the viewer that the film also functions as a critique of the isolation of the suburban woman. In relaying her fears of takeover and inadvertently bringing up the specter of Diz, the mastermind of patriarchal control in Stepford, Joanna does the same; with phrasing that recalls the recurrent trope of her own lost—or stolen—vision, she describes to the doctor what she imagines her replacement will be like: "She won't take pictures and she won't be me. She'll . . . be like one of those robots in Disneyland."[42]

In attempting to effect her flight from Stepford, Joanna must first escape her husband, Walter. She does so by striking him in the forehead with an iron from the fireplace, and Forbes's camera captures Walter's blood as it splatters a nearby *New Yorker* magazine. The sophisticated humor here underscores a secondary but crucial insight of the film—that the confining gender roles found in suburbia are, to a large extent, the product of popular culture discourse. And if, as I have argued, the precise detail characterizing *New Yorker* fiction mirrored the sense of order and propriety to be found in the suburban landscape, then Forbes uses wry humor in this scene to underscore the cultural dynamics of Joanna's flight. In bloodying the *New Yorker,* the guidebook of suburban taste and style, Joanna's deft stroke with the fire iron symbolically suggests her possible escape from the very prison of suburban decorum captured in the *New Yorker* style.

Joanna's escape is short-lived, however, and she ultimately finds herself trapped inside the Men's Association building, where Diz orchestrates her replacement by the robotic other. Interestingly enough, this final conversion scene—toward which the entire plot has been building—leaves behind the suburban landscape featured throughout the film in favor of an intensely gothic setting. Within the stately Victorian mansion owned by the association, on a dark, stormy night, Diz chases Joanna down a series of labyrinthine hallways as the lights of the mansion flicker on and off, casting eerie, expressionistic shadows on the walls. The removal to the gothic here suggests a certain degree of discomfort with pinning the evils of Stepford entirely on the suburban landscape; instead, trappings more suited to a late-eighteenth-century romance displace the heart of Stepford's darkness into a more comfortable world of pure fantasy. Or at least this seems to be the case, until Diz eventually corners Joanna in a room that is an exact duplicate of her own suburban bedroom. The play with simulacra here reinforces the insignificance, even interchangeability, of women in this patriarchal suburban sphere. In the corner of the duplicated bedroom sits another simulacrum, Joanna's replacement, a perfect replica except for her lack of eyes. As the android approaches Joanna, twisting in her hands the rope she will use to strangle her, the camera pulls back to Diz's perspective, displaying in fetishizing fashion the naked body of the android Joanna beneath a transparent negligee. Here, in the climactic scene of the film, the "money shot," as it were, the connections suggested throughout the narrative among sexuality, dominance, and the omnipotent male gaze are fully realized. That this moment transpires in a prefabricated, replicated space, while featuring the ascendance of a manufactured, subservient female entity, only emphasizes the central insight of the film: that upper-middle-class suburbia, an artificial, overdetermined, and male-centered environment, is no place for a "real" woman.

The depictions of female isolation, alienation, and subservience offered in Beattie's *Falling in Place* and Forbes's *The Stepford Wives* stand as telling manifestations of our cultural anxiety over suburbia and its relationship to gender identity in the pivotal decade of the 1970s. Set in a time when the suburbs were in the process of becoming the dominant landscape of the country and the women's movement was at its peak of political power, these texts reflect an ongoing concern over the nature of women's experience in a terrain predicated on the centrality of the domestic experience. Drawing on Friedan's groundbreaking analysis of suburbia and female disempowerment, both Beattie's novel and Forbes's film offer what might now appear to be somewhat dated, if not irrelevant, critiques of gender inequity in the suburban landscape. More recent depictions of suburban womanhood in popular culture, after all, tend to focus less on a sense of purposelessness and isolation than on the strivings of what is presented as an increasingly aggressive and driven sector of the society. But as Susan Faludi has demonstrated, such contemporary antifeminist attacks are part of a recurrent reactionary tendency in American culture against social advances made by women. *The Stepford Wives* and *Falling in Place,* set at the height of the women's movement of the 1970s, also suggested as much, picturing the suburb as an alienating environment for women, much as previous chroniclers of suburban life had imagined it to be for men.

Color Adjustment

African American Representations
of Suburban Life and Landscape

In 1968, in the wake of three summers marked by rioting in urban African American communities across the United States, the National Advisory Commission on Civil Disorders (also known as the Kerner Commission) released its influential report on race and demographics in the United States, warning that the nation was "moving toward two societies, one black, one white—separate but unequal." At the heart of this separation, the report concluded, was a growing demographic disparity between "white" suburbs and increasingly "black" inner cities. As Stephan and Abigail Thernstrom point out in their study *America in Black and White*, the Kerner report presents an interesting problem: Although the report "captured headlines," it "received remarkably little critical scrutiny, then or since," as a majority of cultural commentators have tended to accept the veracity of the Kerner Commission's findings.[2] But with more than thirty years passed since the Kerner report's dire warnings of a deepening racial

people tend to accept Kerner findings

and spatial rift in the United States, one might be prompted to question the extent to which these warnings have come to pass. Do inner cities continue to house a disproportionate number of black Americans? Or, conversely, have African Americans followed the demographic trend of whites, moving out to the suburbs and in the process altering the erstwhile image of suburbia as the enclave of lily-white America? The answer to both of these questions is, oddly enough, yes and no. Looking only at the numbers, the past three decades have seen a massive expansion of the African American community into the American suburbs. But as I have argued throughout this study, suburbia as a social phenomenon is irreducible to numbers and demographic trends, as it is also a landscape heavily invested with cultural aspirations and anxieties. Race issues figure prominently in the cultural dynamics of suburbia; for this reason, to gauge matters of race in the suburban context, one needs to look beyond merely "the numbers," to the symbolic understandings of race and identity as they have been constructed in the popular imagination and, indeed, as they have been inscribed on the very landscape of suburbia itself.

To be sure, the Kerner Commission's central notion—that the suburb/city split has been informed by, among other things, a drive toward racial separatism and exclusion—was indisputably an accurate reflection of American suburbia, at least in its developing years. A case study of this phenomenon can be found in the story of the various Levittowns, where Levitt and Sons chief Bill Levitt simply refused to sell any homes to African Americans for fear of racial strife in his new towns. While noteworthy for his outspoken defense of such selective selling practices, Levitt was otherwise by no means a unique case, as racial restrictions and covenants (legal agreements between buyer and seller that no person of African descent could ever be allowed to live on the property) were common practice in the postwar suburban housing market.[3] Government programs meant to help facilitate the mass movement to suburbia were complicit in fostering the homogeneous racial makeup of the new suburban landscape. The Federal Housing Administration (FHA), formed in 1934 to support a shaky housing market by providing federal insurance to private lending institutions, followed practices that served to insure the racial segregation that quickly emerged as the norm in postwar suburbs. Exhibiting an antiurban bias, the FHA tended to back mortgages for homes in new, all-white suburbs, while offering less attractive terms or no backing at all for inner-city housing.[4] Historian Kenneth Jackson, who claims that "no agency of the United States government has had a more pervasive and powerful impact on the American people over the past half-century than the Federal Housing Administration," reads the discriminatory lending practices of the FHA in explicitly racial terms and notes the disastrous effects of such policy: "FHA . . . helped to turn the building industry against the minority and inner-city housing market, and its policies supported the income and racial segregation of suburbia. For perhaps the first time, the federal government embraced the discriminatory attitudes of the marketplace. Previously, prejudices were personalized and individualized; FHA exhorted segregation and enshrined it as public policy."[5]

Perhaps taking a cue from such government-sanctioned environmental racism, developers and real estate agents generally restricted sales of suburban homes to white, middle-class families, and the continued use of racial covenants insured the whiteness of the emerging suburbs.[6] As Charles Abrams argues in *Forbidden Neighbors: A Study of Prejudice in Housing,* such practices served to create a social landscape predicated on fear and exclusion of racial "others." Arguing that the concept of "neighborhood dignity" became synonymous with a vision of "neighborhood homogeneity," Abrams concludes that the suburban neighborhood "was turned into a breeding ground of bias, fear, and discrimination."[7] And while racial covenants were outlawed by the U.S. Supreme Court's *Shelley v. Kraemer* decision in 1948, this decision "had little effect on the evolving pattern of racial segregation of postwar private housing development in suburbia."[8] Instead, the suburbs remained, at least throughout the 1950s and most of the 1960s, a landscape both populated by whites and associated in the collective cultural imagination with whiteness.[9] And if, as literary critic Valerie Babb has argued, in various periods of American history "a variety of symbols, laws, and institutions have been mobilized to sustain the concept of whiteness, and over time . . . have cemented its identity," then the landscape of postwar suburbia might be considered as one such reminder of white hegemony in the United States.[10] Imagined in television and other vehicles of postwar popular culture as the naturalized setting of the white middle class, the suburbs to this day retain more than a trace of this symbolic meaning. As historian Samuel Kaplan points out, racial homogeneity was, from the outset, a crucial component of the "dream vision" of suburbia sold to white Americans: "It is important to keep in mind that the prevailing myth in suburbia is the Protestant Ethic, which, simply defined, is that an individual through hard work shall reap his reward—and that reward according to the ethic and embellished by advertising and the media is ownership of a single, detached house on a plot of landscaped ground in an economically, socially, and racially homo-geneous community free of the turmoil of the evil city."[11] Kaplan's obser-vation, coming as it did in 1976, serves as testament to the lasting power of a vision of suburbia—one shaped by governmental policy, discriminatory real estate practices, and popular culture imagery—as a landscape not only racially homogeneous, but indeed symbolically central to the experience of middle-class white Americans.

As I have suggested throughout this study, twentieth-century Ameri-can literature set in suburban environments has tended to reflect this larger cultural vision of the suburbs as a bastion of whiteness. Suburban fiction as a subgenre composes a decidedly white canon, with the various writers of *New Yorker* fiction—a style targeted toward a white, upper-middle-class readership—emerging as the central voices. In the majority of literary works set in the suburbs, racial "others" are either entirely absent—as in much of Cheever's fiction set in the upper-middle-class suburbs of Westchester—or are demonized as threatening urban dwellers, the "bar-barians at the gate" of the white protagonists' suburban worlds. Hence in *The Great Gatsby,* a novel whose racial politics anticipated the phobic drive toward community homogeneity in postwar suburbs, the influx of racial others from Manhattan and Queens is offered as evidence of the deterioration of the exurban fantasy worlds of East and West Egg; in *Rabbit Redux,* the "angry black revolutionary," Skeeter, emerges from the ghettos of Brewer to become the "blot of black" within Rabbit's home that identifies the house as a corrupting influence on the suburban neighborhood, one that must be removed; and in Cheever's one novel set in the suburbs, *Bullet Park,* the slums adjacent to the affluent suburb of Bullet Park are both demonized and exoticized, presented as home to drug dealers, thieves, rioters, and one black swami with mystical powers. In all of these cases, racial others in general and African Americans in particular are rigorously positioned as city dwellers; their appearance in the suburbs marks a disturbance in the order of things, and the response is either a violent reaction against such infiltration—as in *Rabbit Redux*—or the resigned acceptance that the social landscape has been irrevocably altered and corrupted, as in *The Great Gatsby* and *Bullet Park.*

Place-bound treatments of racial identity have been handled in a similar manner in both television and film of the last half century. Indeed, the television industry has helped to sustain the cultural perception of racial demographics from the postwar years on. As Robert Fishman has argued, white suburban sitcoms of the 1950s and 1960s "glorified the single family house as the standard American home, enshrined the low-density neighborhood, and (perhaps not coincidentally) . . . provided an unrelentingly negative picture of the city as the haven of crime and violence."[12] That such "glorification" of suburban life has been a matter intertwined with presentations of racial identity becomes apparent with a consideration of race-bound treatments of landscape on TV. In the 1950s and 1960s, when the suburban sitcom reigned on television, African Americans were, with a few notable exceptions, almost entirely absent from TV programming.[13] Even in the 1970s, as African Americans began to receive some representation on popular television, black characters and families were still confined to the urban sphere, as on such popular comedies as *The Jeffersons, Good Times,* and *Sanford and Son.* While *The Jeffersons* found its humor in the loudmouthed pretenses of nouveau-riche George Jefferson, who with his family had, as the theme song reminded us, "moved on up to the East Side," in both *Sanford and Son* and *Good Times,* the plight of urban African Americans living in poverty formed the basis for a new type of domestic comedy. Despite their differences, these TV comedies of the 1970s reinforced for the white suburbanite viewer the notion that the "place" of African Americans was, undeniably, the city.

And in more recent years, black sitcoms still have maintained the link between blackness and the urban sphere. Even the seeming exceptions to this phenomenon from the past three decades—programs such as *Diff'rent Strokes, The Fresh Prince of Bel Air,* and *The Cosby Show*—actually support traditional racialized readings of landscape. While in *Diff'rent Strokes* two African American brothers do relocate to the suburbs, they do so only courtesy of the munificence of their adoptive father, Mr. Drummond, an utterly paternalistic, if benign, imparter of white, middle-class values. In *The Fresh Prince of Bel Air,* Will, a young, streetwise rapper from tough West Philadelphia, comes to live with his aunt and uncle's affluent family in Bel Air, and the humor of each episode derives from the clash between Will's values and those of his wealthy new "family." Lest one miss the point that urban Will possesses the somehow more "genuine" African American identity, a recurring source of humor in the show stems from Will's interactions with his cousin Carlton, who has so fully adopted the attitudes and tastes of affluent, "white" America that his greatest joy comes in singing and dancing along to a recording of Tom Jones's "It's Not Unusual." A recurring comic device throughout the program's six-year (1990-96) run, Carlton's "whiteface" song-and-dance number only served to reinforce the distinction the program built between "genuine," urban blackness and what were presented as the diluted, comical sensibilities of exurban, "bougie" blacks.[14] By contrast, *The Cosby Show,* which Shelby Steele suggestively refers to as "a blackface version of the American Dream," celebrated the sensibilities of an affluent black family, while carefully positioning its characters within the urban sphere: Even though the program perfectly captured the mise-en-scene of the traditional suburban sitcom, with nearly all of the action of every episode transpiring in the living room of the Huxtable family's home, the viewer was periodically reminded that the action was taking place in New York City, not its suburbs.[15]

Hollywood cinema of the last several decades has served to reinforce this binary racial division between the urban and suburban environments. On the whole, African American cinema, with several notable exceptions I will discuss shortly, has tended to focus on the urban milieu; indeed, a commercially successful tradition initiated by the urban "blaxploitation" films of the early 1970s and continuing with the wave of ultraviolent, "gansta" films of the late 1980s and 1990s has, if anything, contributed to continuing racial and environmental stereotypes through its thoroughgoing association of African Americans (and particularly young black men) with a hyperviolent urban world of crime and drugs. Such portrayals have drawn harsh criticism from many African American film critics, who see in these films the perpetuation of the worst type of image for black Americans. Characteristic in this regard is the assessment of Jacquie Jones, who argues that, with the success of the "new blaxploitation" films of the 1990s, "the age-old ghettoization of black products remains unchanged. The industry's wholesale investment in films that explore only ghettoes and male youth ignores the existence of a black community beyond these narrow confines."[16]

As for primarily "white" films set in the suburbs, racial homogeneity on screen has tended to confirm the cultural vision of all-white suburbs; in the few white suburban movies focusing on racial interaction, portrayals of racial others have been strikingly negative. Consider Frank Oz's 1986 musical remake of Roger Corman's *Little Shop of Horrors.* Seemingly a whimsical musical comedy about the dreams of working-class whites in the postwar era looking to escape the city and find a better life in the suburbs, the film takes the form of an allegory of postwar "white flight" to the suburbs, as its protagonist, Seymour, a meek clerk at a florist's shop, must run for his life from a creature named "Audrey 2," a massive and powerful man-eating plant he has raised, named, and fed by hand. Shocked when he discovers the plant can talk—in a raunchy and confrontational, black-urban dialect (the voicing was done by the front man of the musical group the Four Tops, Levi Stubbs)—Seymour becomes further terrified as the plant grows more aggressive, displaying an insatiable appetite and, when his demands for food are not met, eventually destroying the florist's shop and ravaging the surrounding working-class neighborhood before he is finally killed. The paranoid allegorical rendering does not end there, however; after Seymour and his love, Audrey, manage to escape to their dream home in suburbia, the final frame of the film reveals a small army of "Audrey 2" plants growing amid the crabgrass of their front yard. A shockingly paranoid fantasy of racial conflict and flight, *Little Shop of Horrors* closes by confirming its own worst fears: that blacks might manage to escape the city just like whites and eventually "sprout up" on the suburban landscape.[17]

The reactionary racial message of this seemingly innocuous comedy may have much to do with the time at which it was made. By the 1980s, the African American population in the suburbs was steadily increasing. As James Blackwell and Philip Hart note, the Omnibus Housing Bill, part of the Civil Rights Act of 1968, opened the door to black emigration to the suburbs, helping to spur the movement of "some 800,000 blacks into suburbia between 1970 and 1977" alone.[18] This migration was significant enough that the so-called opening up of the suburbs to African Americans became a topic of heated debate throughout the 1970s—in *Newsweek* magazine's terms, "the major domestic social and political battle of the decade."[19] On one side of this debate were anti-integration "community rights" advocates, who attempted to use zoning restrictions to enforce what one observer in the early 1970s called a "white barricade" against black suburbanization.[20] On the other side were civil rights and fair housing advocates who lobbied for governmental intervention to integrate

Mt. Laurel/MsWACP - followwicker

the suburbs.[21] A potentially landmark decision of the New Jersey State Supreme Court in the Mount Laurel case of 1975 (*Southern Burlington County N.A.A.C.P. v. Township of Mount Laurel*) seemed to offer precisely what the fair housing advocates were calling for: a judicial mandate that new and developing suburbs zone in an inclusive, rather than exclusionary, manner. Nonetheless, the battle over suburban integration continued, as subsequent court decisions across the country backpedaled from the Mount Laurel decision, leaving it, in one historian's terms, a "hollow" victory.[22] Paradoxically, by the 1980s the pace of black suburbanization was continuing to accelerate, even while suburban segregation remained more the norm than the exception.

Several factors have contributed to the continued segregation of suburbia in ensuing decades, including the perpetuation of informal covenants among homeowners' associations and the unwillingness of municipal governments to push for integration on the local level.[23] In addition, the illegal but common practice among real estate agents of racial "steering"—the directing of black prospective home buyers toward largely black neighborhoods—has reinforced patterns of residential segregation.[24] Perhaps the most significant contributing factor in the perpetuation of suburban segregation has been the continued phenomenon of "white flight" toward ever more distant suburbs. This white migration away from the urban center has helped to facilitate the movement of African Americans and immigrant groups into older, "inner-ring" suburbs. The flourishing in the 1980s and onward of affluent black suburbs such as Prince George's County, Maryland, also suggests a desire among black suburbanites—similar to that of their white counterparts—for racially homogeneous communities.[25] Despite persisting patterns of segregation, the fact remains that beginning in the 1970s, black suburbanization effected significant demographic changes. By 1980, census figures showed a decrease in the percentage of black Americans living in the inner city, while the suburbs for the first time claimed 20 percent of the black population.[26] This initial movement was part of a larger trend of suburbanization among African

Americans that continues in the present. Calling African American suburbanization of the last three decades a "huge demographic shift . . . even larger than the Second Great Migration," Thernstrom and Thernstrom note that the proportion of African Americans living in suburbia nearly doubled, from less than one-sixth to nearly one-third, between the years 1970 and 1995.[27] Nevertheless, despite this very real shift in the racial makeup of suburbia, the prevailing cultural image of the suburbs continues to be tied to the white experience; in cultural anthropologist Constance Perin's terms, when it comes to race matters, "suburban systems of meaning" remain "frozen in place."[28]

There have been efforts in popular culture in recent years to address the African American suburban experience; a number of films by black filmmakers have explored black suburban life, and several current television programs have followed suit. Most notable among these programs is *The Hughleys,* a sitcom featuring comedian D. L. Hughley as a suburban dad. The program began its run in 1998 on ABC, where early episodes focused squarely on issues of racial alienation experienced by the Hughleys as newly arrived black suburbanites. The program has since moved to the lower-profile UPN network and evolved into more of a standard-issue suburban family sitcom; these developments suggest a growing acceptance of the image of black suburbanites among UPN's target audience of African American viewers, a point supported by the presence in the network's lineup of several middle-class black sitcoms (*Girlfriends, The Parkers, One on One*). At the same time, ABC's cancellation of the show indicates that the major networks might not yet be ready for the black suburbanite. The fate of this program at ABC, and that of recent black suburban movies, which continue to be overshadowed by crime- and action-oriented urban black films, suggest that, as Robert Lake observed back in 1981, "suburban blacks have constituted one of the nation's invisible populations."[29] Indeed, the "invisibility" of the black suburban experience might be read logically as a consequence of the profound weight of cultural discourse that has for so long aligned African Americans with the urban sphere. But this fact in itself would seem to pose a double-edged problem for those who would chronicle the suburban black experience: how to make visible a racial and ethnic experience that not only runs counter to inherited notions of the geographical "place" of African Americans, but also transpires in a setting long known for its erasure of markers of difference such as class, race, and ethnic affiliation?[30]

That is, given the ingrained image of the urban milieu as the center of twentieth-century African American community identity, from what basis can the black experience be depicted in a landscape so long predicated on the ideals and values of the white community alone? Considered in Homi Bhabha's terms, the sense of "cultural displacement" experienced by nonwhites relocating to suburbia might well mark this landscape as a site of "social and psychic anxiety," a place where, for marginalized minorities, "strangeness and contradiction cannot be negated and must be continually worked through."[31] Two texts from recent years that portray the African American suburban experience—Gloria Naylor's novel *Linden Hills* (1985) and Reginald Hudlin's film *House Party* (1990)—exhibit precisely this "working through" of psychological and cultural anxieties occasioned by their characters' relationship to the suburban environment. While these two works offer widely divergent visions of the black experience in suburbia, I hope to demonstrate that the differences between them prove instructive in assaying various modes of understanding the suburban experience among African American artists. Each work is set in a carefully delineated, heterogeneous social landscape that positions elite suburbs alongside poor, inner-city neighborhoods. In Naylor's novel, the boundary line between a working-class, urban neighborhood and an elite black suburb signifies the split between a vision of well-defined racial identity and community and that of a rigidly patriarchal, vacuous bourgeois society whose members have lost all sense of their own blackness; in Hudlin's film, by contrast, the suburban terrain is valorized as representing the very promise of African American achievement. Despite their differences, both works present the suburban landscape as a rigorously controlled environment whose exclusivity belies a rigid, even forbidding, social structure.

🏠 🏠 🏠

Published in 1985, Gloria Naylor's *Linden Hills* emerged as the second novel in what would become a series of thematically related and interconnected works, which also includes her first novel, *The Women of Brewster Place* (1982), and the subsequent works *Mama Day* (1988), *Bailey's Cafe* (1992), and most recently *The Men of Brewster Place* (1998). Like its predecessor, *Linden Hills* chronicles the lives of a number of characters positioned within a carefully delineated geographical space, with Naylor again interweaving a number of plot lines in a narrative that shifts perspective throughout, capturing through a polyvocal approach the variety of experiences that shape the dynamics of a particular lived environment. But this is where the similarities between *Brewster Place* and *Linden Hills* end, for otherwise the two novels differ dramatically in their treatments of landscape and community. The most immediately discernible difference has to do with environment itself: Brewster Place is an urban ghetto, and Linden Hills an elite, upper-middle-class suburb. Further, Naylor's vision of community differs sharply in the two works: Whereas the beleaguered African American women of Brewster Place eventually construct some sense of community—however troubled and tenuous—in *Linden Hills* Naylor portrays the complete absence of an abiding sense of community among the inhabitants of an all-black suburb. The isolation of these affluent suburbanites, Naylor suggests, is tied to their relentless pursuit of the "American Dream" of wealth and social advancement.

Indeed, Naylor herself has noted that capturing the sense of isolation and broken community ties among upwardly mobile black Americans was her primary goal in *Linden Hills*. She notes that her objective in the novel was to portray "what happens to black Americans when they move up in

America's society. They first lose family ties . . . then there are the community ties. You can create a whole different type of community around you—mostly of a mixture of other professional, middle-class people—but you lose ties with your spiritual or religious values. And ultimately, the strongest and most difficult ties to let go of are your ties with your ethnocentric sense of self. You forget what it means to be an African American."[32] Setting this drama of ethnic and racial "forgetting" precisely in an affluent suburban milieu, Naylor implies that the suburban landscape itself—and its association in the broad cultural imaginary with a lifestyle dictated by the drive for "status" and the attainment of material signs of wealth—fosters in her African American protagonists a sense of anomie, a dislocation from the very ties of ethnicity and shared experience that sustain the bonds of community in a locale such as Brewster Place. And this despite the fact that the neighborhood of Linden Hills is presented as an historically all-black suburb, a place that lures potential homeowners from all across the country with its image as a model of upper-middle-class African American community. What quickly becomes apparent, instead, is that the only vestige of "community" spirit remaining among the residents of Linden Hills is to be found in the unified actions of the civic association, who together work to keep "undesirables" out of the area surrounding their elite neighborhood. Linden Hills, as a landscape of social prominence and success, becomes then the antithesis of a community, as its residents—adherents to the American master narrative of success through material advancement—willingly neglect, even shun, community ties for the sake of personal gain, exchanging ethnic integrity for a piece of the American dream as embodied in the landscape of the affluent suburb. Naylor uses her fictional suburb to play out the tension between a fading sense of racial identity and the assimilationist dreams of the black bourgeoisie.

So insistent is Naylor on using the suburban landscape to illustrate the corrupting influences materialistic striving has on the African American community that she consciously and carefully lays out the topography of Linden Hills as a direct parallel to the vision of Hell Dante constructs in the *Inferno*. Extant critical work on *Linden Hills* has, following the close and extended analysis of Catherine Ward, made much of the Dantean parallels, and rightly so.[33] Naylor's novel, in contrast to the prevailing style of most suburban fiction, is heavily steeped in allegory and emerges less as a critique of manners in suburbia—although it is that as well—than an apocalyptic vision of the corrupting influence of bourgeois values, effected through the interweaving of mythical and realist techniques.[34] While no reading of the novel can fail to account for the strong and suggestive parallels to Dante's *Inferno* that run throughout, forgoing extended recitation of these connections will allow for a closer examination of what critic Virginia Fowler has aptly noted to be the "underlying concept" of Naylor's realist allegory: "the death of the (black) human soul occasioned by pursuit of the (white) American dream of material prosperity."[35] In focusing on landscape itself as a defining element in the novel, a more profitable approach might lie in examining the extent to which the suburban landscape fosters in Naylor's characters what W. E. B. Du Bois had, a century earlier, termed the "double-consciousness" of African Americans. If, as Du Bois argued, the African American "ever feels his two-ness—an American; a Negro; two souls, two thoughts, two unreconciled strivings; two warring ideals," then Naylor's use of the suburban landscape serves to emplace this drama of double-consciousness in a landscape resonant with the larger conflicts and contradictions of American bourgeois life.[36] Ultimately, Naylor depicts suburban Linden Hills as a place where the "warring ideals" of racial identity and assimilationist desire converge, and the lure of the American dream of financial success—as represented by an ever-present desire to advance in Linden Hills' socially stratified society—eventually effaces the ideal of racial identity and, consequently, the hope for community altogether.

These "warring ideals" or "unreconciled strivings" are inscribed on the face of the landscape itself from the opening of the novel, when Naylor begins with an extended description of the history and topography of Linden Hills. Founded in 1820 by Luther Nedeed, a Mississippi freeman rumored to have "sold his octoroon wife and six children for the money he used to come North and obtain the hilly land," Linden Hills, a "worthless" valley of "hard sod" that at its terminus was "hemmed in by the town cemetery," had remained under the control of the Nedeed family ever since.[37] More specifically, the landscape had, at least in the eyes of the surrounding community, remained perpetually in the hands of Luther Nedeed: The founder of Linden Hills, after marrying a woman of light skin, fathered a child nearly identical to himself, whom he named Luther, and his son, grandson, and great-grandson did exactly the same, ensuring the perpetual presence of a Luther Nedeed to maintain control over the landscape and inhabitants of Linden Hills. Indeed, Luther I's many descendants emulate him in more than merely marriage and child-rearing practices: Each Luther, unconsciously mimicking his father, subjugates and psychologically abuses his wife, exploiting her for the sole purpose of bearing an heir to the Nedeed throne. In this sense, Luther I's sale of his first wife and children amounts to a founding act in the establishment of what would become a phallocentric economy in Linden Hills, a place characterized as much by masculine dominance as it is by a mounting sense of racial and spiritual dislocation.

Financed by the family undertaking business begun by Luther I—and this source of income suggests the "spiritual death" that would haunt latter-day residents of Linden Hills—each successive generation of Luther Nedeeds contributed to shaping the environment into the affluent suburb it had eventually become by the time of the narrative's action. While Luther I could only dream of the day when he would exercise dominion over inhabitants of his land, Luther II turned this dream into a reality, selling the land "practically for air to the blacks who were shacking there," and providing them with a "thousand-year-and-a-day lease—provided only that they passed their property on to their children" (7). Sensing that the "future of America . . . was going to be white" (8), and fearing the encroachment of whites from surrounding Wayne County onto his increasingly valuable land, Luther II initiated the construction of what he felt would be an oppositional landscape, a place whose very blackness would serve as counterpoint to the materialistic strivings of the affluent dominant culture. On his dying bed, with his son, Luther III, by his side,

Luther reflects on the landscape he hopes to have created: "He had given his people some of the most expensive land in the county. They had the land for a millennium. Now just let them sit on it and do what they do best: digging another man's coal, cleaning another man's home, rocking another man's baby. . . . Nedeed's last vision when he closed his puffy eyelids, with his image bending over him, was of Wayne County forced to drive past Linden Hills and being waved at by the maids, mammies, and mules who were bringing the price of that sweat back to his land and his hands. A wad of spit—a beautiful, black wad of spit right in the eye of white America" (9).

While Luther II's millennial vision was predicated on the subjugation of his tenants—he sold them the land but continued to provide the only home insurance as well as funeral services for the town, in the process taking all of the disposable income of the residents of Linden Hills—it nevertheless stressed a vision of the landscape as a counterpoint to the dominant narrative of success in white America. Under the tenure of his grandson, however, Linden Hills changed dramatically; while Luther IV still wanted his landscape to represent a torment to white America, he believed that in order to do so he had to create a black society that reflected the values of the white bourgeoisie: "His grandfather's dream was still possible—the fact that they had this land was a blister to the community, but to make that sore fester and pus over, Linden Hills had to be a showcase. He had to turn it into a jewel—an ebony jewel that reflected the soul of Wayne county but reflected it black" (9) So in the years following World War II, in the era of mass suburbanization, Luther IV formed a realty corporation and set out to remake the landscape of Linden Hills. Dreaming of a place of "smooth curved roads . . . long sloping lawns and manicured meridians," and anchored by showplace homes whose residents "wanted nothing better than to forget and to make the world forget their past" (10), Luther IV pitched to the residents his plan to suburbanize Linden Hills. In contrast to his grandfather, who had wanted Linden Hills to remain forever tangible evidence of the racial inequities of American society, Luther IV sought to efface the legacy of racial oppression—indeed, he sought to suppress a sense of racial identity altogether—through the creation of a landscape that reflected only the gleam of prosperity. In effecting this divorce from racial and communal history, Luther first needed to "weed out" those who would disrupt his vision, and he quietly bought out or forced out of the new community those residents who "rooted themselves in the belief that Africa could be more than a word; slavery hadn't run its course; there was salvation in Jesus and salve in the blues" (11). Having no use for those who subscribed to any notions of "black power," Luther IV instead sold his dream vision of the landscape of Linden Hills—as well as the notion of his new realty corporation and its low-interest mortgages—to those willing simply to forget the past:

> As he placed his polished wing-tip shoes on their sagging front porches, he watched them watching the crisp lines in his linen suit, counting the links in his gold watch chain, and measuring the grade of his son's gabardine knickers. . . . Come, look, listen and perhaps you will learn how to turn the memory of our iron chains into gold chains. The cotton fields that broke your grandparents' backs can cover yours in gabardine. See, the road to salvation can be walked in leather shoes and sung about in linen choir robes. Nedeed almost smiled at their simplicity. Yes, they would invest their past and apprentice their children to the future of Linden Hills, forgetting that a magician's supreme art is not in transformation but in making things disappear. (12)

As the action of the novel commences, the fifth Luther Nedeed has inherited this landscape from his father, a place that lures potential black residents from all over Wayne County and beyond, for as everyone knows, "making it in Linden Hills meant 'making it'" (15). Now fully developed and landscaped as a "zoned district of eight circular drives that held some of the finest homes" (13) in the county, Linden Hills also had become characterized by a strict sense of social stratification. The dream of each resident of Linden Hills is to move eventually farther "down the hill," as increasing *"damne will"*

proximity to the residence of Luther Nedeed—the richest man in the county—at the bottom of the valley signifies heightened social status. Naylor thus uses landscape as a means of critiquing what she presents as the unreflective striving for social advancement among the black bourgeoisie; that is, the upside-down topography of class in Linden Hills—with the bottom signifying ultimate advancement and elite class status—inverts, as Keith Sandiford notes, "conventional rules of order," in the process "cynically subverting a (mainly black) middle-class's faith in the possibility of racial progress."[38] Indeed, Naylor's treatment of landscape, considered on an allegorical level, does more than this: As the "circular drives" of Linden Hills directly parallel the levels of Dante's Hell, social advancement toward the realm of Luther Nedeed—whose street address, 999 Tupelo Drive, reads in this "upside-down" world as the number of the beast—also suggests a loss of spiritual direction if not an inexorable march toward damnation.

Naylor suggests that this loss of spiritual direction is tied directly to the loss of racial identity, and both have been fostered by the commodification of the landscape itself. Luther V considers this fact as he ruminates on the troubled connections between race, materialism, and the land that has become his dubious inheritance:

loss of spiritual identity people

> Tupelo Drive and Luther Nedeed: it became one cry of dark victory for blacks outside Linden Hills or inside Linden Hills. And the ultimate dark victor sat in front of his home and behind his lake and looked up at the Nedeed dream. It had finally crystallized into that jewel, but he wore it like a weighted stone around his neck. Something had gone terribly wrong with Linden Hills. He knew what his dead fathers had wanted to do with this land and the people who lived on it. These people were to reflect the Nedeeds in a hundred facets and then the Nedeeds could take those splintered mirrors and form a mirage of power to torment a world that dared think them stupid—or worse, totally impotent. But there was no torment in Linden Hills for the white god his fathers had shaken their fists at, because there was no white god, and there never had been. (16)

Witnessing the materialistic drive of his residents, Nedeed is left to conclude instead that the "omnipresent, omnipotent, Almighty Divine is simply the *will* to possess" (17). The dream of Luther's "dead fathers" had—as the Nedeeds developed the landscape from a "worthless" terrain supporting a small collection of shacks to a high-end suburban enclave—been subverted and stripped of its racial essence. No longer an oppositional landscape characterized by its blackness, Linden Hills had become, in Luther's mind, simply a reflection of the larger, materialistic American middle-class experience: "Linden Hills wasn't black; it was successful. The shining surface of their careers, brass railings, and cars hurt his eyes because it only reflected the bright nothing that was inside of them. Of course Wayne County had lived in peace with Linden Hills for the last two decades, since it now understood that they were both serving the same god. Wayne County had watched his wedge of earth become practically invisible—indistinguishable from their own pathetic souls" (17).

The phrasing in this passage is telling; by portraying the landscape as both a mirroring surface (as Updike does throughout *Rabbit Redux*) and, ultimately, an "invisible" place devoid of the color that once distinguished it from its white surroundings, Naylor suggests that the landscape itself reflects the dissolution of racial identity among its inhabitants. The passage recalls a phrase uttered by Grandma Tilson—a contemporary of Luther II's and the one person who fought the Nedeed plans to create a glittering "jewel" of Linden Hills—that serves as an epigraph to the novel and recurs throughout the narrative; cautioning her grandson that hell can be found here on earth, she warns him that to find it, "you just gotta sell that silver mirror God propped up in your soul." And in the gleaming suburban landscape, Naylor offers a counterpoint to the spiritual struggle her African American characters face; so driven toward assimilation into the mainstream culture represented by their terrain that they sacrifice their very "blackness," the denizens of Linden Hills exchange the "mirror in their souls" for a piece of a landscape has been manufactured to "reflect" the values of middle-class white America.

The action of the narrative proper centers on the journey of Willie Mason, a young street poet from the adjacent lower-class black community of Putney Wayne, and his friend and fellow aspiring poet Lester Tilson, a descendant of Grandma Tilson who lives with his mother and sister in one of the less elite sections of Linden Hills, as they traverse Linden Hills during the week before Christmas, working odd jobs to raise money for the holidays. As Willie and Lester pass through the various levels of Linden Hills' topography and society, they discover hypocrisy and alienation behind the shining facade of success. Counterparts in Naylor's allegorical scheme to Dante and Virgil, Willie and Lester function to uncover the mystery of the affluent life of the black bourgeoisie: that "to rise socially is to fall spiritually toward dehumanization, self-extinction and spiritual death."[39] In counterpoint to this main plot is the story of Willa Nedeed, wife of Luther, who is locked in the basement of the Nedeed home for the crime of bearing what Luther feels to be a "white" son. Linked to the series of Nedeed wives preceding her—all of whom have been similarly abused— Willa epitomizes the plight of disenfranchised women in a landscape characterized by masculine ambition and power. Luther, enraged by his sense that his wife has given birth to a white man's child—or, conversely, seeing in the "whitened" image of the sixth Luther Nedeed, his own son, not only the dissolution of his family's racial identity, but by extension the final "whitewashing" of the Linden Hills dream itself—has imprisoned Willa and the son, who eventually starves to death in the basement. As Willie, an outsider from poor Putney Wayne, makes his way down the terrain of Linden Hills, Willa, who slowly discovers her connection to the other abused Nedeed wives, eventually makes her way up from the basement; their meeting marks the climax of the novel, in a moment that exposes, and eventually destroys, the Nedeed family's destructive hold on the black community of Linden Hills.

By structuring her plot in the form of a symbolic journey down through the inverted class ranks of Linden Hills, Naylor effects a stringent critique of the alienating effects of bourgeois society on African American identity. In this regard, her novel conforms to what critic Jerome Thornton has noted to be a tradition in African American literature, in which a protagonist "takes a journey in an effort to forge a bond that identifies the protagonist with the African American opposition to existing social conditions of black bourgeois life."[40] While Willie Mason does eventually forge such a bond with Willa Nedeed, over the course of his journey through Linden Hills he observes a series of characters who evidence an increasingly apparent estrangement from racial community in this elite society. Through the journey motif, Naylor reveals Linden Hills to be a society characterized by obsessive control of both landscape and inhabitants, restrictive codes of gender and sexual identity, and, above all, a single-minded pursuit of financial and social gain. *restrictive covering description*

At the beginning of Willie's journey, Naylor suggests the striking difference between the elite suburb and the surrounding working-class community by contrasting his visit to the home of Ruth and Norman Anderson in Putney Wayne to his overnight stay with the Tilson family on First Crescent Drive in Linden Hills. Topography provides the key to understanding the distinction Naylor creates between the two homes and families: The Andersons represent the lifestyle of the working-class poor who reside on the urban fringe surrounding Linden Hills, while the Tilsons, who live on the "first house in" on the first street of Linden Hills—the entryway to Naylor's allegorical suburban hell—embody the least offensive brand of the relentless social snobbery that will become more pronounced as Willie and Lester make their way farther down the valley. Ruth and Norman, old friends of Willie and Lester, invite the pair in for a drink to their "dilapidated garden-apartment" that features only "three pieces of furniture . . . in three large rooms: one sofa in the living room, one kitchenette set with plastic-bottomed chairs on uncertain chrome legs, one bed" (33). Despite their poverty, Ruth and Norman are idealized as the moral force of the novel; Norman's assessment of their home and life together—"Love rules in this house" (38), he proclaims at one point to his wife—emerges as the standard against which the hypocrisy of Linden Hills is measured.

Ruth had once lived in Linden Hills, but she will not be lured back by its promise of material comforts: "I've had that life, Norm, and I lasted six months. Those folks just aren't real" (39), she explains. Like Beattie's Tiffy Adamson, Ruth sees through and resists the surface appeals of the suburban lifestyle. Vowing she will "never go back down there again" (39), she instead remains with Norman, despite the fact that he suffers from a psychological disturbance that afflicts him "every other spring," sending him into a hallucinatory state he can only endure by destroying all the material furnishings in their home.[41] Naylor thus presents the pair as the antithesis of Linden Hills society: Trapped in perpetual poverty, they nonetheless construct a worthwhile life together. And although they are employed to contrast the empty materialism of the Linden Hills residents, Ruth and Norman Anderson nonetheless raise a potentially troubling aspect of Naylor's treatment of race and class, suggesting that the only "genuine" black experience is to be found among the poverty-stricken urban underclass. As Fowler notes, the novel "fails to offer any positive, morally sound character who is not poor or dangerously close to it."[42]

Consider, by contrast, the treatment of the Tilson family; although they are the descendants of Grandma Tilson, known in Linden Hills lore as the one person who steadfastly opposed the development efforts of the domineering Nedeed family, the Tilsons have become enamored of the Linden Hills mystique and hope one day to move "downward" from their position on the fringe of the Hills to a more elite position. Their adherence to the Linden Hills ethos is evidenced by their home and possessions, all of which are the color of money: "It was the smallest house on a street of brick ranch houses with iron picket fences. Its two-story wooden frame had been covered with light green aluminum siding, and three brick steps led up to a dark green door. . . . Willow-green print furniture sat on jade carpeting and there were green-and-white Japanese porcelain vases arranged on the tables in the living room. The curtains in the hallway and the living room had avocado stripes and fern prints, and with the light coming through them, they gave a whisper-green tint to the white walls"

(47-48). Mrs. Tilson's drive to advance in Linden Hills society takes the form of pride of place; as she explains to Willie, the materialistic color scheme of her decoration is only part of a larger desire to transcend what she has for years felt to be the limiting nature of her surroundings: "I was never one for keeping up with the Joneses, but it's pretty embarrassing to have the worst house on the block and to just settle for that" (51). Willie's friend Lester despises the materialistic strivings of his family, invoking his grandmother's admonition about "selling the mirror in your soul" to explain the connections between his family and the Linden Hills elite; his family, like all the residents of the Hills, he claims, have "lost all touch with what it means to be *them*" (59). The specifically racial overtones of Lester's observation apply to the case of his sister, Roxanne—Lester describes her as a "true prodigy of the Hills (57)—who "felt comfortable with the fact that she had paid her dues to the Civil Rights Movement by wearing an Afro for six months and enrolling in black history courses in college" (53). This debt to her racial identity behind her, Roxanne hopes to move "down the hill" through a strategic marriage to a rising star in Linden Hills society, Xavier Donnell.

Through her presentation of Xavier and his colleague Maxwell, Naylor crystallizes her critique of the deadening influence material gain has on a sense of racial identity. Xavier, who has advanced to the status of vice president of minority marketing at General Motors, occupies an untenable position with regard to his racial identity. Hailed by those at GM as a "Super Nigger" for his meteoric rise to prominence in the corporation, Xavier nonetheless feels himself to be a "fragile god," one who cannot afford to emphasize his blackness for fear of losing his position in the corporation: If his carefully deracialized image "ever crumbled," Xavier muses, "his own fate wasn't too far behind" (99). Hence the fact that he is falling in love with Roxanne, a lower-class black woman from the very fringes of Linden Hills, becomes for Xavier "one of the most terrifying experiences of his life" (97). He turns for advice to Maxwell Smyth, the only other black man "on the tenth floor at GM" and his superior in both the corporation and Linden Hills society. As Willie and Lester clean out Xavier's garage, Maxwell visits with Xavier to offer his counsel. So estranged from his racial identity that his speech is marked equally by his two "pet passions," "French and ghetto dialect," Maxwell responds to Xavier's various queries with rejoinders such as "No sweat, *mon ami,*" and "*Sacre Dieu,* blood."

Epitomizing Naylor's vision of dehumanized black suburban affluence, Maxwell shuns human interaction, avoids sex, and so strictly regulates his dietary intake as to render toilet paper obsolete in his home; instead, his "daily ritual" in the bathroom "could have taken place on the seat of a theater or concert hall, with absolutely no clues to tip off even the nearest party about his true nature" (105). Maxwell's comically exaggerated fastidiousness links him to the suburban ideal of rigidly maintained appearances. Through her depiction of Maxwell, Naylor offers an image of the orderly, superficial sheen of suburbia that recalls both Cheever's homes where "nothing had not been burnished" and Beattie's vision of distorted suburban propriety—where even a shooting is written off as a "*faux pas,*" its bloodstain efficiently cleaned up as if it were nothing more than a glass of spilled wine. Maxwell's connection to such notions of ill-conceived suburban propriety is only underscored by his terse reaction to the question of Xavier's marrying Roxanne. After meeting Lester, he pronounces his verdict: "So that's Roxanne's brother. . . . That family has one foot in the ghetto and the other on a watermelon rind. There's no question of your marrying into something like that. You wouldn't have a snowball's chance in hell" (116). Maxwell's advice has as much to do with Xavier's position in Linden Hills society as it does with his future in the corporation: to marry "down" ("up" in inverted Linden Hills) to a lower-prestige, "blacker" family would, for Xavier, spell the end of his dreams of social advancement; his only other choice is to emulate Maxwell, who lives an existence so devoid of racial identity that he spends "every waking moment trying to be no color at all" (106).

The painstaking manipulation of image that Maxwell both lives and preaches to Xavier is, Naylor suggests, the legacy of the Nedeed family's tradition of control over the social landscape, a phenomenon that becomes more apparent to Willie and Lester as they progress farther down the Hills. As the pair work the back room of the elaborate wedding reception of Winston—a closeted gay man who goes through with an unwanted marriage in order to advance "down" Linden Hills (Nedeed rewards him with a home at the bottom of the Hills, the most elite section of town)—Willie notices the artificiality of this lavish "celebration." Sensing that the affected joviality of the expensively attired guests masks a complete lack of "spontaneity," Willie concludes that "he was actually watching them watch themselves having this type of affair" (83).[43] The celebration of exclusivity apparent in this scene takes a decidedly political turn in a subsequent event Willie and Lester work, a memorial service for Lycentia Parker, once a leading figure in Linden Hills politics who had most recently served with the Wayne County Citizens Alliance (described by Willie as the "Ku Klux Klan without a Southern accent") to prevent a low-income "housing project" from being built in neighboring Putney Wayne. On learning at the memorial the news that the housing project has been provisionally approved by the county government, the affluent black guests react heatedly, predicting a future for Linden Hills of barred windows, "overcrowded schools," and TVs and stereos "walking out the door." The late Lycentia has the final word in the conversation, as her husband, exhibiting the seamless melding of exclusivity and social grace that is the hallmark of Linden Hills society, announces to the guests, "'Lycentia . . . would often say to me, "Chester, I'm going to do everything in my power to keep those dirty niggers out of our community." And this evening is in her honor.' He smiled weakly around the table. 'So please, there's more roast beef, folks'" (135). Steeped in overtly racist rhetoric, the vision of the Linden Hills landscape offered by Lycentia and the guests at her memorial suggests the utter inversion of racial sensibilities in Linden Hills.

The dissolution of racially understood bonds of community apparent in this scene bespeaks a larger loss of identity among the residents of the elite suburb, one that contributes to a sense of "facelessness" in the community that Naylor exposes as Willie continues farther down toward the Nedeed residence. One resident, Laurel Dumont, has become so alienated by her single-minded pursuit of professional and material advancement that she commits suicide, diving off the high diving board into her empty swimming pool—Willie finds her crushed, "faceless" body at the bottom of the pool. Willa Nedeed, imprisoned in her basement, discovers the mementos of generations of Nedeed wives, and she finds that all were psychologically imprisoned by their husbands. In a fate paralleling those of the women of Levin's and Forbes's Stepford, each wife was essentially "disposed of" after producing an heir to the Nedeed family concern. Still, the Nedeed wives left evidence of their former selves, recording their travails in the pages of Bibles, recipe books, and photo albums that Willa discovers. The most striking case is that of Priscilla McGuire Nedeed, whose family photo album reveals a series of photos of herself, her husband, and son; as the photos progress chronologically, Priscilla becomes "overshadowed" by the presence of the two Luther Nedeeds, until finally Willa discovers that in late photos Priscilla's entire face has been removed.[44] Willie, too, suffers from a nightmare in which a woman accosts him and worriedly tells him that he has "no face." As Grace Collins has argued, Naylor's extended metaphor of facelessness, in suggesting the "theme of invisibility, a constant in African-American fiction, provides the clue to the events of the novel."[45] That is, the thematic link among Willie's nightmare, Laurel's suicide, and the Nedeed wives' plight lies in their common relationship to a landscape that works to render blackness invisible. By subverting racial integrity and the bonds of community for the sake of creating a terrain that reflects only the veneer of wealth and prestige, the Nedeed dream— intentionally or not—served, literally, to efface the essence of its inhabitants; this point is made near the end of the novel by the town historian, Dr. Braithwaite: "'If you must fault them [the Nedeeds] for anything, fault them for wanting power. But it was *black* power they wanted. These were to be black homes with black aspirations and histories—for good or evil. But that's not what Luther inherited. Put yourself in the place of a man who must reign over a community as broken and disjointed—as faceless—as Laurel Dumont's body. If he could have stopped her, he would have. But what he saw diving off that platform was already a shattered dream'" (261).

Luther Nedeed himself reflects on this "shattered dream" on Christmas Eve, the night that would later, after Willa's emergence from the basement, see the deaths of both Willa and Luther in a fire that destroys their home. Shortly before the arrival of Willie and Lester, who are fulfilling the last of their Linden Hills odd jobs by helping him trim his Christmas tree, Luther ruminates on the total failure of the Nedeeds and their residents to construct a sense of black community in Linden Hills: "All of those sacrifices to build them houses and they refused to build a history. Father, forgive me, Luther almost whispered aloud, but sometimes I wish you had left me another dream" (286). This brief, almost sympathetic glimpse into the psyche of Nedeed—who throughout had been characterized as the devil incarnate—constitutes a curious turn near the close of Naylor's narrative. Emerging as a figure akin to a Jay Gatsby or Neddy Merrill—another "dreamer" whose idealized vision of his landscape was only to be corrupted—Luther almost seems, in his final hours, to be as much or more of a victim than the alienated inhabitants of Linden Hills. Nevertheless, the extent of Nedeed's pathology comes home to him later in the evening when his wife finally emerges from the basement to announce "Luther, your son is dead" (299). As Luther tries to wrest the body of the son away from Willa, Willie and Lester watch in horror as the three Nedeeds lock in a macabre embrace, in the process upsetting a nearby candle and becoming engulfed in flames.

The denouement features a curious blend of the suburban and the gothic, recalling Forbes's gothic turn at the close of *The Stepford Wives*.[46] As Willie and Lester run from the burning house, they turn in time to see "smoke billowing from the side of the house as the den draperies went up in flames." Then Willie stands in front of the blazing house as its "darkened windows" loom at his back "like gutted eyes" (302). Naylor's gothic atmosphere is shattered, literally, when Willie—frustrated in his efforts to rouse neighbors into calling the fire department—throws a rock through the picture window of a nearby home, and he prepares to do the same to the remaining houses on the street until Lester stops him. What Willie fails to understand, until Lester informs him, is that the neighbors are intentionally letting the house burn, presumably sensing a kind of liberation in the destruction of the Nedeed estate. Lester and Willie eventually escape the scene, scaling the fence of the Nedeed yard out of Linden Hills and into an adjacent apple orchard. And while Naylor's closing image of Willie and Lester crossing hand in hand into the orchard suggests a transcendent close, an escape from the suburban "hell" of Linden Hills, it is nonetheless a problematic finish.

To be sure, the residents of this "community" do finally act as such—banding together, if only in their decisive nonaction, to allow the Nedeed house and all it stands for to burn to the ground. But if this is a positive development at the close of the novel, it still leaves unanswered the question of how the Linden Hills residents will live their lives in the future: Does Naylor suggest that the destruction of Nedeed and his home mark the beginning of racially understood community in Linden Hills, or will the exclusionary, bourgeois status quo prevail? And does Willa's defeat of Luther suggest an awakening of resistance to Linden Hills' patriarchal culture, or—given her demise as well—signify little change at all in prevailing sexual politics? The apocalyptic finish leaves cause to wonder about these matters, for as Fowler has pointed out, Naylor's depiction throughout of "middle-class black suburbia as a kind of hell seems to preclude the possibility of a solution beyond destruction" (88). Ultimately, this cautionary allegory about the alienating effects of bourgeois life on African American identity and community paints the middle-class suburbs in no uncertain terms as a living hell, a place that subordinates women and dissolves racial identity and community within a miasma of unreflective American materialism.

🏠 🏠 🏠

The alarmist, dystopian view of black suburbanization Naylor offers in *Linden Hills* finds few counterparts in African American cinema; indeed, with the exception of such very recent films as Rick Famuyiwa's *The Wood* (1999), a nostalgic look at four black friends who grew up in suburban Inglewood, California, and Steve Carr's *Next Friday* (2000), a sequel to the 1995 urban party film *Friday* that finds its protagonist relocated to the Southern California suburb of Rancho Cucamonga, one is hard pressed to find works by black filmmakers that are predominantly set in the suburbs. As Karen Ross has noted, the consistent choice of the urban milieu by black filmmakers both reflects and helps to reinforce notions of the city as the only center of African American identity.[47] Nevertheless, as far back as Lorraine Hansberry's classic 1959 play *A Raisin in the Sun* (adapted for the screen by Hansberry and director Daniel Petrie in 1961), one can sense a tension between African American visions of the city and the suburb. In Hansberry's drama of a poor black family's dreams of buying a house of their own—in an all-white neighborhood—outside the urban center, the suburban sphere is portrayed as both a promised land of sorts and a threatening, rigorously defended white enclave. Nearly coerced into abandoning their hopes of relocating through the threats and bribes offered by a representative of the white "neighborhood association," Hansberry's protagonists ultimately decide to press on with the purchase of their new home, albeit fully aware of the dangers the move poses to their very existence. Despite its central importance, the suburb remains an absent force in Hansberry's influential play, with the action of the narrative transpiring entirely within the family's cramped, inner-city apartment. Over the next two generations, suburbia would remain largely uncharted territory in dramatic depictions of the black experience.

Nevertheless, while the mainstream of African American cinema has continued to explore the (often violent) dynamics of urban existence—as witnessed by the blaxploitation genre of the 1970s and its revival in late-

1980s' and 1990s' "gangsta" films—a recent trend among black filmmakers has shifted focus to depictions of middle-class African American communities. Works such as Forest Whitaker's *Waiting to Exhale* (1995), George Tillman Jr.'s *Soul Food* (1997), and Kevin Rodney Sullivan's *How Stella Got Her Groove Back* (1998) have, by situating romantic and familial melodramas within an atmosphere of comfortable affluence, offered a much-needed corrective response to the monolithic vision of the "new blaxploitation" of the violent, crime-ridden ghetto as the center of black lives. Other films have been less sanguine about the dynamics of black affluence: Reginald Hudlin's *Boomerang* (1992) and Matty Rich's *The Ink Well* (1994), for example, feature protagonists struggling psychologically with issues driven by class identification and its impact on the protagonist's sense of self. In *Boomerang,* a powerful executive loses himself amid the machinations of a devious, striving corporate world and must come to terms with his alienation from friends and community; in *The Ink Well,* a young man of working-class roots confronts what he feels to be the hypocrisy and duplicity of the black bourgeoisie. Both films reflect a growing interest among black filmmakers in portraying material success and its impact on African American identity and modes of community.

In Hudlin's first film, 1990's *House Party,* class issues similar to these are played out among a group of African American high schoolers who set out to have the blow-out party of the year. Essentially a teen coming-of-age/ party movie in the tradition of such white teen party films of the 1980s as *Sixteen Candles* and *Risky Business,* *House Party* overlays a number of serious social issues with popular music, dance, and broad, youth-oriented comedy. *House Party* differs from the canon of 1980s' white teen party films in its use of setting: *Sixteen Candles* and *Risky Business* are resolutely suburban tales chronicling the foibles of affluent kids growing up, while *House Party* is set in more of a socially diverse urban milieu; as the variety of characters move between their houses and apartments over the course of the film, they traverse a landscape that runs the gamut from inner-city "projects" through lower- and middle-class suburban fringe neighborhoods to the upper-middle-class suburbs. The physically and socially heterogeneous terrain provides more than backdrop for the action of the narrative; instead, it becomes a crucial element in relaying the film's social dynamics. Indeed, the central drama, [involving the "choice" the protagonist must make between two potential love interests, one from the lower-class projects and the other from the elite suburbs, is metonymically rendered through the treatment of landscape. As in films such as *Boomerang* and *The Ink Well,* this romantic plot opens out into a series of concerns over the protagonist's identity and how it is impacted by matters of race, class affiliation, and landscape.]

In a classic teen party film plot, the protagonist, Kid (Christopher Reid), grounded for getting into a fight with a trio of hoodlums at his high school, must escape from the watchful eye of his father to attend the party of the season being thrown by his friend Play (Christopher Martin). [Among the throng of attendees from Kid and Play's all-black high school are Kid's two love interests, Sharane (A. J. Johnson) and Sidney (Tisha Campbell).] As the evening unfolds, Kid finds himself in one tight spot after another, as he is pursued throughout town by his father, the school bullies, and the police. But over the course of the evening, Kid is also confronted with a number of conflicts centering on his racial identity (he is light-skinned, the son of an African American father and now-deceased white mother) and class status (being raised by a conscientious, if in Kid's mind "overprotective," working-class father, he aspires to attend college and advance beyond his father's position in society). [The primary conflict Kid faces concerns his attraction to both Sharane, a lower-class, sexually provocative dark-skinned girl, and Sidney, the lighter-skinned, conservative daughter of affluent parents, as he finds himself falling for both at Play's party.] "Sharane and Sidney, the two finest women in here. Now how could a man choose?" Kid asks the two at one point during the party. "He better choose right," Sharane cautions; later, when Sidney reminds him that he needs to make a decision on the matter, she flatly declares, "I'm not asking you for anything. It's about what you want." And indeed, the "choice" between Sharane, a "girl from the projects," and Sidney, the daughter of well-heeled suburban parents, is about more than romantic interests: Overlaid with issues of racial identification and class affiliation (and also more than a bit reminiscent of George Bailey's "choice" between Mary Hatch and Violet Bick in Capra's *It's a Wonderful Life*), this romantic subplot metaphorically stands for the life choices facing Kid as he navigates the literal and figurative landscapes of his present and future.

Hudlin's treatment of physical terrain itself is crucial to understanding the social dynamics surrounding Kid's "choice." What becomes apparent from early in the film is the way that Hudlin sets up a class-bound hierarchy of landscape. At the bottom of the socioeconomic ladder is Sharane, who lives with at least seven other extended family members in a cramped apartment located in a fenced-off, forbidding row of redbrick projects. Headed by an immensely overweight father who dresses in ill-fitting sweatsuits and ceaselessly consumes "Dick Gregory's diet shakes," Sharane's family is presented as a collection of loafers whose only notice-able activity—aside from lying around the living room watching televi-sion—is mixing pitchers full of sugar-laden Kool-Aid. Kid, though considerably better off than Sharane, occupies the next rung in this class ladder: his conscientious father works two jobs as a laborer to maintain their single-family home, but as Hudlin's camerawork reveals, they exist on the working-class fringe. Hard by a major urban thoroughfare, Kid's house is set on a plot of dying grass and withering shrubbery, protected by a rusty, dilapidated metal fence. By contrast, the homes of Play and friend Bilal (Martin Lawrence) sit on shaded, tree-lined streets, their position and architecture signifying higher class status; still, a variety of markers—the ancient television and well-worn furnishings of Play's home, the metal security bars on the doors and windows of Bilal's—indicate that they too are far from affluent. The one elite member of the group is Sidney, who resides with her upper-middle-class parents in the most recognizably suburban section of the city. Several extended scenes transpire in front of her house, a large, pillared white colonial shaded by a massive oak and set far back from the street on a lush, manicured lawn. With each sequence shot at Sidney's house, the prevailing hip-hop soundtrack is replaced by soothing, easy-listening background music—a leitmotif that not only signals, but indeed valorizes, Sidney's bourgeois existence. This tendency for extended sequences in front of Sidney's home suggests the value afforded the suburban landscape, which is presented—primarily through contrast to Sharane's projects—as a sought-after environment.

Given Hudlin's precise "mapping" of class identity, Kid's problematic attraction to both Sharane and Sidney becomes intertwined with a class-bound politics of landscape. Kid's friend Play reveals as much when he advises the protagonist that the proper object of his affections ought to be Sidney, because "you can't be dealin' with no project girl." When Kid objects to his friend's derisive labeling of Sharane, Play clarifies his position: "But Sidney, she has a *home*, you know what I'm sayin'? A *house*." While Play's rationale behind this advice is that his friend will have more privacy with Sidney, his admiration of her social stature and environment is echoed by the film's cinematography and ultimately its linking of Kid and Sidney: Sidney's suburban home signifies black success, while Sharane's apartment in the projects is consistently portrayed as a threatening environment, a place to be avoided at all costs. Hence, in direct contrast to Naylor's valorization of urban poverty and indictment of suburban bourgeois life, Hudlin—through his treatment of Sidney and Sharane and their respective environments—embraces the suburban dream. The defining moment in establishing these dynamics of landscape comes after Kid leaves Play's party to escort both Sharane and Sidney back to their homes. Although he hopes to make a romantic connection with Sharane, he is frightened by her description of life in the projects, where a neighbor recently "went crazy and started sniping people from the roof." As Kid and Sidney leave Sharane's, their romantic relationship begins. In a telling use of landscape, Hudlin offers a long shot of the couple exiting the grounds of the projects; as they pass through the gate that fences off the forbidding apartment complex, they are talking animatedly about their future plans—both are busy filling out college applications, Sidney hopes to attend an Ivy League school. This conversation, marking the beginning of their romance, ties dreams of social advancement to an escape from the landscape of the inner city, with Hudlin capturing through his use of setting an image of Kid's larger journey toward Sidney, the suburbs, and middle-class sensibilities.

As critic Donald Bogle has rightly argued, the sustained contrast between inner-city and suburban lifestyles is also intimately tied to racial concerns; arguing that Hudlin's film expresses "traditional attitudes on women and class," Bogle notes that the casting of a lighter-skinned actress to play Sidney and a dark-skinned actress for the role of Sharane works to conflate class and racial identity. As in Naylor's novel, where the inexorable "whitening" of the Nedeed family pairs social advancement with the loss of racial identity, Hudlin draws noticeable parallels between skin tone and class position. This tendency is reinforced, as Bogle points out, by the modes of humor directed at the families of the two women: While Hudlin's satirical humor aimed at Sidney's bourgeois family is handled in "restrained, even deferential terms," Sharane's family are characterized as "lowlifes" by whom the viewer is meant to be "comically appalled."[48] The protagonist as well becomes a part of this racially informed treatment of class and landscape: As the "half-white" son of a father who describes himself as a "poor black man," Kid exists on the margins of both racial and class identity.[49] In this sense, his attraction to both Sidney and Sharane becomes more than a mere romantic entanglement: As an ill-fitting, liminal figure in a film featuring otherwise carefully constructed connections among class, race, and landscape, Kid faces a decision that will integrate him into a fixed, definable position within the narrative. His decision at the close of the film to begin seeing Sidney, then, amounts to an affirmation of the suburban lifestyle.

Nevertheless, despite the eventual endorsement of Sidney's bourgeois existence, the suburban environment is also presented as a rigidly controlled place, protected by modes of surveillance and discipline that range from Play's incessant worrying about the trashing of his mother's house to the domineering, even brutal actions of two white police officers who appear repeatedly over the course of the narrative. In comic fashion, Hudlin portrays the paranoid fears of Play, who—though he attempts to play the role of the easygoing party host—desperately fears that the insurgent crowd of partygoers will destroy his parents' comfortable home. A scene before the party itself finds Play hastily removing all of his mother's glassware from the china cabinet, replacing it with plastic cups so his guests do not have the opportunity to "break mom's good stuff." The end of the party is occasioned by Play finding his mother's toilet broken; in an extended bit of scatological humor, Play and several assembled friends look in horror at the pile of shit left behind. The symbolic weight of this discovery is too much for Play to bear: Sensing the ultimate corruption of his parents' home, he angrily lectures his guests—"I put you in my house and you dog me," he yells—before calling an abrupt end to the party and throwing everyone out. During the party, the trio of men who are chasing Kid—trash-talking urban toughs—attempt to enter the party, but Play, advising them that "no hoods are allowed at my party," instead suggests, "Why don't you go rob a liquor store or something?" While an innocuous enough bit of humor, a scene such as this suggests the extent to which the sensibility Hudlin creates in this film differs from that offered by urban, "new blaxploitation" cinema; the very character types who figure at the center of black urban crime dramas are here barred from the party altogether. Their response is both explosive and comic: They attempt to burn down Play's house, but do so by pouring gasoline on the brick outer walls and in the process are immediately accosted by the seemingly omnipresent white police.

In his characterization of the local police, Hudlin creates a portrait of surveillance and abuse that is at once comic and subtly scathing. Thoroughly stock figures, the two white cops who patrol the area surrounding Play's party seem to exist solely for two reasons: to eat doughnuts and to abuse the local black residents. Over the course of the narrative, several times they accost Kid and the "hoods" who are pursuing him and also verbally harass Kid's father as he walks down the street in search of his son. In a provocative assessment, Richard Dyer has argued that this perpetual police presence contributes to an atmosphere of "ghettoization" in the film; as Dyer suggests, "the fact that the middle-class and . . . all-American streets of *House Party* are a ghetto is emphasized by the at once comic and sadistic, racist cop duo who patrol and keep the inhabitants in line."[50] While an interesting reading, Dyer's analysis fails to consider two important points about the landscape Hudlin creates: First is the fact that the action occurs on a noticeably diverse terrain that ranges from an actual "ghetto" to the elite sections of the city; second, and more important, the police surveillance is confined to the more upper-class neighborhoods. In the several scenes that transpire at Sharane's projects, the police are not to be found anywhere; indeed, the almost total silence and sense of calm prevailing at the projects suggests not so much a peaceable environment as a place that is utterly neglected by law enforcement. Such a reading is supported by another telling comic moment in the narrative, when a black neighbor of Play's dials the police and we hear him say, "911? Yeah, I'll hold." What Hudlin suggests through his treatment of police activity is that the cops' central role is not to "protect and serve" but, as Dyer rightly suggests, to "keep the inhabitants in line." Indeed, one might rephrase this assessment to suggest that the police strive to keep inhabitants "in their place"; their laissez-faire approach to the projects and intense surveillance of wealthier parts of town signifies not only a willing neglect of black poverty but also a concern over black affluence that has the effect of marking the suburban areas as proscriptive environments.

A number of sequences highlight this sense of the suburbs as an environment of surveillance and control. The first features Kid being accosted by the two white cops as he walks down a tree-lined street en route to Play's party. The scene seems to resolve in benign comedy, as the cops leave Kid alone after realizing they are "out of doughnuts" and thus have more important business to tend to; still, it ends with the cops cautioning Kid, "Hey you, watch yourself, you understand, 'cause we are." These words prove prophetic, for the police continue to maintain intense scrutiny of the higher-class environments. In a subsequent appearance, they accost Kid's father, Pops, on what looks like the same street. To their blunt demands to know where he is going, Pops responds, "I'm going to mind my fuckin' business, that's where I'm going. Do you have a problem with that, officer?" Yelling "Freeze!" the cops pull their guns on him and instruct him to put his hands on top of his head. Grudgingly complying, Pops accurately assesses the cops' motives: "I know why you stopped me. I know why. 'Cause I'm a poor black man in a black neighborhood, on a black block, and y'all just wanna bust my black ass." To this one cop responds, "No, no; you look suspicious," while the other adds, "Yeah, you look suspicious, and you definitely look black." Cautioning him, "Watch your attitude," the cops drive off, but not before they have underscored a message the film as a whole presents about race and landscape: that higher-class, suburban environments remain under the watchful, domineering eye of white authority.[51]

The psychologically and physically abusive nature of this authority is revealed in a pair of scenes centering on Kid and the trio of "hoods" pursuing him. At one point, the three thugs chase Kid onto the grounds of a magnificent estate playing host to the social gathering of a successful black fraternal organization. The attendees—including Sidney's parents—watch in horror as the two white cops appear out of nowhere and hold the four youths at gunpoint, making them repeat in unison one cop's sarcastic affirmation, "I . . . am . . . somebody." The hypocrisy of white law enforcement receives a telling satirical treatment here, as a phrase seemingly meant to underscore the importance of the black individual is coerced from the youths with a threat to their very lives. Later this threat of police violence is realized when the cops, after again accosting the thugs pursuing Kid, take them down to "the docks," where "nobody can hear 'em scream," for a beating. Although this moment is not pictured on-screen, the trio's subsequent appearance finds them aching from the

physical abuse, having suffered bruises and broken ribs. The nonappear-
ance of the beating scene raises some potentially troubling issues; critic
Tommy Lott, for example, argues that Hudlin suppresses the scene "in
order not to offend the potential white audience," a crucial compromise
that in Lott's terms renders the film little more than another example of
"blaxploitation cinema."[52] At the same time, it is worth considering the
notion that Hudlin's decision not to portray the police brutality directly
only heightens the mystique of the police as a silent force, an invisible but
omnipresent power capable of punishing with impunity.

The closing of the film brings together the separate but related
thematic concerns over class, race, and landscape control. Finally arrested
along with his trio of pursuers, Kid is taken to the city jail, where —in a
bizarre and unsettling scene—he is fondled by other inmates and nearly
raped before finally being bailed out by his friends. While Kid languishes
in prison, Play and Bilal go to Sharane and Sidney in an attempt to come
up with bail money; while Sharane has nothing to offer and can be coerced
into going down to the prison only with the promise that the group will go
to "Burger King" afterward, the question of bail money is solved after the
visit to Sidney's. Sidney's "bailing out" of Kid can, given their respective
class affiliations and growing romantic relationship, be read in metaphori-
cal terms as well. In rescuing him from the potential violence of the prison
cell, Sidney represents in the broadest terms the lifeline by which Kid also
can escape his perilous position on the fringe of poverty. Not surprisingly,
the bailout scene is followed by a final sequence featuring Kid and Sidney
in front of her suburban home; as the romantic easy-listening music plays
in the background, their growing romance is precisely located within the
comfort and promise of her suburban surroundings.

🏠 🏠 🏠

The final sequence of *House Party* features Kid finally getting his comeup-
pance from Pops, whose old-fashioned sense of discipline is manifested in

the vicious beating he gives Kid with his belt. After the initial credits begin to roll, a final scene appears out of nowhere; an echo of the very first sequence of the film, in which Kid in his sleep dreams of Play's party being so good that the roof literally blows off the house, this final scene shows where the roof finally lands—directly on the heads of the two white cops, crushing them. Following this startling shot, the remainder of the credits roll. As critic Ed Guerrero notes in his excellent study *Framing Blackness: The African American Image in Film,* this closing reflects a satirical tendency in contemporary African American cinema to "mask and express . . . discontents that, if depicted otherwise, might make the suburban moviegoer uneasy." That is, in imagining the killing of white cops, an image that, as Guerrero notes, caused rapper Ice-T "to be so vilified in the national media for the release of his song 'Cop Killer,'" *House Party* closes by turning the sadistic impulses of white authority back on itself.[53] Nonetheless, this closing image remains a fantasy; in the world of the film, the suburban enclaves of the wealthy black community are depicted as rigorously controlled by the white power structure. And in the end, this sense of prohibitive control impinges on Hudlin's otherwise glowing vision of black suburban life: In contrast to Naylor, whose suburban allegory indicts the sensibilities of the growing black bourgeoisie, Hudlin depicts the lure of the suburban dream for African Americans, all the while emphasizing the notion that access to this dream remains under the control of reactionary and unforgiving white authority.

Cue the Sun

Soundings from Millennial Suburbia

In a crucial scene from Peter Weir's hit 1998 film *The Truman Show*, protagonist Truman Burbank, after discovering the (un)reality of his situation, makes a break for freedom. As Truman attempts to escape his imprisoning sound-stage suburban world under the cover of night, his omnipotent foe, the creator/director of "The Truman Show," Christof, directs his minions to "cue the sun" and flood the area with sunlight, even though it is the middle of the night. A climactic moment of sorts, Christof's order—and the wee-hours sunrise that follows—makes plain the utter artificiality of Truman's universe, while at the same time highlighting the forces massed to keep Truman in his place. Read metaphorically, this sequence in Weir's film depicts suburbia not only as an artificial recon-struction of small-town America but also, more tellingly, as a landscape of imprisonment and control. And while the conceit of *The Truman Show* may have been clever (if not, perhaps, entirely original—as fans of Philip K. Dick's 1959 novel *Time Out of Joint* might argue), its thematic message was by no means unique: As I hope to have demonstrated, American fiction and films from the past half century that depict the suburbs have painted a consistently negative environment.[1] Almost without fail, the major novels, stories, and films chronicling suburban life have envisioned suburbia as a contrived, dispiriting, and alienating place. Even today, at a time when more Americans live in the suburbs than either the city or the country, and when the success of "gated communities" and "neotraditional" towns suggests that the process of suburbanization continues to evolve in new ways, the major recent films about suburbia (*The Truman Show, Pleasantville, American Beauty,* Todd Haynes's *Far from Heaven*) nonetheless represent this environment as an entrapping and debilitating place to live. I hope to have shown that this consistent focus on suburbia as an American dystopia is more than coincidence and instead reflects our uneasy relationship to an environment heavily invested with, even defined by, middle-class America's cultural aspirations and anxieties.

Lacking the established cultural meanings of the more knowable terrains of city, country, or small town, the suburb has assumed meaning and cultural significance largely through its representations in the popular arts and media. And, as any viewer of Nickelodeon's "TV Land" network can attest, perhaps the most enduring cultural impression of suburbia was cast during the massive wave of postwar suburbanization in the 1950s. Evidence of the lasting power of TV's vision of suburbia can be found in the success of *The Truman Show* and *Pleasantville,* both of which look back in time to invoke 1950s'-style suburban situation comedy as a metaphor for exploring the repressions and assorted neuroses of contemporary American suburbia. Other popular suburban movies of recent years, ranging from Robert Zemeckis's *Back to the Future* films of the 1980s to Hugh Wilson's 1999 comedy *Blast from the Past,* use a similar motif of time travel to 1950s' suburbia as the source of their humor and light social commentary. In a quite different vein, Todd Haynes's acclaimed melodrama of suburban repression, *Far from Heaven* (2002), continues the look back at suburbia in the 1950s. In fact, Haynes's film, a remake of Douglas Sirk's 1955 drama *All That Heaven Allows,* most clearly suggests the prolonged cultural afterlife of the image of suburbia constructed during the postwar years.[2] Meticulously re-creating the look and feel not necessarily of 1950s' suburbia, but rather of Sirk's *depiction* of that bygone landscape, Haynes's film intentionally and self-referentially toys with distinctions between real and imagined history, highlighting the sense of suburbia as a culturally constructed environment. And if, as Frederic Jameson argues, nostalgia films on the whole train us to "consume the past in the form of glossy images," then it is also worth noting that the nostalgia mode in these suburban films confirms the extent to which this terrain has been, since the postwar years, very much an imaged environment, a landscape of the mind.[3]

The oddly transhistorical look at suburbia offered by these films also underscores how firmly the vexed cultural perception of the suburbs remains tied to visions of suburbia in post–World War II America. Hollywood's anachronistic vision in this regard stands as testament to the profound cultural influence of the suburban landscape in the postwar years, a point *The Truman Show* seems to treat in self-reflexive fashion. What makes this film's handling of the suburbs distinct, however, and what lends particular relevance to its intentional melding of contemporary and postwar visions of suburbia, is the extratextual matter of its having been shot on location. The movie was filmed in Seaside, Florida, the crown jewel of the contemporary "New Urbanism" architectural movement, a postsuburban, neotraditional urban design philosophy centered on planned communities and described by its leading practitioners as an antidote to suburban sprawl. The ironies abound: Weir's choice of the master-planned, presumably postsuburban Seaside as the physical setting to depict his make-believe suburban sitcom set, which in turn was meant to mirror old-fashioned American suburbia, suggests a metatextual commentary on neotraditionalism, nostalgia, and planned (or enforced) community that is potentially explosive, but accessible only to those viewers aware of Seaside's history and philosophy. In a broader sense, *The Truman Show*'s Seaside locale suggests the convergence of contemporary and postwar visions of suburbia at the turn of the millennium and the end of America's suburban century. In that sense, this film serves as an apt starting point for looking at the state of suburbia—and its representations—at the beginning of the twenty-first century.

In many ways, *The Truman Show* is a movie very much of its times, as turn-of-the-century America has continued to struggle with ever-expanding suburbanization, as well as the dubious legacies—physical, demographic, and philosophical—of a half century's worth of massive suburbanization. Not coincidentally, Weir repeatedly draws from *It's a Wonderful Life*—sometimes subtly, other times directly and explicitly—as he relays the story of Truman Burbank. In self-consciously echoing Capra's proto-suburban fantasy of fifty years earlier, Weir seems to be inviting his audience to reassess Capra's look at the suburban future, in light of the ensuing half century of suburbanization. That he ultimately glosses his suburban satire with layers of horror/fantasy—as did Levin and Forbes (*The Stepford Wives*) and Naylor (*Linden Hills*) before him, as well as contemporary Gary Ross (*Pleasantville*)—does not take away from the elements of the film that do resonate with contemporary suburban experience. In fact, in its emphasis—however heavy-handed—on control and imprisonment masquerading as old-time community, *The Truman Show* evokes the two latest (and among the most philosophically complex) movements in American suburbanization: the neotraditional developments of the New Urbanists and the rising popularity of the "gated community."

Both gated communities and New Urbanist neotraditional developments stand as responses, in differing manners, to suburban sprawl, the filling up of the countryside with what recent antisuburban observers have called "jive-plastic commuter tract home wastelands" and "sea-to-sea parking lots."[4] For developers and residents of gated communities, creating a separate, walled-off community space provides not only security but also a measure of cultural distinction from the surrounding populace. Of course, gated communities—which by the mid-1990s housed some 3 to 4 million Americans—also raise fundamental questions regarding the relationship between individual and society.[5] Representing the ultimate in privatization, gated communities typically provide their own security, street maintenance, trash collection, and the like, thus establishing a degree of independence from the surrounding municipality. In return, homeowners' associations in gated communities reserve the right to divorce themselves entirely from the denizens of the world outside the gates. It is not difficult to read the rise of gated communities as representing the culmination of certain patterns in suburbanization from the postwar years onward; if one impetus for the move to the suburbs has always been "flight" from the travails of urban existence and escape into a safe haven of sorts, then the gated community is merely the logical extension of this tendency. Nonetheless, the hyper-exclusivity of gated communities raises genuine social and even legal concerns; legal scholar David J. Kennedy has recently argued that the barring of public access to previously public roads raises concerns regarding freedoms of speech and assembly, and also raises the specter of "Jim Crow–type" enforced segregation of municipal spaces.[6] On the other side of the coin, if fear of outsiders drives the building of walls around communities, it requires little foresight to see that the gated community ought to become, as New Urbanist Peter Calthorpe argues, a "self-fulfilling prophecy," as enforced isolation will breed yet more fear of the increasingly unknown outsiders.[7] As "landscapes of fear," in Yi-Fu Tuan's phrasing, the oxymoronically labeled gated communities figure "community" through a system of locks, guards, and barricades—which is eerily reminiscent of the philosophy of *The Truman Show*'s evil mastermind, Christof.

As opposed to the privatizing drive of the gated community movement, for the New Urbanists, community planning and design "must assert the importance of public over private values."[8] Leaders of the New Urbanist movement such as Andres Duany and Elizabeth Plater-Zyberk, the design team who created Seaside, believe that a community ethos can be facilitated through architectural and landscape design. Specifically,

Duany and Plater-Zyberk counter traditional suburbia's emphasis on private property with a focus on communal spaces: Master-planned communities such as Seaside and Celebration, Florida, feature pedestrian-friendly streets oriented toward identifiable town centers that support both recreational and employment opportunities, thus offering at least the possibility of organic community building.[9] For some critics, the New Urbanism holds the promise of righting the wrongs of suburbia while at last realizing the utopian dream of community that the suburbs once seemed to offer. Vincent Scully, for example, argues that Seaside has "succeeded, more fully than any other work of architecture in our time has done, in creating an image of community."[10] Others would counter that Scully's phrasing is all too accurate and that all that has been created in Seaside, the hometown of Truman Burbank, is just that: the "*image* of community." Certainly the New Urbanists are vulnerable to the charge of design fanaticism, a naïve belief that managing such elements as architectural design, street orientation, and visual perspective will somehow inherently instill a sense of community.[11] More significantly, New Urbanism has been challenged as being almost exclusively geared toward the bourgeoisie: Although leaders of the movement argue passionately for the potential renewal of abandoned urban centers and decaying inner-ring suburbs through New Urbanist principles, the fact remains that the great majority of their major projects have been higher-end enclaves such as Seaside. As Andrew Ross argues in his recent work *The Celebration Chronicles*, "New Urbanist towns are 'commentaries' on urban problems, they do not provide a solution to them."[12]

Ross's phrasing puts one in mind of Bill Levitt, who had noted a half century earlier that he could address either a housing problem or a larger social problem, but not both. Levitt's hands-off stance toward prevailing social issues epitomized the escapist mentality of postwar suburbia, and the legacy of such a philosophy unfortunately seems to live on today, even in high-minded movements such as the New Urbanism. That is, until the New Urbanist movement succeeds in offering residential designs that are truly open to the urban working class, their project will continue to be seen—fairly or not—as merely the latest spin on the tried and true formula of escapist suburbanization. This might be another way of saying that the more things change in suburbia, the more they stay the same. And much the same might be said about our broader cultural perception of the suburbs: Although suburbia itself has continued to evolve, its image in the popular media has remained relatively static.

This is a point D. J. Waldie captures in his recent work *Holy Land: A Suburban Memoir*, as he recounts an event of particular significance that transpired shortly after the founding of his postwar suburban town of Lakewood, California. In 1950, after the houses were built but before residents had moved in to Lakewood—to that point the largest pre-planned suburban development town in the nation—a photographer shot a series of stark, aerial photographs of the new landscape, capturing the discomforting vision of a terrain as desolate as it was orderly; his work, as Waldie notes, would retain symbolic resonance for generations to come: "Four of the young man's photographs became the definition of this suburb, and then of suburbs generally. . . . Architectural critics and urban theorists reprinted the photographs in books with names like *God's Own Junkyard.* Forty years later, the same four photographs still stand for the place in which most of us live."[13] Waldie concludes that, in the years since its founding, those same theorists and critics have not "looked again" at Lakewood, instead accepting the implication raised by the aerial photographs of an unpopulated, meticulous terrain: that the suburban "grid, briefly empty of association, is just a pattern predicting itself."[14] This observation raises interesting issues related to the study of suburbia as a lived environment—for the suburb, at the beginning of the twenty-first century, is no longer an emergent environment "empty of association," but rather a fixture of American landscape and society. Indeed, suburbia has, over the past half century, become the dominant landscape in the United States, and yet it remains, as Waldie suggests, an underscrutinized terrain. *it is not empty of association, but a fixture, it is inscrutable yet terrain*

From what impulses does this broad cultural resistance to the landscape of suburbia spring? As I have suggested throughout this study, the suburb remains a vexing element of American topography because of the extent to which it became invested with remarkably durable symbolic meanings in the postwar years. The mass production techniques of firms like Levitt and Sons created a place marked by homogeneity of architecture and landscape design, and even as the suburbs were rightly celebrated for opening home ownership opportunities to a massive new segment of the population, they also evoked cold war–era fears over mounting social conformity. While the low cost of postwar suburban housing helped to fuel an unprecedented expansion of the American middle class, supporting "the structural mobility of an entire generation," the consequent aura of classlessness in the new suburbs raised the specter of a disturbing, pervasive new type of social homogeneity.[15] Indeed, concerns over *sameness* in the suburbs extended beyond the realm of class issues, as the much-touted harmonious social dynamics in postwar suburbs—a mystique supported by the images of suburban living disseminated in popular magazines and television—only contributed to the split in cultural perceptions of the suburb as either a haven of old-fashioned community values or a bastion of limiting and potentially dangerous groupthink.

The outpouring of reaction—both positive and negative—to the suburbs in the postwar years was inextricably tied to the nature of this new landscape itself. While proponents of suburban living saw in their environment the perfect "marriage of town and country," critics of the new suburbia voiced what Waldie would later aptly refer to as the "anxiety of the grid": the sense that the new suburbs were not really *places* at all, but rather interchangeable, placeless locales that would foster not only individual alienation, but a broader sense of cultural dislocation. The primary fear that postwar suburban development provoked, then, was an *Invasion of the Body Snatchers*-type image of a soulless, conformist populace whose disturbing homogeneity reflected that of their landscape. Moreover, I would argue that this reactionary take on suburbs and suburbanites is alive and well today, as evidenced by the central message of the recent, popular film *Pleasantville*: suburban homogeneity equals dangerous cultural conformity.

But one is tempted to ask what, if any, relevance the postwar view of suburbia as an American dystopia holds today. One would be hard pressed, after all, to find a suburban town in the early-twenty-first-century United States that resembles the faceless uniformity and austerity of Lakewood in 1950 or Levittown in 1947. Indeed, even Levittown does not look like "Levittown" anymore; after decades of residents' additions and personalizing alterations to the homes of this first mass-produced suburban town, few if any of the original Bill Levitt home designs remain in their original form.[16] Given this "humanization" of a once-forbidding landscape, and the continued demand for suburban housing that facilitates the ongoing growth of suburbia across the country, one would imagine that America would have, by this point, made peace with the suburbs. And yet this is not the case: Sociologists, environmental critics, and laypersons (including established suburbanites) continue to decry the seemingly inexorable process of suburban "sprawl," rightly seeing in suburban expansion the loss of more elemental, natural terrain and the withering social and economic importance of the American city. Perhaps the suburb, then, is the environment we as a culture want even when we know it is not good for us. Or perhaps the very process of suburbanization amounts to an exercise in self-loathing, a point humorist P. J. O'Rourke broaches in the title of a recent essay: "I Hate the Suburbs—Sort of. . . . But What I Really Hate Is Myself."[17] Either way, such paradoxical relationships to lived place suggest that the suburb continues to reflect both the desires and fears of American culture at large. "do we want it" "everywhere it is no good for us?"

Another way of approaching this vexed relationship to suburbia is to return to Michel Foucault's notion of "heterotopic" spaces. The suburb, I believe, functions as a heterotopic "mirror" to mainstream American culture in its invocation of a utopian dream of middle-class community and security and its constant reminder of the social realities undercutting such a fantasy vision. The dynamics of fiction and film set in the suburbs tend to reinforce the sense that this landscape reflects a wide array of social aspirations and concerns. A review of the writers and filmmakers I have discussed reveals the variety of cultural ideals and anxieties with which they invest the suburban landscape. While Fitzgerald and Cheever, for example, depict the wealthy suburbs as the last, already-compromised haven of an imperiled elite class, Nichols and Naylor portray a world where class prerogative leads only to a stifling materialistic impulse. Capra envisions the postwar suburbs as the site that would re-create traditional, small-town values, while Updike's work reveals the dissolution of any sense of community values and cohesion. Naylor suggests that suburban life compromises notions of racial identity for African Americans, while Hudlin sees in the suburbs the promise of black success. And while Perry, Updike, and Nichols view the suburb as an emasculating environment for the middle-class American male, Beattie, Forbes, and Naylor represent the same terrain as a sphere of patriarchal control where women are robbed of any social identity outside the home and family. Family discord and dysfunction are thematic constants throughout almost all of the works I have examined, and they continue to figure as central factors in contemporary depictions of suburbia: Among the major suburban novels of recent years, Richard Ford's *Independence Day* (1995), Jeffrey Eugenides's *The Virgin Suicides* (1993), and Rick Moody's *The Ice Storm* (1994) all revolve around families that have become broken or damaged— sometimes for mysterious reasons.

The increasingly complex picture of suburban life suggested by these works reminds us that the terms of the "suburban question" have shifted over the years. While Fitzgerald's and Capra's works, along with Lewis's *Babbitt*, in some sense anticipated the social concerns that would be common to subsequent fictional and cinematic treatments of the suburbs, each of the works I have discussed reflects prevailing social concerns of its era, using the suburban setting as the field on which these concerns are played out. Cheever's suburban works, along with Perry's adaptation of "The Swimmer," reflect anxieties over the seeming classlessness of postwar America, portraying affluent suburban societies whose sense of community is compromised by the need to maintain a fading class prerogative. Updike and Nichols both depict the perils of suburban masculinity, in an era when prevailing social turbulence undercut the postwar dream of suburbia as the material manifestation of the "American dream." Beattie's and Forbes's works, in explicitly critiquing the restrictive gender roles common to suburban America, suggest the emergent strength of the women's movement in the 1970s while emphasizing the backlash against feminist progress by a reactionary patriarchal culture. Naylor and Hudlin both approach the issue of racial identity in suburbia at a time when African American migration out of the city was beginning to alter the ingrained image of the suburbs as a bastion of white America. The progression of social concerns in these works suggests that the suburbs became an ever more embattled terrain throughout the century.

For all of their differences, these various texts also work through similar themes and motifs that might be said to characterize the suburban experience. For example, nearly all of the works I have discussed imagine the suburb as an intensely visual environment. The anonymous eyes peering through the picture window of Rabbit Angstrom's "apple-green" house might serve as the most apt symbol of the theme of surveillance common to all of the works I have discussed. This recurring motif reflects a cultural perception of the suburbs as a place where the distinctions between public and private lives have become blurred, a "picture window" world of visibility and compromised privacy. That this perception remains alive today is evidenced by the use of televisual, photographic, and surveillance motifs as central factors in three of the most popular and well-received suburban films of recent years, *Pleasantville*, *The Truman Show*, and *American Beauty* (1999). Related to this notion of suburbia as an intensely public sphere is a recurring sense in suburban works of the landscape itself as heavily commodified, self-consciously fashioned to reflect a veneer of affluence. For Beattie's Louise Knapp, the manufactured appeal of suburbia simply falls flat—"It's so beautiful here," she notes, but that "doesn't seem to help us be happy." In other texts, the critique of environmental commodification is more pointed; the nostalgic strain running through Fitzgerald's, Cheever's, and Updike's works is a direct reaction to a landscape whose hypermateriality renders it devoid of abiding qualities. The loving attention directed toward a plastic garbage bag floating through the streets of affluent suburbia in Mendes's *American Beauty* conveys, in ironic fashion, a similar message. The quintessential symbol of a materialistic suburban landscape, the backyard swimming pool, recurs throughout the works I have discussed; signifying alienation, disconnection, spiritual and even physical death, the use of the swimming pool captures in microcosmic form an ongoing critique of suburban materialism.

If the recurrent nostalgia mode in suburban fiction and film signals an attempted psychological retreat from the alienating, commodified landscape of suburbia, it also works in a broader sense to question the nature of place identification in the suburbs. A yearning for a "place apart" characterizes much suburban fiction and film, and this recurring theme reflects a sense of discomfort with an environment situated between the more knowable terrains of the city and the countryside. To be sure, the city in some suburban works connotes the unavoidable presence of a "corrupting" urban influence—as it does for Fitzgerald's Tom Buchanan and Cheever's Neddy Merrill, whose downfall is foretold through his vision of a cloud resembling "Hackensack" lurking on the horizon. But for others—Beattie, Forbes, Naylor—lost connections to the city convey, by contrast, a sense of isolation, even placelessness, in suburban living. Moreover, in nearly all of the works I have discussed, the act of commuting between suburbs and the urban center has a dislocating effect on characters. As Naylor's Dr. Braithwaite observes, the people in Linden Hills became psychologically displaced through their need to live the commuter's lifestyle; "they had to keep going out and coming back . . . but with less and less of themselves" (260). Braithwaite's comment could apply to the characters of any one of a number of works I have discussed in this study; this recurring focus on

[handwritten margin note: relationship to city + country / no longer subordinate / to central city]

the dislocating place dynamics of suburbia reflects a historically specific reaction to the understanding of place in an age of commutation.

But what happens to this equation when the relationships to both the countryside and the central city cease to be defining characteristics of suburban place? Without question, the ongoing process of suburbanization is rendering the rural sphere an ever more marginal environment. Perhaps a more telling development is that the role of suburbs as bedroom communities to larger urban centers is clearly on the wane: By the mid-1990s, suburb-to-suburb commutes accounted for up to 40 percent of total commutes in the United States, while the once-traditional suburb-to-city commute accounted for only 20 percent of all such trips.[18] With the increasing decentralization of businesses and services has come the development of what have been called, variously, "centerless cities," "technoburbs," "edge cities," or "multinucleated metropolitan regions": densely developed and populated "suburban" areas that feature sufficient employment opportunities—typically in industrial, technological, retail, and service sectors—to render the break from the city complete.[19] Simply put, many suburbs no longer maintain a subordinate relationship to a central city, a fact that has led some commentators to question whether suburbs, in the strict definition of the term, really exist anymore.[20] This spatial development would seem to have far-reaching ramifications for the understanding of suburban place in contemporary America. If the emergent suburbs of the postwar years threatened to homogenize American experience, their ties to distinct urban centers nonetheless suggested an enduring metropolitan and regional identity; by contrast, the autonomous "technoburbs" of today, free of regional, metropolitan associations, convey a heightened sense of cultural homogenization. The office parks, shopping malls, "Super Wal-Marts," and "Price Clubs" that share today's suburban space know no regional identification; they look the same in New Mexico as they do in New York. How does this phenomenon—a kind of corporate "suburbanization of America"—affect place identification in general and representations of the suburban landscape in particular?

A good place to look for an answer to this question might be in contemporary fiction and films that attempt to present a realistic depiction of the suburbanized landscape. In contrast to grand suburban allegories such as *Pleasantville* or *The Truman Show*, any number of recent films use minimalistic detail to convey the sense of suburbia as an interchangeable anyplace. Consider, for example, the 1996 Richard Linklater/Eric Bogosian film *SubUrbia*, in which strip mall and convenience store parking lots come to define the boundaries of both environment and experience for a group of young friends. Perpetually "hanging out" at the 7-Eleven parking lot, the youths of *SubUrbia*, in their utter lack of direction, are meant to be representative of a generation raised in a landscape flattened by an inexorable, desultory standardization. A similar evocation of placelessness in contemporary America can be found in the fiction of writers from what has come to be called the "New South." Arguably no region of the United States has witnessed the phenomenon of homogenizing suburbanization more fully than the South over the past several decades, and realist fiction from contemporary Southern writers tends to reflect this fact. A case in point can be found in the work of Bobbie Ann Mason, who provides a particularly compelling example because of her close affiliation with the *New Yorker* magazine, long associated with suburban fiction. An inheritor of the *New Yorker* tradition of precise, ironic realism, Mason uses her keen eye for detail to capture a Southern landscape notable not for its regional qualities, but for its sense of placelessness. Although her stories typically are set in Kentucky, one has the sense that they could be taking place anywhere in "technoburb" America, filled as they are with references to Wal-Marts, strip malls, and nondescript housing developments. In a sense, Mason's brand of hyperrealism takes the *New Yorker* tradition of suburban fiction to its logical conclusion; in contrast to Cheever and Beattie, for whom the tepid suburban environment provokes a longing for places from the past, Mason's interchangeable fictional settings emphasize, above all, the homogenization of place and experience in contemporary America.

And perhaps this is the fate of suburban place: Confirming the worst fears of postwar social critics, the suburbs may well be flattening the landscape of America, fostering homogeneity of experience through the "displacement" of place itself. Nevertheless, other contemporary chroniclers of the suburbs present a different picture, invoking history as the factor that saves the suburbs from the fate of placelessness. Waldie's compelling memoir, a pastiche of autobiography and environmental and community history, concludes by presenting suburban Lakewood, California, as more a sacred landscape than a profane one. Although tempered throughout by recognition of the shortcomings of this postwar suburb—a place of shoddy homes financed by dubious and restrictive selling practices—Waldie's *Holy Land* suggests the values that inhere to a generationally rooted place, even if that place is a suburban development town. Eugenides's *The Virgin Suicides*, despite the mysterious sadness that drives it, casts a wistful glance back at American suburbia of the 1970s, as does Mark Salzman's recent memoir, *Lost in Place: Growing Up Absurd in Suburbia* (1995). A similar fondness for the suburbs fuels Pam Conrad's *Our House: The Stories of Levittown* (1995), a short story sequence for children that relays the stories of children growing up in Levittown, New York, from the postwar years through the 1990s. Like Waldie, Conrad suggests that, through the sheer passage of time and the development of community ties and place associations, the postwar suburb has become what no cold war–era commentator ever thought it would be: the American small town.

In contrast to these visions of suburban community and continuity, the recent spate of successful and celebrated films chronicling contemporary suburban life tend to view the history of the suburbs in a different light. Both *Pleasantville* and *The Truman Show* eschew notions of generational ties in the suburbs, figuring suburban history instead as a compendium of social anxieties that have changed little over the past fifty years.

Hollywood's most recent look at contemporary suburbia, Mendes's *American Beauty*, also focuses on the darker side of the suburban experience, invoking essentially traditional, dated critiques of suburban life: Both the presentation of the protagonist as a beleaguered, emasculated head of household and the publicizing of his illicit sexual desires have a distinctly postwar feel; the caricatured depiction of his wife as an aggressively driven real estate agent amounts to 1980s'-style antifeminist backlash masquerading as contemporary satire; and the nod to sexual plurality in the suburbs offered through a positive depiction of the protagonists' gay neighbors is undercut by the film's conclusion, in which another neighbor—a confused, closeted army colonel—shoots and kills the protagonist in a fit of rage and passion. But the most interesting—and perhaps most conflicted—aspect of *American Beauty* lies in its treatment of the suburban landscape. After the film completes its unqualified condemnation of suburbia, the narrator's final, posthumous voice-over exhorts viewers to "look closer" and find the beauty in life—even, one is led to believe, in so wretched an environment as the suburb.

Ultimately, *American Beauty* seems as appropriate a summation of this study as it is a compelling look at turn-of-the-century American views of the suburban landscape. Although the film at times hints at embracing both the "family values" associated with suburban living since the postwar years and the cultural pluralism of fin-de-siecle America, it finally undercuts both of these visions, retreating into a caricature of suburban life as hyperbolic as any offered by postwar novelists and social commentators. Nevertheless, Mendes critiques the particular social woes of suburbia in decidedly contemporary terms, demonizing the suburbs as embodying the worst aspects of modern American culture—superficiality, violence, aggressive and unreflective professional striving, and the complete absence of abiding familial and community ties. Needless to say, Mendes's vision of the specific problems besetting contemporary suburbia (and America) is a far cry from that of the postwar social critics, but the difference between these views only underscores the extent to which the suburbs have, for half a century, served as a mirror to the fantasies and phobias of the culture at large. For all of its faults, *American Beauty* suggests through its broad social critique that the suburban question has become increasingly complex. Indeed, the film's dramatic, if often strained, look at the suburbs as the backdrop for a host of contemporary social ills forcefully reminds us of what suburbia has by now become for most Americans—not an alien, nondescript "noplace" lurking on the margins of the landscape and the culture, but in fact someplace far more intimate, the most profound and vexing of all environments: home.

Notes

INTRODUCTION

1. As historian of the suburbs Kenneth Jackson notes in *Crabgrass Frontier: The Suburbanization of the United States* (New York: Oxford University Press, 1985), the growth of cities in the later nineteenth and early twentieth centuries entailed continuing urban expansion outside the bounds of city centers, a phenomenon that occurred in major cities across the nation. While this expansion itself was in demographic terms a process of "suburbanization," the trend throughout the nineteenth and into the early twentieth centuries was for cities to annex the villages into which they expanded. When annexation efforts began to fail in the early twentieth century, commuter suburbs as independent, autonomous entities began to sprout up across the nation. See Jackson, especially chapter 8, pp. 138-156, for an extended discussion of this demographic and political trend.

2. According to analyses of U.S. census data, the suburbs, which as of the 1950 census were nearing parity with urban and nonmetropolitan areas in terms of population, by 1960 were clearly the most populous type of landscape in America, claiming over 33 percent of the total population. This percentage has steadily risen in subsequent decades. Analyses of recent census figures indicate that the trend toward suburbanization continues: G. Scott Thomas, in *The United States of Suburbia: How the Suburbs Took Control of America and What They Plan to Do With It* (Amherst, NY: Prometheus, 1998), notes that as of the 1990 census, 41.1 percent of Americans lived in the suburbs. Minnesota's McKnight Foundation reports that the 2000 census reveals that 43 percent of American voters live in the suburbs. William Lucy and David Phillips, authors of the recent survey "Suburbs and the Census: Patterns of Growth and Decline" (The Brookings Institution Center for Urban and Metropolitan Policy, December 2001), offer an analysis of the 2000 census figures indicating that, notwithstanding evidence of some population gains by urban centers, "decentralization of economic and residential life remains the prevailing trend in metropolitan American today." Bruce Katz and Alan Berube, in their recent essay for *The American Enterprise Magazine*, "Cities Rebound—Somewhat" (June 2002), echo this observation, noting that 2000 census figures indicate gains for some central cities, but a larger continuation of the trend toward decentralization and suburbanization.

3. Roger Silverstone, ed., *Visions of Suburbia* (New York: Routledge, 1997), ix.

4. J. Nicholas Entrikin, *The Betweenness of Place: Towards Geography of Modernity* (Baltimore: The Johns Hopkins University Press, 1991), 7.

5. Geographer E.V. Walter, in *Placeways: A Theory of the Human Environment* (Chapel Hill: University of North Carolina Press, 1988), offers a useful summary of Plato's distinction between the concepts of *topos* and *chora*. In contrast to *topos*, a

term Plato uses to designate physical space itself, *chora* refers to lived space, or what I will refer to throughout this work simply as "place." Interpreting Plato's reading of the dynamics of *chora*, Walter suggests, "[p]eople and things in a place participate in one another's natures. Place is a location of mutual immanence, a unity of effective presences abiding together" (121). As Walter's interpretation suggests, place emerges as something psychologically and emotionally invested, something far more than and indeed entirely different from mere neutral, physical space.

6. Entrikin, 20.

7. As prominent ecocritic Lawrence Buell notes in his contribution to the recent PMLA Forum on Literatures and the Environment, *PMLA* 114 (October 1999): 1090-1092, ecocriticism at this point remains a loosely defined theoretical/critical movement, encompassing work deriving from conservationist/ecological, platial, and sociological bases. And despite the presence of the recent *Ecocriticism Reader*, edited by Harold Fromm (Athens: University of Georgia Press, 1996), a collection of essays in which an ecological sensibility proper dominates, Buell suggests the value of leaving the field open to a plurality of approaches, noting that "the phenomenon of literature-and-environment studies is better understood as a congeries of semioverlapping projects than as a unitary approach or set of claims" (1091).

8. D. W. Meinig, ed., *The Interpretation of Ordinary Landscapes* (New York: Oxford University Press, 1979), 6.

9. Clifford Clark, "Ranch-House Suburbia: Ideals and Realities," in *Recasting America: Culture and Politics in the Age of the Cold War*, ed. Lary May, 171-191 (Chicago: University of Chicago Press, 1989), 171.

10. Kim Ian Michasiw, "Some Stations of the Suburban Gothic," in *American Gothic: New Interventions in a National Narrative*, ed. Robert K. Martin and Eric Savoy, 237-257 (Iowa City: University of Iowa Press, 1998), 253. In this fascinating article, Michasiw suggests that the suburb has emerged as a gothic terrain in that the contemporary suburban landscape is symbolic of American cultural anxieties. The author uses the example of the gated community to make this point: While those living within such a landscape certainly live in literal fear of the barbarians at the gate, those on the outside of the gate (presumably, the rest of us) can only speculate on the individuals who could choose to reside *within* such a self-consciously gothic environment.

11. Ada Louise Huxtable, "An Alternative to 'Slurbs,'" in *Suburbia in Transition*, ed. Louis H. Masottie and Jeffrey K. Hadden, 185-191 (New York: New Viewpoints, 1974), 186; 188.

12. Michel Foucault, "Of Other Spaces," trans. Jay Miskowiec, *Diacritics* 16 (Spring 1986): 24.

13. Ibid., 26.

14. In many ways, Levittown, New York, and the subsequent Levittowns built in Pennsylvania and New Jersey provide a fascinating case study of the dynamics of the postwar suburban experience. For an excellent extended discussion of the Levittown experience, see William Gans, *The Levittowners* (New York: Pantheon, 1967).

15. As Jackson notes, Levitt and Sons' tight control of Levittown extended to stringent regulations on use of the land: "The Levitts forbade fences (a practice later ignored) and permitted outdoor clothes drying only on specially designed, collapsible racks. They even supervised lawn-cutting for the first few years—doing the job themselves if necessary and sending the laggard families the bill" (236).

16. Quoted in David Halberstam, *The Fifties* (New York: Fawcett Columbine, 1993), 141.

17. Max Lerner, in *America As a Civilization* (New York: Henry Holt & Co., 1987), argues that in the suburbs one finds a sort of "new Fourierism," where "standardization and conformism" are the price residents pay for establishing a sense of community, rather than suffering the isolation resulting from pure individualism. Lerner's qualified defense of the suburbs on these grounds makes sense, but it is interesting to consider how the latest manifestations of U.S. suburbia—the gated community and the neotraditional communities favored by the movement known as "New Urbanism"—invite a reconsideration of the balance between individualism and community being sought by today's suburbanites. While neotraditionalist developers of towns such as Celebration emphasize the ideal of community, the oxymoronically labeled "gated community" phenomenon stresses just the opposite ideal, selling protection from the outside world—through locked and monitored gates—as the ultimate in residential comfort and value.

18. See chapter 11 of David Harvey, *Justice, Nature, & the Geography of Difference* (Cambridge, MA: Blackwell, 1996), for a brief but fascinating case study of Guilford, an upper-class enclave of Baltimore whose residents considered converting to a gated community. Harvey deftly uses this example to set up a discussion of the politics of place and community.

19. Quoted in Russ Rymer, "Back to the Future: Disney Reinvents the Company Town," *Harper's* (October 1996): 68.

20. Ibid., 69.

21. For studies that trace the profound social impact suburban situation comedies of the 1950s and 1960s had on culture in their day and beyond, see Nina Leibman, *Living Room Lectures: The Fifties Family in Film and Television* (Austin: University of Texas Press, 1995); Dana Heller, *Family Plots: The De-Oedipalization of Popular Culture* (Philadelphia: University of Pennsylvania Press, 1995); and Lynn Spigel, *Make Room for TV: Television and the Family Ideal in Postwar America* (Chicago: University of Chicago Press, 1992).

22. Samuel G. Freedman, "Suburbia Outgrows Its Image in the Arts," *New York Times*, February 28, 1999, section 2, p. 1.

23. Albert Hunter, "The Symbolic Ecology of Suburbia," in *Neighborhood and Community Environments*, ed. Irwin Altman and Abraham Wandersman, 191-221 (New York: Plenium Press, 1987), 199.

24. Catherine Jurca, *White Diaspora: The Suburb and the Twentieth-Century American Novel* (Princeton, NJ: Princeton University Press, 2001), 4.

25. Evidence that the suburban landscape is beginning to be taken into serious consideration by cultural and place theorists can be found in the recent collection edited by Roger Silverstone, *Visions of Suburbia* (New York: Routledge, 1997), which contains a number of compelling essays on the political and cultural dynamics of the suburban environment.

26. Freedman, 26.

27. Consider as well in this regard the revivification of the suburban sitcoms from the 1950s and 1960s on the Nickelodeon network. Claiming to celebrate "our TV heritage," Nickelodeon nightly offers viewers the chance to revisit programs of the golden age of suburbia, an opportunity the network promotes as a gently ironized form of nostalgia. Nickelodeon's promotional strategy—positing the terrain of the

postwar sitcom as the fantasy version of our "heritage"—seems a profound (if unintentional) statement about the dislocation of the "TV generation."

28. Walter, 123.

29. Barbara Ching and Gerald W. Creed, eds. *Knowing Your Place: Rural Identity and Cultural Hierarchy* (New York: Routledge, 1997), 3.

30. Pierre Bourdieu, *Distinction: A Social Critique of the Judgment of Taste*, trans. Richard Nice (Cambridge, MA: Harvard University Press, 1984), 170.

31. Martyn Lee, "Relocating Location: Cultural Geography, the Specificity of Place and the City Habitus," in *Cultural Methodologies*, ed. Jim McGuigan, 126-141 (London: Sage, 1997), 132.

32. Frederic Jameson, *The Political Unconscious: Narrative as a Socially Symbolic Act* (Ithaca, NY: Cornell University Press, 1981), 82.

33. In this sense, the suburban landscape presents, in the apt phrasing of Terrell Dixon, "a kind of denatured nature . . . shaped for high-end commodification" (80). See Dixon's "Inculcating Wilderness: Ecocomposition, Nature Writing, and the Re-greening of the American Suburb," in *The Nature of Cities: Ecocriticism and Urban Environments*, ed. Michael Bennett and David W. Teague, 77-90 (Tucson: University of Arizona Press, 1999).

34. Frederic Jameson, *Postmodernism: or, The Cultural Logic of Late Capitalism* (Durham, NC: Duke University Press, 1991), 44.

35. D. J. Waldie, *Holy Land: A Suburban Memoir* (New York: W. W. Norton & Co., 1996), 118.

36. Gaston Bachelard, *The Poetics of Space*, trans. Maria Jolas (Boston: Beacon Press, 1994), 4.

37. Philip Y. Nicholson, "The Elusive Soul of the Suburbs: An Inquiry into Contemporary Political Culture," in *Suburbia Re-examined*, ed. Barbara M. Kelly, 207-213 (New York: Greenwood Press, 1989), 207.

38. Yi-Fu Tuan, *Landscapes of Fear* (Minneapolis: University of Minnesota Press, 1979). In this compelling study Tuan examines a number of different types of landscapes, their psychological and cultural resonances, and the ways in which they inspire fear. While he does not include a section on the suburbs, given the profound sense of apprehension toward this landscape, at least in the United States, he might well have.

39. Harvey, 293-294.

CHAPTER ONE

1. Kenneth Jackson identifies Brooklyn, New York, as the nation's first commuter suburb, noting that the first four decades of the nineteenth century saw Brooklyn's transformation from a primarily rural to suburban environment. See *Crabgrass Frontier: The Suburbanization of the United States* (New York: Oxford University Press, 1985), chapter 2, pp. 20-44, for Kenneth Jackson's discussion of early suburbanization.

2. For excellent, extended discussions of the first century of American suburbanization, see Margaret Marsh, *Suburban Lives* (New Brunswick, NJ: Rutgers University Press, 1990), and John R. Stilgoe, *Borderland: Origins of the American Suburb, 1820-1939* (New Haven, CT: Yale University Press, 1988).

3. Stilgoe makes historical and qualitative distinctions between the "borderlands" of the early suburbs and what he terms the "front-lawn" suburbs of development suburbia. While this distinction is important, I borrow his compelling notion of the suburb as a "borderland" to reinforce the impression that suburbs—even in their post–World War II, development incarnation—remain a vexing, ill-defined landscape of the United States.

4. Landscape theorist J. B. Jackson, in *Landscapes: Selected Writings of J. B. Jackson,* ed. Ervin H. Zube (Amherst: University of Massachusetts Press, 1970), suggests that the developing suburban landscape was heavily invested with utopian American beliefs regarding the relationship between individual and environment, reflecting both the Jeffersonian ideal of "human perfectibility" through egalitarian landscape design and a romantic, Thoreauvian celebration of the natural environment. See "Jefferson, Thoreau & After," 1-9.

5. Marsh, 129.

6. Marsh notes that in the decade of the 1920s, when American suburbanization noticeably intensified, "working class Americans . . . began to find themselves priced out of the housing market" (133).

7. As Marsh argues, "The policies of the national government during the New Deal . . . institutionalized the process of suburbanization for middle-class, white Americans" (155).

8. Catherine Jurca, *White Diaspora: The Suburb and the Twentieth-Century American Novel* (Princeton, NJ: Princeton University Press, 2001), 13.

9. Sinclair Lewis, *Babbitt* (New York: Harcourt, Brace & Co., 1922), 92. Future references to this novel will be indicated parenthetically in the text.

10. Jurca, 46.

11. K. Jackson, *Crabgrass Frontier*, chapter 5, pp. 87-102.

12. And, in this regard, these stately landscapes helped to inspire the future shape of suburbia. Rosalyn Baxandall and Elizabeth Ewen argue this point in their recent suburban history *Picture Windows: How the Suburbs Happened* (New York: Basic Books, 2000): "Though the idea of mass suburban living had not yet taken hold [early in the century], the fantasy world that Gold Coasters created and popular media described in such detail would have a profound impact on the American landscape. While the building of suburbia in the postwar era was indeed the triumphal outcome of modern methods of production and a response to a serious housing crisis, its imaginative origins go back much further; suburbia also was the attempt to realize visions and fantasies that had been percolating for decades" (13).

13. See chapters 2 and 3 (pp. 14-33) of ibid. for an interesting discussion of how automobiles and highway construction shaped the development of suburbia in this region.

14. Gaston Bachelard, *The Poetics of Space*, trans. Maria Jolas (Boston: Beacon Press, 1994), xxxi.

15. F. Scott Fitzgerald, *The Great Gatsby* (New York: Scribner's, 1925), 182. Subsequent references will be indicated parenthetically in the text.

16. As E. V. Walter argues in *Placeways*, "we internalize . . . environment not only materially but also emotionally and symbolically" (150). Clearly part of the difficulty facing all of the major characters in this novel is an incongruity between internal and external conceptions of environment. While the eastern environments the characters

inhabit are certainly rife with materialistic and symbolic overtones, an emotional connection to these places is lacking.

17. One could argue that the drama of this novel is driven by the characters' *homelessness*. While not referencing *Gatsby* in particular, Jurca makes a similar general point in *White Diaspora*: "In a paradox that is fundamental to novels about the suburb, white middle-class characters are homeowners, as the expression goes, who are plagued by the problem of homelessness" (4).

18. Specifically, the historical referents for West and East Egg are, respectively, the towns of Great Neck and Sands Point, situated on the northwest shore of Long Island. Fitzgerald had rented a house in Great Neck during the summer of 1923, when he began the writing of this novel.

19. Monica Randall, *The Mansions of Long Island's Gold Coast* (New York: Hastings House, 1979), 14.

20. As landscape theorist Denis Cosgrove reminds us in *Social Formation and Symbolic Landscape* (Totowa, NJ: Barnes & Noble, 1985), "Landscape . . . is an ideological concept. It represents a way in which certain classes of people have signified themselves" (15).

21. Randall, 11.

22. Ronald Berman, *The Great Gatsby and Modern Times* (Chicago: University of Illinois, 1994), 41.

23. Jan Cohn, *The Palace or the Poorhouse: The American House as a Cultural Symbol* (East Lansing: Michigan State University Press, 1979), 239.

24. It is worth considering the extent to which Tom's insecurity as a homeowner drives his intense interest in Gatsby's financial affairs and the means by which Gatsby was able to obtain his West Egg mansion. In his analysis of Hawthorne's *House of the Seven Gables*, from *The Gold Standard and the Logic of Naturalism* (Berkeley: University of California Press, 1987), Walter Benn Michaels notes that one of the lessons of that novel is that "property that has been earned is just as insecure (and, in the end, illegitimate) as property that has been appropriated by some capitalist trick" (98). It seems that Tom Buchanan faces this very dilemma: His drive to "out" Gatsby as a criminal may stem from nothing so much as an attempt to legitimate his own questionable sense of propriety in East Egg.

25. Geographer Anthony King, in "The Politics of Vision," in *Understanding Ordinary Landscapes*, ed. Paul Groth and Todd W. Bressi, 133-144 (New Haven, CT: Yale University Press, 1997), argues that cultures depend on the proliferation of visual images for their very sense of self. He identifies *visualism* as a state that results from the overascendance of the visual code. When the visual becomes separated from the "culture as a whole," the result is "a particular kind of conceit, a reification" of prominent visual imagery. In addition to the narrative technique in this passage, Tom's muteness with regard to his own landscape would also seem indicative of such a visualistic reification of that environment.

26. It is difficult to overstate the central importance of the act of commuting between city and suburb in this novel (or, for that matter, its central importance to suburbanites over the course of the twentieth century, at least until the current age of decentralization). In this novel and in later suburban works by authors such as Cheever, Beattie, and Naylor, the daily commute between suburb and city both highlights and ultimately works to dissolve the distinction between the urban and nonurban realms. In all of these works, the commuting life contributes to a sense of dislocation

experienced by the protagonists. John Stilgoe, in a compelling argument, reminds us that "*to commute* also means to mitigate or lessen, and . . . suburbs began and developed as a spatial means of grappling with and lessening the difficulties of urbanization" (5). But what Fitzgerald suggests in this novel is that the rise of the commuting lifestyle has the opposite effect, bringing the corrupting influences of the urban realm into the pristine exurban environment.

27. K. Jackson, 176.

28. Perhaps this juxtaposition of housing types is not as incongruous as it seems. As Baxandall and Ewen note in *Picture Windows*, "the estates of the robber barons set the precedent for suburban sprawl. Instead of generating clustered villages, Long Island grew rambling, isolated estates surrounded by vast tracts of private property" (5).

29. Richard Lehan, *The Great Gatsby: The Limits of Wonder* (Boston: Twayne, 1990), 7.

30. Ibid., 38.

31. Tom's resistance to automobile culture marks him as a timely representative of the Gold Coast millionaire society. During the 1920s and 1930s, New York parks commissioner Robert Moses was in the process of transforming Long Island from a land of farms, estates, and pristine wilderness into a bustling commuters' haven served by a sprawling network of highways. Moses's proposal to build a highway (the Northern State Parkway) to run through the Gold Coast region, connecting New York City to more easterly regions on the island, met with stiff resistance from the Gold Coast tycoons. Ultimately, Moses compromised and rerouted the Northern State so as not to interfere with the Gold Coast landscape; nonetheless, the writing was clearly on the wall for the Tom Buchanans of Long Island, as Baxandall and Ewen note in *Picture Windows*: "The North Shore elite may have won the battle to preserve their dominion, but they lost the war. . . . In 1920 there were no highways on Long Island; but twelve years later there was a modern interconnected parkway system linking the various Long Island communities and allowing easy access to the city" (27).

32. Brian Way, "*The Great Gatsby*," in *New Essays on The Great Gatsby*, ed. Matthew J. Bruccoli (New York: Cambridge University Press, 1985), 190.

33. Roger Lewis, "Money, Love, and Aspiration in *The Great Gatsby*," in *New Essays on The Great Gatsby*, argues that Gatsby's love for Daisy is represented in "commercial" terms and is thus reflective of "postwar America, of a society that consumes" (46).

34. Berman, 102.

35. Leonard Lutwack, in *The Role of Place in Literature* (New York: Syracuse University Press, 1984), takes the argument a step further. Arguing that the automobile is the "instrument of destiny" in this novel, Lutwack notes that the "relationships of characters are framed by their racing from one . . . [place] to another" (221).

36. Felipe Smith, "The Dark Side of Paradise: Race and Ethnicity in the Novels of F. Scott Fitzgerald," Ph.D. dissertation, Louisiana State University, 1988, 194.

37. Smith goes further than this, identifying the bridge scene as the crucial moment in the novel. In a fascinating line of argument, Smith suggests that this scene works to align Gatsby with the novel's racial and ethnic others, in that both represent to Nick "phenomena of social deterioration" (162). Hence for Smith, Gatsby's "tan counte-

nance, coupled with his ethnic name (Gatz) and his mysterious origins, makes him racially indeterminate (a crucial factor in his demise)" (168).

38. Marsh suggests that "white flight" to the suburbs, as the process came to be known later in the century, has its origins in the post–World War I era, when whites who had been unsuccessful in barring black residents from their urban neighborhoods took advantage of a boom in suburban housing development and, in large numbers, "moved into more outlying areas" (130).

39. Kaja Silverman, *Male Subjectivity at the Margins* (New York: Routledge, 1992). Silverman argues that the historically traumatic experience of World War II threatened to render returning veterans, at least in a psychological sense, redundant. She reads *It's a Wonderful Life* as one of a number of postwar films that worked to reinstate what she calls the "dominant fiction" of masculine agency in the postwar period.

40. For a thorough discussion of the postwar housing boom, see Kenneth Jackson, chapter 13 (pp. 231-245). The sheer numbers of new housing starts are indicative of the landscape revolution underway at this time. As Jackson notes, "Single-family housing starts spurted from only 114,000 in 1944, to 937,000 in 1946, to 1,183,000 in 1948, and to 1,692,000 in 1950, an all-time high" (233).

41. Patrick McGee, *Cinema, Theory, and Political Responsibility in Contemporary Culture* (New York: Cambridge University Press, 1997), 11.

42. A general proximity to the New York metropolitan area is suggested by Sam's relocation there and his ability to just "drop by" before heading off on a trip to Florida; also, Violet's proposed move to the city suggests its nearness. But a shot that was cut from the film but reprinted in Jeanine Basinger's *The It's a Wonderful Life Book* (New York: Knopf, 1986) clearly demonstrates the northern Westchester setting. It is a still of George, during his triumphant run through the streets of Bedford Falls near the end of the film, passing a street sign with directional cues pointing toward "Aspetuck" and "Kitchawan" in one direction and "Katonah" and "Chappaqua" in the other. While the geography is a bit skewed on the whole, the positioning between the neighboring towns of Katonah, Chappaqua, and Kitchawan, New York, on one hand and Aspetuck, Connecticut, on the other would indisputably situate Bedford Falls in northeastern Westchester County, around the location of Bedford Hills.

43. See Kenneth Jackson, chapters 5 and 9. As Jackson points out, southern Westchester County had become, over the course of the second half of the nineteenth century, a collection of fashionable, "high-status, high-prestige" commuter suburbs (95). But with the increasing popularity of the automobile in the 1920s and 1930s and the creation of an extensive network of highways over those decades, the area was opened up to increasing numbers of residents and increasing development.

44. This is not a particularly popular view. Most critics tend to deride the film's "nostalgic" sensibility for presenting a single, old-fashioned view of the town and its people. For example, Robert B. Ray, in an otherwise insightful essay on the film in *A Certain Tendency of the Hollywood Cinema, 1930-1980* (Princeton, NJ: Princeton University Press, 1985), argues that the film presents "a nostalgic, unchanging place existing outside of time" (179). But to make such an argument seems to me to be neglecting some fairly important images and sequences in the film: The bank run scene and the contrasting landscapes of Potter's Field, Bailey Park, and Pottersville

are all used to show a town whose fate is very much up in the air and subject to the force of history.

45. Gilles Deleuze, *Cinema 1: The Movement Image*, trans. Hugh Tomlinson and Barbara Habberjam (London: Althone, 1986), 146.

46. James Agee, "It's a Wonderful Life," in *Frank Capra: The Man and His Films*, ed. Richard Glatzer and John Raeburn (Ann Arbor: University of Michigan Press, 1975), 158.

47. George Toles, "No Bigger Than Zuzu's Petals: Dream-Messages, Epiphanies, and the Undoing of Conventions in *It's a Wonderful Life*," *North Dakota Quarterly* 52.3 (1984): 62.

48. Raymond Carney, for example, in *American Vision: The Films of Frank Capra* (New York: Cambridge University Press, 1986), 392-393, argues that the use of the heavenly frame implicates both the angels and the viewers of the film in a form of "cosmic voyeurism" which is selectively directed by Joseph, the "cosmic moviola operator."

49. Toles, 63.

50. Carney, 397.

51. Randall Fallows, "George Bailey in the Vital Center: Postwar Liberal Politics and *It's a Wonderful Life*" *Journal of Popular Culture* 25:2 (Summer 1997): 56.

52. For a discussion of this fascinating redirection into the social sphere of Freud's oedipal model of desire, see Gilles Deleuze and Felix Guattari, *Anti-Oedipus: Capitalism and Schizophrenia*, trans. Robert Hurley, Mark Seem, and Helen R. Lane, section 4.5, esp. 353-357 (Minneapolis: University of Minnesota Press, 1983).

53. Indeed, even Capra's casting choices for the roles of Violet and Mary seem significant in this regard: While Gloria Grahame went on in the 1950s to star as the femme fatale in a string of noir films, in the process helping to create the genre's vision of the darkly sexual and fetishized woman, Donna Reed went on to portray, in *The Donna Reed Show* (1958-66), the embodiment of the utterly domestic, stay-at-home suburban mom and an icon of the wholesome, even antiseptic, television family.

54. Joseph McBride, *Frank Capra: The Catastrophe of Success* (New York: Simon & Schuster, 1992), 523.

55. For an in-depth discussion of the social and psychological effects of feminine enclosure within the domestic sphere in the age of suburbia, see Betty Friedan, *The Feminine Mystique* (New York: W. W. Norton & Co., 1963).

56. Silverman also considers *The Best Years of Our Lives* and *The Guilt of Janet Ames*.

57. Silverman, 106.

58. Carney, 397. Carney deftly elucidates the recurring entrapment theme with a number of compelling examples.

59. Ray actually notes three such American "cultural oppositions" that the film works through: adventure/domesticity, individual/community, and worldly success/ordinary life.

60. Carney, 388.

61. In this sense, the film resonates with the plight of many returning veterans of this time, who struggled to construct an identity for themselves in the faceless business world while at the same time adjusting to life in what was often seen as the

"feminized" space of the suburbs. For an analysis of this dilemma, see William H. Whyte Jr., *The Organization Man* (Garden City, NY: Doubleday Anchor, 1956).

62. Robert Schultz, "Postwar Society in Postwar Popular Culture," *American Studies* 31.1 (Spring 1990): 49.

63. Carney, 381.

64. While George may be remaking the community in his own image, of course he does so as a product of the milieu itself. As Deleuze argues, the relationship between the hero and his environment is always reciprocal, in that the power with which a hero is able to save the community is something generated by the collective in the first place: "the milieu . . . encompasses the collectivity. It is as representative of the collectivity that the hero becomes capable of an action which makes him equal to the milieu and re-establishes its accidentally or periodically endangered order" (146).

65. Agee, 158.

66. Schultz, 48. Schultz's observation gets at the sense that postwar suburbs functioned according to the logic of what C. B. Macpherson terms "possessive individualism," or the elevation of private property ownership as the measure of not only personal dignity, but indeed political power. See Macpherson, *The Political Theory of Possessive Individualism: Hobbes to Locke* (Oxford, UK: Clarendon Press, 1962).

67. Martini's phrasing calls to mind the analysis of the cultural significance of the pig offered by Peter Stallybras and Allon White in *The Politics of Poetics of Transgression* (Ithaca, NY: Cornell University Press, 1986). Noting that the pig has metaphorically functioned in western societies as the "symbolic analogy of scapegoated groups and demonized 'Others,'" Stallybras and White argue that symbolically the pig serves as a focus of *"displaced abjection,* the process whereby 'low' social groups turn their figurative and actual power, not against those in authority, but against those who are even 'lower'" (53). Martini's derisive labeling of his erstwhile neighbors as "pigs"— his last words before leaving the ghetto—exhibits just such a demonization of his inferiors. His comment and demeanor suggest that the glowing vision of cohesive community the film presents is restricted to the property-owning class.

68. For a good discussion of the profound impact the GI Bill had on housing and the American landscape, see Kenneth Jackson, chapter 11.

CHAPTER TWO

1. Jean Murray Bangs, "How American Is Your Way of Living?" *House Beautiful* 92 (September 1950): 80.

2. Recently a number of interesting scholarly studies have focused on the influence of magazine culture. Two such works that consider how popular journals helped shape middle-class identities in the early decades of the twentieth century are Jennifer Scanlon's *Inarticulate Longings:* The Ladies' Home Journal, *Gender, and the Promises of Consumer Culture* (New York: Routledge, 1995) and Richard Ohmann's *Selling Culture: Magazines, Markets, and Class at the Turn of the Century* (New York: Verso, 1996). Scanlon offers a thorough, multifaceted discussion of how the *Ladies' Home Journal* helped to solidify for its readers a middle-class, "consumerist definition of womanhood" (6). Ohmann examines the way magazine advertisements and journalism helped establish an urbane, privileged identity for readers from the professional managerial class at the turn of the twentieth century.

3. Margaret Marsh, in her thorough and excellent study of suburbanization in the nineteenth and early twentieth centuries, *Suburban Lives* (New Brunswick, NJ: Rutgers University Press, 1990), suggests that the social climate in post–World War I America made suburban home ownership particularly appealing to the middle class. While "in the first decade and a half of the century . . . it was important for a middle-class family to be in the suburbs, not necessarily to own a house" (133), by the 1920s home ownership was considered to be not only a marker of success for the middle-class family, but indeed a "sign of good citizenship" (134). With the advent in the postwar years of mass-produced development towns such as Levittown, which offered monthly mortgage payments equal to or lower than apartment rental costs, along with little or sometimes no downpayment required, this middle-class ideal became a pervasive reality.

4. With the end of the war, housing starts in 1946 tripled, and the number of new housing starts continued to rise steadily for the next ten years. For an excellent overview of the extent of suburban development in the postwar years, see Kenneth Jackson, *Crabgrass Frontier: The Suburbanization of the United States* (New York: Oxford University Press, 1985), chapter 13 (pp. 231-245). See also chapters 11-12 (pp. 190-230) for an extended discussion of the impact of federal housing subsidies and the subsequent spread of suburbia in the postwar years.

5. Elaine Tyler May, in *Homeward Bound: American Families in the Cold War Era* (New York: Basic Books, 1988), takes this point a step further: Emphasizing the tight connections between suburbanization and the baby boom, May argues that "[b]y stimulating . . . suburban housing developments (such as Levittown) and providing subsidies to homeowners, the federal government effectively underwrote the baby boom" (171).

6. "Up From the Potato Fields," *Time,* July 3, 1950, 68.

7. Rosalyn Baxandall and Elizabeth Ewen, *Picture Windows: How the Suburbs Happened* (New York: Basic Books, 2000), 147.

8. Even Robert Moses, the onetime New York State parks commissioner and master planner, the man more responsible than anyone else for shaping Long Island suburbia, weighed in vocally in an *Atlantic Monthly* essay against thoughtless home construction and the "rage to subdivide," which he described as "destructive practices which in many cases amount to sheer vandalism" (40). See Robert Moses, "Build and Be Damned," *Atlantic Monthly* 186 (December 1950): 40-42. For a thorough, insightful look at Moses and his legacy, see Robert Caro's definitive biography, *The Power Broker: Robert Moses and the Fall of New York* (New York: Knopf, 1974).

9. Catherine Jurca, *White Diaspora: The Suburb and the Twentieth-Century American Novel* (Princeton, NJ: Princeton University Press, 2001), 136.

10. Keats was quite blunt on this point in his essay "Compulsive Suburbia," *Atlantic Monthly* 205 (April 1960): 47-50, where he argued that it is a "short step" from the acceptance of development suburbia, in all its mediocrity, to "acceptance of crime in the cities, thievery in government, knavery in labor unions, unconscionable business practices, mindlessness in the public schools, and the disappearance of anything that could remotely be called the national will" (50). Given the variety of social ills Keats ascribed to suburbia, it is little wonder that he concluded that "a development is an environment that cannot be altered for the better by any means short of

dynamite and bulldozing; if anything is to be salvaged out of suburbia, it must be the people who live there" (50).

11. John Cheever, "The Country Husband," *The Stories of John Cheever* (New York: Knopf, 1978), 345. All future Cheever story references will be to this collection, and page number citations will be in text.

12. C. B. Macpherson, *The Political Theory of Possessive Individualism: Hobbes to Locke* (Oxford, UK: Clarendon Press, 1962). MacPherson claims that twentieth-century western societies continue to be structured by the notion of "possessive individualism," the "conception of the individual as essentially the proprietor of his own person or capacities, owing nothing to society for them." Explaining the social ramifications of this phenomenon, Macpherson argues, "The human essence is freedom from dependence on the wills of others, and freedom is a function of possession. . . . Political society becomes a calculated device for the protection of . . . property" (3).

13. Arguing that "there is an economy of cultural goods" that functions according to a "specific logic" (1), Bourdieu, in *Distinction: A Social Critique of the Judgment of Taste*, trans. Richard Nice (Cambridge, MA: Harvard University Press, 1984), suggests that markers of cultural distinction, such as refined taste in cultural products and artifacts, serve to reinforce social distinctions between economic classes. His compelling argument transposes particularly well to a fictional milieu such as Cheever's, where one's "place" in the social landscape is dictated by the ability to demonstrate possession of discriminating taste and propriety, or what Bourdieu refers to as "cultural capital."

14. A testament to the power of such cultural capital—and to Cheever's accuracy in depicting his subjects—can be found in *Newsweek* magazine's gushing description, from a June 1957 special feature on exurbia, of the lending library in haute-exurban Westport, Connecticut: "The new $350,000 library, equipped with a smoking lounge, reflects Westport's intellectual appetites. Some 9,000 of its customers—half the population—are active users. Light love stories and Westerns get no play, but the philosophy and psychology shelves are boom territories" (89). "Exurbia: It's Not Just a Place, It's This," *Newsweek*, June 3, 1957, 83-90.

15. Scott Donaldson, "The Machines in Cheever's Garden," in *The Changing Face of the Suburbs,* ed. Barry Schwartz, 309-321 (Chicago: University of Chicago Press, 1976), 309.

16. As David Halberstam notes in *The Fifties* (New York: Fawcett Columbine, 1993), the mass production techniques of Levitt and similar firms can be thought of as not only a response to the growth of the middle class and their subsequent need for housing, but indeed as a force behind the growth of the new middle class itself: "These techniques made it possible to provide inexpensive, attractive single-unit housing for ordinary citizens, people who had never thought of themselves as middle-class before" (132).

17. Vance Packard, *The Status Seekers* (New York: David McKay Company, 1959), 4.

18. Nina Leibman, *Living Room Lectures: The Fifties Family in Film and Television* (Austin: University of Texas Press, 1995).

19. As Dana Heller argues in *Family Plots: The De-Oedipalization of Popular Culture* (Philadelphia: University of Pennsylvania Press, 1995), suburban family sitcoms tended to "naturalize" the white, middle-class suburban experience, serving as

models of "familial normalcy" (45), idealized visions of what suburban middle-class family life ought to be like.

20. Lynn Spigel, *Make Room for TV: Television and the Family Ideal in Postwar America* (Chicago: University of Chicago Press, 1992), 111.

21. Barbara Ehrenreich, *Fear of Falling: The Inner Life of the Middle Class* (New York: Pantheon, 1989), 4. Ehrenreich points to such popular sociological works as Riesman's *The Lonely Crowd*, Whyte's *The Organization Man*, and Betty Friedan's *The Feminine Mystique* as examples of commentary that tended to universalize middle-class experience.

22. Moses, 42.

23. "Moses and the Jackals," *Life*, September 26, 1955, 49.

24. Neil P. Hurley, "The Case for Suburbia," *Commonweal*, August 28, 1959, 440, 441.

25. William M. Dobriner, "The Natural History of a Reluctant Suburb," *Yale Review* 49 (March 1960): 400.

26. William Zeckendorf, "Fluid Suburbia," *Yale Review* 48 (Autumn 1958): 29.

27. "Exurbia: It's Not Just a Place, It's This," *Newsweek*, June 3, 1957, 90.

28. Dobriner, 404.

29. "Toward Pleasanter, More Efficient Communities" (excerpts from the Joint Committee report, "A Housing Program for Now and Later"), *American City* 63 (September 1948): 122.

30. The recurrence of labels such as these calls to mind both cold war–era concerns over proliferating conformity and 1950s' science fiction films, phenomena that were often interrelated. Indeed, films such as *Invasion of the Body Snatchers* (1956), with its vision of soulless alien pod people replacing the American populace, and *The Blob* (1958), in which an amorphous ooze swallows small-town Middle America, resonate with much of the criticism voiced over the spread of suburbia. It is difficult, in fact, not to envision a scene from a mid-1950s' science fiction film when perusing some descriptions of suburbia's destructive powers. Consider this excerpt from Hurley's "The Case for Suburbia": "Today, entire generations are growing up with no vital contact with city life. They are the products of neither a rural milieu nor an urban one, but of a new phenomenon called 'subtopia,' a monster that is devouring in its bulldozer jaws some three thousand acres of green countryside daily" (439).

31. Clarence S. Stein, "Greendale and the Future," *American City* 63 (June 1948): 106-109; "Flight to the Suburbs," *Time*, March 22, 1954, 102.

32. William H. Whyte, *The Organization Man* (Garden City, NY: Doubleday Anchor, 1956), 341. Whyte's groundbreaking and influential work considers the many ways in which organizational/corporate structure shapes the individual and society in the postwar years. Included is a section on the nature of suburban living, with a particular focus on social dynamics in the suburb of Park Forest, Illinois.

33. C. Wright Mills, *White Collar: The American Middle Class* (New York: Oxford University Press, 1956), 240.

34. Dubbed in one famous disparaging critique as "those Connecticut stories," the *New Yorker* stories of Cheever and others were often considered to be little more than flatly realistic and ultimately tepid renderings of the travails of life in the commuter suburbs of New York City. For a collection of representative reviews and essays, both positive and negative, see R. G. Collins's *Critical Essays on John Cheever* (Boston: G. K. Hall, 1982).

35. Rollene Waterman, "Interview with John Cheever," *Saturday Review,* September 13, 1958, 33.

36. As Mary Corey points out in her excellent study *The World Through a Monocle: The New Yorker at Midcentury* (Cambridge, MA: Harvard University Press, 1999), for the new, educated postwar middle class, "The *New Yorker* possessed an almost magical authority" (2). Corey argues that the magazine, directed toward "middle-class readers with upper-class aspirations" (6), benefited from the process of suburbanization, as it represented "a civilized subculture separated by taste and affinity from the presumed vulgarities of the mass culture which surrounded it" (13). For another recent study that examines the cultural significance of the *New Yorker,* see Ben Yagoda, *About Town: The* New Yorker *and the World It Made* (New York: Scribner, 2000).

37. Alwyn Lee, "Ovid in Ossining," *Time,* March 27, 1964, 66-72.

38. As a writer who consistently drew from autobiographical experience, Cheever had ample experience to help him illustrate the "borderline" existence of the Westcotts. As Scott Donaldson notes in *John Cheever: A Biography* (New York: Random House, 1988), at the time of the writing of "The Enormous Radio" and the other stories of that collection, the Cheevers were living in a rented apartment at 400 East 59th Street, "in the same neighborhood, if not the same rent district, as Sutton Place" (107).

39. Patrick Meanor, *John Cheever Revisited* (New York: Twayne, 1995), 53. In an intriguing discussion, Meanor suggests that the Westcotts represent a modern, urban Adam and Eve; their eventual "fall" into self-doubt is, then, just punishment for their ill-gotten knowledge of their neighbors' lives.

40. Bourdieu, 498.

41. It is worth considering the extent to which the design of the suburban landscape itself heightens a sense of visibility. In contrast to the verticality of the crowded city and the far-flung isolation of the countryside, the suburban landscape, featuring homes with street-level windows in close proximity to one another, makes scrutiny of the landscape and its inhabitants a relatively easy task.

42. Michel Foucault, *Discipline and Punish,* trans. Alan Sheridan (New York: Vintage Books, 1979), 203. For an extended discussion of panopticism and its relation to modes of societal discipline, see pp. 195-228.

43. Ibid., p. 217

44. As Samuel Coale notes in *John Cheever* (New York: Frederick Ungar, 1977), what Jim reacts against here are the "placid inadequacies of the life of elegant illusion" (40).

45. Scott Donaldson, "Cheever's Shady Hill: A Suburban Sequence," in *Modern American Short Story Sequences: Composite Fictions and Fictive Communities,* ed. J. Gerald Kennedy, 133-150 (New York: Cambridge University Press, 1995).

46. The timeliness of Cheever's publication of this collection is worth noting: Coming as it did near the end of the great decade of suburban expansion, the 1950s, *The Housebreaker of Shady Hill* both consolidated the suburban vision Cheever had been developing throughout the decade and, in effect, made him the official literary voice of the suburban experience. As Donaldson puts it in his *Biography,* after the publication of this collection, Cheever "became known, overnight and always, as a chronicler of suburban life" (170).

47. Meanor, 94.

48. In essence, the difference between the two landscapes has to do with their respective age as well as the income levels of their residents: As Kenneth Jackson has detailed, most of the towns and villages that compose the real life counterpart of "Cheever Country" were incorporated around the turn of the century—long before the physical and symbolic landscape of "suburbia" exploded across the country. See Jackson (321) for a table listing the incorporation dates of these towns and villages.

49. The anxiety over this potential intrusion expressed by some members of Cheever's Shady Hill community has a verifiable historical referent: as Jackson points out, by as early as 1955, "subdivisions accounted for more than three-quarters of all new housing in metropolitan areas" (233). Given this rapid spread of suburban subdivisions in the decade following the end of the war, the reactionary stance of more affluent exurbanites seems inevitable. Geographer Yi-Fu Tuan, in *Topophilia: A Study of Environmental Perception, Attitudes, and Values* (Englewood Cliffs, NJ: Prentice-Hall, 1974), notes that such an insistence on the value and primacy of one's own environment is a generalizable trait that transcends specific historical and geographic boundaries; as Tuan argues, "people everywhere tend to structure space—geographical and cosmological—with themselves at the center and with concentric zones . . . of decreasing value beyond" (27). Nevertheless, given the verifiable distinctions between older main-line suburbs and the new suburbia, it seems clear that the class-bound apprehension expressed by a number of Cheever's Shady Hill characters is indeed the product of a historically specific time and place— the elite yet threatened exurbs of the 1950s.

50. This passage comes from the story "The Wrysons" (p. 319), which appeared in Cheever's subsequent short story collection, *The Brigadier and the Golf Widow* (New York: Harper & Row, 1964). Nevertheless, the story is set in Shady Hill, and Irene Wryson's observation is congruent with those of the more reactionary Shady Hill residents Cheever portrays throughout his *Housebreaker of Shady Hill* collection.

51. Lynne Waldeland, *John Cheever* (Boston: Twayne, 1979), 73.

52. Ibid.

53. As Scott Donaldson reminds us in evoking Leo Marx, the railroad train is always significant in Cheever's fiction, as it represents the "machine" in Cheever's "garden"—a reminder of the rootlessness that characterizes the lapsed eden of suburbia while continually undermining a sense of community and belonging. See Donaldson, "The Machines in Cheever's Garden." On this point, see also Frederick Karl's essay "John Cheever and the Promise of Pastoral," in *Critical Essays on John Cheever*, ed. R. G. Collins, 209-219 (Boston: G. K. Hall, 1982). Karl interprets Cheever's commuter train in similar fashion, referring to it as a "monster of civilization" (215). In his suburban writing and elsewhere, Karl finds Cheever exploring "a major American theme, that of the persistence and, ultimately, the failure of pastoral" (209).

54. Bourdieu, 7.

55. Joan Didion, "The Way We Live Now," in *Critical Essays on John Cheever*, 67-69, argues that Cheever's suburbanites are urban "exiles," separated from their often-fading class stature as much as they are from their urban roots. Commenting on a recurring sense of alienation in Cheever's characters, Didion suggests that a dwindling sense of class affiliation is often the cause: "Lost money, the recollection of better times . . . the twilight world of the old American middle class is indeed a lost

world . . . it has become a dream that in some respects never was, an imagined territory capable of paralyzing its exiles" (68). While this assessment risks oversimplifying Cheever's complex class structure (at least one protagonist, Will Pym of "Just Tell Me Who It Was," feels alienated from his peers in Shady Hill because he is a "self-made man" of working-class roots), Didion's sense that Cheever's characters search in vain for an "imagined territory" of the past perfectly captures the struggles of figures such as Cash Bentley and Neddy Merrill.

56. Bourdieu, 54.

57. Waldeland, 66.

58. Hake's self-description as a "child of darkness" is itself a culmination of Cheever's careful attention throughout the story to contrasting images of light and darkness. Several times Hake describes himself sitting in the dark or staring out into darkness, and at the depths of his despair in New York he encounters an imitation "blind man" begging for money on the streets. This vision of a swindler hiding behind self-imposed darkness—the man serving as a kind of doppelganger to Hake—helps to clarify Cheever's use of the light/dark contrast: What is suggested by this interplay, more than anything else, is the "blind eye" turned to financial hardship by a society governed by proprietary codes of conduct.

59. Meanor, 90.

60. Richard Rupp, "Of That Time, of Those Places: The Stories of John Cheever," in *Critical Essays on John Cheever*, 231-251, 238.

61. Waldeland, 95.

62. Benedict Anderson, *Imagined Communities* (New York: Verso, 1991), 7. Although Anderson's focus is on nationalism and its origins, his notion of the "imagined community" is more widely applicable to the study of various forms of community.

63. Robert Slabey, "John Cheever: The 'Swimming' of America," in *Critical Essays on John Cheever*, 180-191, 188.

64. Meanor, 117.

65. While Perry receives the sole directing credit for the film, the story is a bit more complicated. The film had a troubled history and was shelved for a time by Columbia after Perry completed it. Columbia brought in Sydney Pollack to reshoot some scenes before finally releasing the picture with Perry receiving the director's credit.

66. Neddy thus appears as another incarnation of what by this time was becoming a recognizable figure in literature about or set in the suburbs: the bewildered, ineffectual suburban male. Following in the footsteps of William Whyte's "organization man," Sloan Wilson's "Man in the Grey Flannel Suit" and John Keats's character "John Drone," Neddy is buffeted between the uncaring urban world of business, which treats him as a replaceable cog in the wheel, and the "feminine" space of the suburbs, where he lacks a sense of agency, propriety, and control.

CHAPTER THREE

1. Dana Heller, *Family Plots: The De-Oedipalization of Popular Culture* (Philadelphia: University of Pennsylvania Press, 1995), 54.

2. John Keats, *The Crack in the Picture Window* (Boston: Houghton Mifflin, 1957), 181.

3. In fact, the argument could be made that Keats's bizarre vision of the suburban male as a "woman-bossed, inadequate . . . neuter" is not all that dated after all. The depiction of the male suburbanite cowering, childlike, before his wife, an all-powerful matriarch, remains a staple comic device in contemporary advertising and situation comedy. Magazine pieces describing suburban manners also continue to peddle the stock vision of the castrated suburban male. A recent *New York Observer* story, for example, offered a "behind-the-scenes" look at a suburban cocktail party, where, amid a gaggle of loud, powerful women, their husbands "had the air of stand-up eunuchs as they hid their desperation behind rocks glasses." The author of this piece notes that this party "harked back to at least the 70's . . . or perhaps even further, to the 50's, to ones I'd seen on television and in movies." Imagine that. See D. J. Levien, "So Men Are Back? Not in Suburbia," *New York Observer*, November 5, 2001, 5.

4. Richard E. Gordon, Katherine K. Gordon, and Max Gunther, *The Split-Level Trap* (New York: Bernard Geis Associates, 1960), 28.

5. Lewis Mumford, *The City in History: Its Origins, Its Transformations, and Its Prospects* (New York: Harcourt, Brace, & World, 1961), 494.

6. Mumford was not alone in noting the overzealous attachment to the sporting life among male suburbanites. Philip Roth, for example, in his debut novella, *Goodbye, Columbus* (Boston: Houghton Mifflin, 1959), uses a suburban family's intense devotion to sports and recreation not only as a comic device but also as a trope to help express the alienation experienced by a young man of the city who finds himself thrown into their suburban milieu. Neil Klugman, Roth's narrator, after falling in love with Brenda Patimkin, the teenage daughter of nouveau riche suburbanites, brings his Newark sensibility to their suburban Short Hills surroundings; despite his profound attraction to what he feels to be an almost "heavenly" landscape, Neil is repulsed and frightened by the Patimkin family's fanatical interest in backyard sports. Noting that various family members tend to gorge themselves on store-bought fruit in order to sustain their endless backyard competitions, spirited events that lead to various sporting goods becoming permanently lodged in the branches of their trees, Neil makes a wry observation that suggests the arbitrary, nonsensical, or even inverted order of things in suburbia: "Oh Patimkin! Fruit grew in their refrigerator and sporting goods dropped from their trees!" (53)

7. Mumford, 495

8. Consider, for example, the case of Levittown, New York, the prototypical postwar suburban development town. In the early years of the town's existence, utter control over the landscape remained in the hands of the developers/town planners, Levitt and Sons, who prohibited even minor alterations to individual plots. For a description of life in the early days of Levittown, see William Gans, *The Levittowners* (New York: Pantheon, 1967).

9. See Nina Baym's classic essay "Melodramas of Beset Manhood: How Theories of American Fiction Exclude Women Authors," *American Quarterly* 33 (1981): 123-139, for her discussion of how and why novels depicting the plight of the embattled male have been embraced as the "classic" texts of American literature. As Baym argues, in the typical "melodrama of beset manhood," the male protagonist longs for escape from the restrictions of domesticity and society, which are coded as feminine, and to prove his manhood through conquest of the natural environment, also

depicted in feminized terms. This is precisely the thematic template of Lewis's *Babbitt*.

10. Stephen Birmingham, *The Golden Dream: Suburbia in the Seventies* (New York: Harper & Row, 1978), viii.

11. In a more recent theoretical formulation of "corporate" placelessness, Gilles Deleuze and Felix Guattari have argued that the global spread of capitalism has entailed a process of "deterritorialization" that effaces connections to landscape even as it inducts workers into the machinery of corporate culture. While Deleuze and Guattari's argument centers on the "schizophrenic" effects of capitalist expansion into developing nations, their argument resonates with the spread of "placeless," corporate suburban landscapes in the postwar United States. They see deterritorialization as part of the "cruelty" of the capitalist system, in that it serves to efface the distinction between the individual and the corporate altogether: "Cruelty is the movement of culture that is realized in bodies and inscribed on them . . . [making] men or their organs into the parts and wheels of the social machine." For the authors' discussion of territoriality and deterritorialization, see Gilles Deleuze and Felix Guattari, *Anti-Oedipus: Capitalism and Schizophrenia*, trans. Robert Hurley, Mark Seem, and Helen R. Lane (Minneapolis: University of Minnesota Press, 1983), 145-153.

12. The suburban situation comedy ruled the airwaves in the late 1950s and early 1960s, with *Leave It to Beaver* running from 1957 to 1962; *Father Knows Best* from 1954 to 1963; and *The Donna Reed Show* from 1958 to 1966.

13. As Douglas Miller and Marion Nowak note in *The Fifties: The Way We Really Were* (Garden City, NY: Doubleday, 1977), a sense of isolation, estrangement from society, and a kind of free-floating subjectivity was a recurrent theme in fiction of the 1950s. Miller and Nowak aptly point out that this feeling of estrangement from a bland and alienating consumer culture was perfectly captured in the strange, solitary mantra of Saul Bellow's Eugene Henderson—"I Want, I Want, I Want" (377).

14. Peter Schwenger, *Phallic Critiques: Masculinity and Twentieth-Century Literature* (London: Routledge & Kegan Paul, 1984), 9.

15. The real-world counterparts of these fictional locales are, respectively, Updike's childhood town of Olinger, Pennsylvania, and the nearby city of Reading, Pennsylvania.

16. The four novels, slightly revised, were eventually repackaged and published as component parts of a single volume entitled *Rabbit Angstrom: A Tetralogy* (New York: Knopf, 1995). Subsequently, Updike would publish the sequel "Rabbit Remembered," a novella appearing within the collection *Licks of Love: Short Stories and a Sequel* (New York: Knopf, 2000).

17. Donald J. Greiner, "No Place to Run: Rabbit Angstrom as Adamic Hero," in Lawrence R. Broer, ed., *Rabbit Tales: Poetry and Politics in John Updike's Rabbit Novels*, 8-16 (Tuscaloosa: University of Alabama Press, 1988), 9.

18. Paula R. Buck, "The Mother Load: A Look at Rabbit's Oedipus Complex," in *Rabbit Tales*, 150-169, 151.

19. Mary O'Connell, *Updike and the Patriarchal Dilemma: Masculinity in the Rabbit Novels* (Carbondale: Southern Illinois University Press, 1996), 2.

20. This sort of "double consciousness" is typical of the classic American male fictional protagonist in general; nevertheless, such a simultaneous identity as insider and outsider seems a particularly relevant characteristic for the suburban male protago-

nist, one who is living in a setting that purports to be the environmental realization of the "American dream" itself while at the same time often functioning to confound and suppress the very qualities of differentiation and self-definition long seen as the sine qua non of American manhood.

21. Sandy Finkelstein, *Existentialism and Alienation in American Literature* (New York: International Publishers, 1965), 244.

22. Howard M. Harper, *Desperate Faith: A Study of Bellow, Salinger, Mailer, Baldwin and Updike* (Chapel Hill: University of North Carolina Press, 1967), 171.

23. Indeed, in more than one interview, Updike has expressed the feeling that *Rabbit, Run* was, in some ways, a reaction to Kerouac's *On the Road*, a novel that he felt espoused an unrealistic, doomed wanderlust.

24. Gordon E. Slethaug, "*Rabbit Redux*: Freedom Is Made of Brambles," in *Critical Essays on John Updike,* ed. William R. Macnaughton, 237-253 (Boston: G. K. Hall and Co., 1982), 240.

25. O'Connell, 103.

26. John Updike, *Rabbit Redux* (New York: Knopf, 1971), 3. Subsequent references will be indicated parenthetically in the text.

27. Robert Detweiler, *John Updike,* revised ed. (Boston: Twayne, 1984), 132.

28. As Detweiler argues, these references act "as the context for metaphoric uses of space. . . . The spectral figures of the astronauts on the moon set the tone for the strong ghost imagery, which stands for the insubstantial quality of American life and for the haunting memory of better times" (128).

29. Greiner, "No Place to Run," 11, 12.

30. J. Gerald Kennedy, *Imagining Paris: Exile, Writing, and American Identity* (New Haven, CT: Yale University Press, 1993), xii.

31. Ralph C. Wood, *The Comedy of Redemption: Faith and Comic Vision in Four American Novelists* (South Bend, IN: University of Notre Dame Press, 1988), 202.

32. Donald J. Greiner, *Adultery in the American Novel: Updike, James, and Hawthorne* (Columbia: University of South Carolina Press, 1985), 38.

33. Robert Fishman, *Bourgeois Utopias* (New York: Basic Books, 1987), 153.

34. Matthew Wilson, "The Rabbit Tetralogy: From Solitude to Society to Solitude Again," in *Rabbit Tales*, 89-110, 95.

35. Dana Nelson, *National Manhood: Capitalist Citizenship and the Imagined Fraternity of White Men* (Durham, NC: Duke University Press, 1998), 180.

36. Julia Kristeva, *Strangers to Ourselves,* trans. Leon S. Roudiez (New York: Columbia University Press, 1991), 181.

37. A number of critics have offered insightful Freudian readings of the Rabbit tetralogy and *Rabbit Redux* in particular. For illuminating discussions of this aspect of the work, see Buck, "The Mother Load," O'Connell, "Updike and the Patriarchal Dilemma," and Judie Newman, *John Updike* (New York: St. Martin's Press, 1988).

38. Indeed, Harry's vacillation of interest between his sexual affairs and the state of his dying mother would seem to position him as a virtual case study of the struggle between the death drive and the procreative drive Sigmund Freud analyzes in "Beyond the Pleasure Principle" in *The Freud Reader,* ed. Peter Gay, 594-626 (New York: Norton, 1989). As Freud argues, the instinct toward sexual pleasure and procreation stands as the sole aberration in human instincts, which otherwise tend toward the return to an earlier, more conservative, state of being. Hence the primacy of the death drive; aside from the life-sustaining force of the sexual instinct, for Freud

"the aim of all life is death" (613). In fact, a case could be made—following Peter Brooks's brilliant textual application of "Beyond the Pleasure Principle" laid out in *Reading for the Plot: Design and Intention in Narrative* (New York: Knopf, 1984), and specifically in his chapter entitled "Freud's Masterplot"—that the entire Rabbit tetralogy functions according to the logic of Freud's "Beyond the Pleasure Principle." A massive, four-volume work that appeared over the course of some thirty years, the *Rabbit* tetralogy is throughout haunted by the specter of Harry's death, moving inexorably toward the moment, at the end of *Rabbit at Rest*, when Harry finally expires. What keeps the narrative going for so long are, primarily, Harry's sexual dalliances, encounters that stave off the closure of death while providing yet more generative material for Updike himself.

39. Buck, 150, 153.
40. Slethaug, 244.
41. Indeed, the triangulated desiring relationship among Harry, Jill, and Skeeter is driven primarily by the homosocial desire between Harry and Skeeter. Each trying to best the other and prove himself more of a man, Harry and Skeeter become locked in an antagonistic yet desiring relationship of the sort that Eve Kosofsky Sedgwick examines in *Between Men: English Literature and Male Homosocial Desire* (New York: Columbia University Press, 1985).
42. Freud, "Three Essays on Sexuality," in *The Freud Reader*, 239-293, 269.
43. Indeed, Buck has accounted for Harry's characteristic cruelty in this manner, noting that his "lack of mastery repeatedly evidences itself in acts of cruelty to those over whom he would be lord" (161). Buck's phrasing seems particularly apt in considering the Harry/Skeeter relationship, one that explicitly plays out the dynamics of the master/slave relationship in highly charged political and erotic terms.
44. As Slethaug notes, Harry's second adolescence results from the very feeling of freedom he experiences on losing his house: "The fact that, after he is freed of his property, Rabbit goes back to the room of his childhood, his womb, at first masturbating and then not even being able to arouse himself at all, indicates the truly disastrous effects of such freedom"(248).
45. Robert Kolker, *A Cinema of Loneliness: Penn, Kubrick, Scorcese, Spielberg, Altman*, 2nd ed. (New York: Oxford University Press, 1988), 325.
46. Quoted in Glenn Man, *Radical Visions: American Film Renaissance, 1967-1976* (Westport, CT: Greenwood Press, 1994), 47-48.
47. Ivone Marguiles, "John Cassavetes: Amateur Director," in *The New American Cinema*, ed. Jon Lewis, 275-306 (Durham, NC: Duke University Press, 1998), 280.
48. Leonard Quart and Albert Auster, *American Film and Society Since 1945* (New York: Praeger, 1984), 88-89.
49. Man, 37.
50. Ibid., 38.
51. Contemporary commentator Bennett Berger, in his 1969 essay "Racist Plastic Uptight," uses the same metaphor to sum up the predicament facing Ben Braddock's generation on coming of age in the late 1960s, describing "the emptiness they sense in the complacent images of the good life which underlie the exhortations they get from their liberal middle-class parents and from the mass media to stay in school, to get good grades, to get trained in a salable skill or profession, to sell it and get ahead with the organizations which have bought it; to get married (not on impulse) and to raise a family in a suburban home (a modest one is OK to start) with at least one

sliding glass door and a garage (preferably heated, and wired 220) big enough to contain two cars, a washer, a dryer, and a freezer, all the while being circumspect about one's opinions and heedful of one's reputation: to become, in short, a good commuter-consumer in pursuit of comfort and fun through the acquisition of the products of American technology, through 'plastic'" (218-219). See Berger's *Looking for America: Essays on Youth, Suburbia, and Other American Obsessions* (Englewood Cliffs, NJ: Prentice-Hall, 1971).

52. Ben is an object of intense observation throughout the film; over the course of the narrative he attempts to dodge the inquiring eyes of omnipresent family friends, a vengeful Mrs. Robinson, the entire staff and even some guests at the Taft Hotel, site of his and Mrs. Robinson's assignations, and the dogged if comical surveillance of the manager at the Berkeley boardinghouse where he rents a room. H. Wayne Schuth, in *Mike Nichols* (Boston: Twayne, 1978), points out that Nichols also uses glass imagery throughout the film to emphasize Ben's entrapment. As Schuth astutely notes, Ben is constantly shown behind glass—the glass doors of the airport, the fish tank, the glass phone booth and tabletop of the Taft Hotel, and so on—as a means of emphasizing his position as (or at least his sense of being) an object of a seemingly omniscient gaze (62).

53. As Man argues, "As the underwater camera pulls away from a medium to a long shot, Ben recedes into a little figure in the watery tomb, isolated and insignificant" (35).

54. Schuth, 51.

55. The oedipal overtones of Ben's relationship with his mother reflect an ongoing concern among social critics, since the postwar years, over the extent of maternal influence in the domestic, suburban sphere. Reactionary writers such as Keats and Philip Wylie decried the rise of matriarchal culture in suburbia, fearing the potentially disastrous effects on children of a too-powerful mother figure. Interestingly, Betty Friedan concurred: In *The Feminine Mystique*, Friedan claims that one of the negative effects of confining women to the domestic sphere was an undue influence on child rearing. According to Friedan, due to constant devotion to child care, suburban mothers began to live "vicariously" through their children, leading to the development of an unhealthy, "symbiotic" relationship between mother and child. For Friedan's discussion of motherhood in suburbia, see chapter 12, 282-309, of *The Feminine Mystique* (New York: W. W. Norton & Co., 1963).

56. The thematic connection between the two scenes is further emphasized by Nichols's use of another linking bit of dialogue. After his mother, angry at Ben, storms out of the bathroom, Ben yells "Wait a minute!" As the scene ends and the screen goes black, we here Ben repeating the phrase "Will you just wait a minute?" only to discover upon the opening of the next scene that he is saying this to Mrs. Robinson, in bed. Again, Nichols intentionally disturbs the synchronization of audio and video to make a thematic link.

57. Schuth, 62.

58. Ethan Mordden, *Medium Cool: The Movies of the 1960s* (New York: Knopf, 1990), 180-81.

CHAPTER FOUR

1. Lynn Spigel, "From Theatre to Space Ship: Metaphors of Suburban Domesticity in Postwar America," in *Visions of Suburbia*, ed. Roger Silverstone, 217-239 (New York: Routledge, 1997), 227.

2. Elizabeth Janeway, for example, in *Man's World, Woman's Place: A Study in Social Mythology* (New York: William Morrow and Company, 1971), argues that the postwar suburban migration, whatever appeals it may have presented, was predicated on a totalizing drive toward female enclosure: "No doubt the women who made the move to the suburbs concurred in it, or most of them did; but in fact it was a move based on a view of woman's role as being pretty well nonexistent outside the family" (302).

3. Christopher Lasch, *Women and the Common Life: Love, Marriage, and Feminism*, ed. Elisabeth Lasch-Quinn (New York: Norton, 1997), 105.

4. Kaja Silverman, *Male Subjectivity at the Margins* (New York: Routledge, 1992). See note 21 of chapter 1 herein.

5. Annmarie Adams, "The Eichler Home: Intention and Experience in Postwar Suburbia," in *Gender, Class, and Shelter: Perspectives in Vernacular Architecture*, ed. Elizabeth Collins Cromley and Carter L. Hudgins, 164-178 (Knoxville: University of Tennessee Press, 1996), 164. Note that this passage is not indicative of the tenor of Adams's article as a whole. While recognizing the inherent cultural and psychological limitations placed on women by the suburban migration of the 1950s and 1960s, Adams goes on in this fascinating article to consider the ways in which suburban women reshaped their relationship to their homes and properties, often defying or modifying what were seemingly the rather stringent, even prescriptive, intentions of the architects and home designers. Adams's essay serves as a reminder of the risks of oversimplifying the relationship between gender and the suburban environment; still, as Adams notes, the broad trend toward isolation of the female in the postwar suburban landscape is unmistakable.

6. Brett Harvey, *The Fifties: A Women's Oral History* (New York: HarperCollins, 1993), 70; 88.

7. Judith Butler, *Gender Trouble: Feminism and the Subversion of Identity* (New York: Routledge, 1990), 33.

8. Nina Leibman, in *Living Room Lectures: The Fifties Family in Film and Television* (Austin: University of Texas Press, 1995), points out the ironic result of women's containment within the home in these domestic sitcoms: In shows about not only the family but also their relationship to the neighborhood and community, women are rarely seen acting outside the home or beyond the realm of the family. This is particularly true of June Cleaver, who, Leibman notes, "exists only in conjunction with her sons. Although she is a stay-at-home mom in a suburban neighborhood, we never see her interact with her neighborhood counterparts" (125).

9. Ibid., 182.

10. Mary Beth Haralovich, "Sitcoms and Suburbs: Positioning the 1950's Homemaker," *Quarterly Review of Film and Video*, 11.1 (1989): 61.

11. The tremendous postwar push toward situating women within the domestic sphere is evident not only on suburban television sitcoms but also in representations of women from movies of the 1950s. For an excellent analysis of Hollywood's construction of gender in films of the postwar era, see Brandon French, *On the Verge of Revolt: Women in American Films of the Fifties* (New York: Frederick Ungar, 1978).

12. Philip J. Wylie, *Generation of Vipers* (New York: Rinehart & Co, 1946), 200, 201. In a series of tirades that would be funny if they were not so frightening (or, perhaps, vice versa), Wylie labels women as agents of "Satan" and "spiritual saboteurs," and goes on to liken American women to Adolf Hitler, before finally exhorting his male

readers, "We must face the dynasty of the dames at once . . . and take back our dreams" (203).

13. Ferdinand Lundberg and Marynia F. Farnham, *Modern Woman: The Lost Sex* (New York: Harper & Brothers, 1947), 235, 240.

14. In contrast to the narrow-minded hyperbole that characterized Lundberg and Farnham's work, or the insanity of Wylie's, Mead vacillates between some showings of support for women's endeavors in the public sphere and repeated admonitions that woman's ultimate place is in the home. The relatively tempered tone of her argument as well as her ultimately conservative stance are evident in a characteristic passage such as this: "To-day, the girl of . . . ability is usually willing to admit that she wants to marry, and seems more than willing to sacrifice her career to marriage than to sacrifice a chance for marriage to her career. Because it is now more and more accepted that girls should work until they marry—and if one is unlucky, this means all one's life. . . . If they have brains and ability, sheer virtuosity plus the need to succeed may lead them to become engrossed in their work, but seldom so engrossed that the desire for marriage is blocked out" (323). Margaret Mead, *Male and Female: A Study of the Sexes in a Changing World* (New York: William Morrow & Co., 1949).

15. Catherine Marshall, "An Introduction by Mrs. Peter Marshall," *Life,* December 24, 1956, 2.

16. Cornelia Otis Skinner, "Women Are Misguided," *Life,* December 24, 1956, 73.

17. Mary Ellen Chase, "She Misses Some Goals," *Life,* December 24, 1956, 24; Robert Coughlon, "Changing Roles in Modern Marriage," *Life,* December 24, 1956, 116.

18. Betty Friedan, *The Feminine Mystique* (New York: W. W. Norton & Co., 1963), 15.

19. As to the durability of this argument, one thinks of the connections to recent work by a feminist thinker such as Lauren Berlant, who, in *The Queen of America Goes to Washington City: Essays on Sex and Citizenship* (Durham, NC: Duke University Press, 1997), makes a compelling, extended argument concerning what she labels the "infantilization" of U.S. citizenship. Arguing that a revivified cult of domesticity and obsession with child rearing bespeaks a nation obsessed with a "familial politics of the national future," Berlant pessimistically concludes of contemporary American society that, "in the process of collapsing the political and the personal into a world of public intimacy, a nation made for adult citizens has been replaced by one imagined for . . . children" (1). Although Berlant makes no specific connections between her analysis of contemporary U.S. citizenship and that of the postwar era, I would suggest that the stringent positioning of women in the domestic sphere that accompanied the postwar migration to suburbia was a significant factor in the unfolding of the process of "infantilization" of citizenship that she describes. That is, while the new "republican mother" of 1950s' suburbia may now be reduced to the status of historical footnote, the very force of political, economic, and cultural discourses that carved out the limiting domestic space for the women of postwar suburbia is evidence of a culture focused on, in Berlant's terms, a "familial politics of the national future."

20. Lasch, 94.

21. Nancy Walker, "Humor and Gender Roles: The 'Funny' Feminism of the Post-World War II Suburbs," *American Quarterly* 37 (Spring 1985): 98-113.

22. Phyllis McGinley, *A Short Walk from the Station* (New York: Viking, 1951), 12; 13; 79.

23. Margaret Marsh, "(Ms)Reading the Suburbs," *American Quarterly* 46 (March 1994): 43.

24. Susan Faludi, *Backlash: The Undeclared War Against American Women* (New York: Crown, 1991). While Faludi's work focuses specifically on antifeminist discourse and media imagery of the 1980s, she notes that such a reactionary cultural attack on women's rights is "a recurring phenomenon: it returns every time women begin to make some headway toward equality, a seemingly inevitable early frost to the culture's brief flowerings of feminism" (46). As Faludi notes, the first half of the 1970s marked such a flowering of attention to women's rights, but as the 1980s approached, a pronounced cultural backlash was taking shape.

25. Mark Baldassare, *Trouble in Paradise: The Suburban Transformation in America* (New York: Columbia University Press, 1986), 1. Noting the demographic emergence of suburbia as the dominant landscape of the nation as of the 1970 census, Baldassare rightly suggests that, in many ways, the decade of the 1970s marked a "turning point" for American suburbia.

26. Linda Greenhouse "Isolation in Suburbia," in *Suburbia in Transition*, ed. Louis H. Masotti and Jeffrey K. Hadden, 32-35 (New York: Viewpoints, 1974), 33.

27. Stephen Birmingham, *The Golden Dream: Suburbia in the Seventies* (New York: Harper & Row, 1978), 187.

28. As critic Pico Iyer argues in "The World According to Beattie," *Partisan Review* 50.4 (1983): 548-553: "The surface details of Beattie's stories so strikingly resemble Cheever's that one might almost read them as a sequel" (548).

29. Joseph Epstein, "Ann Beattie and the Hippoisie," *Commentary* 75 (March 1983): 58; John W. Aldridge, *Talents and Technicians: Literary Chic and the New Assembly-Line Fiction* (New York: Charles Scribner's Sons, 1992), 63.

30. M. P. Baumgartner, *The Moral Order of a Suburb* (New York: Oxford University Press, 1988). Arguing that a sense of dislocation and detachment from community makes nonconfrontation the standard mode of interpersonal behavior in the suburb, Baumgartner concludes that "a kind of moral minimalism pervades in the suburbs" (3). In a compelling argument, Baumgartner suggests that, since increasing numbers of people live in environments characterized by "transiency and fragmentation of social networks," the "culture of avoidance" that characterizes suburban life may become more widespread. In this sense, claims Baumgartner, "suburbia may thus provide a study in the moral order of the future" (135).

31. Ann Beattie, *Falling in Place* (New York: Vintage Books, 1991), 59. Subsequent references will be indicated parenthetically in the text.

32. Iyer, 549; Carolyn Porter, "Ann Beattie: The Art of the Missing," in *Contemporary American Women Writers: Narrative Strategies*, ed. Catherine Rainwater and William J. Scheick, 9-25 (Lexington: University Press of Kentucky, 1985). As Porter argues, the lives of Beattie's characters "do not adhere to a city or town. Instead, they are attached to cars, plants, dogs—that is, not only to objects but to transitory ones" (12).

33. Aldridge, 57.

34. Stacey Olster, for example, in "Photographs and Fantasies in the Stories of Ann Beattie," in *Since Flannery O'Connor: Essays on the Contemporary American Short Story*, ed. Loren Logsdon and Charles W. Mayer, 113-123 (Macomb: Western

Illinois University Press, 1987), argues that in general, Beattie's characters "remain incapable of admitting . . . into their consciousness" either the "passing of time" or the "acceptance of change" (114). Olster examines the role that photographs play in Beattie's fiction, as a constantly idealized reminder of a past no longer accessible. While her analysis centers on Beattie's short fiction, Olster's insights are certainly relevant to a reading of *Falling in Place* , a novel that features recurring references to photographs of the Knapp family from (happier) years past.

35. Susan Janet McKinstry, "The Speaking Silence of Ann Beattie's Voice," *Studies in Short Fiction* 24.2 (Spring 1987): 112.

36. Laura Mulvey, "Visual Pleasure and Narrative Cinema," in *Feminism and Film Theory*, ed. Constance Penley, 57-68 (New York: Routledge, 1988).

37. The connection between Disney World and suburbia as a fantasy land predicated on intense control is a provocative one. As Russ Rymer explains in "Back to the Future," as early as the 1960s, Walt Disney dreamed of creating EPCOT (or Environmental Prototype Community of Tomorrow) "as an actual town, a living experiment in urban habitat" (66). While this vision did not come to pass, the Disney Corporation's recently completed, residential "company town" of Celebration, Florida, stands as a compelling instance of an ultramodern, utterly preplanned, and regulated landscape designed to resemble (and, one assumes foster a sense of) an old-fashioned community. The connections run deep between the fantasies behind the creation of Celebration and those behind the first wave of suburban development in the postwar years. See Rymer's excellent article for an extended discussion of this eerily fascinating experiment in landscape control and behavioral psychology: "Back to the Future: Disney Reinvents the Company Town," *Harper's* (October 1996): 65-78.

38. This reading of the android Carol's breakdown as a transgressive mode of resistance springs from the ideas Donna Haraway put forth in her influential essay concerning identity, resistance, and feminist practice, "A Manifesto for Cyborgs: Science, Technology, and Socialist Feminism in the 1980s," in *Feminism/Postmodernism*, ed. Linda J. Nicholson, 190-233 (New York: Routledge, 1990).

39. Thomas B. Byers, "Kissing Becky: Masculine Fears and Misogynist Moments in Science Fiction Films," *Arizona Quarterly* 45 (Autumn 1989): 86, 91.

40. For such a reading of the politics of *Invasion of the Body Snatchers*, see Stuart Samuels, "The Age of Conspiracy and Conformity: *Invasion of the Body Snatchers*," in *American History/American Film: Interpreting the Hollywood Image*, ed. John E. O'Connor and Martin A. Jackson, 203-217 (New York: Frederick Ungar, 1979).

41. Only reinforcing this sense of inherited gender bias is the way in which the men of the town program the android replacements to become spokeswomen for the pleasures of this "conversion" process. In one of the most riveting scenes of the film, Joanna encounters Bobbie for the first time since Bobbie's "change," and she is filled with both terror and rage as her friend attempts to convince her of the pleasures of life as a "Stepford wife." Vivian Sobchack has argued—in *Screening Space: The American Science Fiction Film* (New Brunswick, NJ: Rutgers University Press, 1997)—that a characteristic feature of "takeover" or "infiltration" films is the "definite emotional appeal to the idea of being 'taken over'. . . . That added emotional attraction is 'no more responsibility'" (123). In the case of *The Stepford Wives*, and in particular Bobbie's final speech, this "emotional appeal" comes in the form of the android replacement mouthing praises to the life of the stay-at-home

suburban housewife that sound as if they have come straight from *Life* magazine, or any of the vehicles of popular culture espousing the new suburban domesticity in the days of the feminine mystique. The men of Stepford, it seems, have learned their cultural history lessons well. Joanna, however, is immune to Bobbie's appeal; she stabs her friend with a kitchen knife, drawing no blood but causing a "shortcircuit" that temporarily disables the android Bobbie. As we are soon to learn, Joanna's victory here is short-lived.

42. Worth noting as well is the film's complicity in the theft of Joanna's vision as an artist. A recurring subplot throughout the narrative centers on Joanna's efforts to find her vision as a photographer. She takes a number of trips to the city in attempts to present her artwork to gallery owners and is consistently turned down. Only after she takes a series of photographs of the children frolicking in the suburban yard does she finally sense that she's "on to something" as an artist; the gallery owner in New York agrees, judging that these new, domestic photographs are "really quite nice." In a film concerned primarily with the detrimental effects of a rigorous positioning of women in the domestic sphere, this curious turn in the subplot of Joanna's search for artistic vision is politically troubling, to say the least.

CHAPTER FIVE

1. National Advisory Commission on Civil Disorders, *Report* (New York: Bantam, 1968), 1; 10.

2. Stephan Thernstrom and Abigail Thernstrom, *America in Black and White: One Nation, Indivisible* (New York: Simon & Schuster, 1997), 204.

3. See chapter 11, pp. 190-218, of Kenneth Jackson, *Crabgrass Frontier: The Suburbanization of the United States* (New York: Oxford University Press, 1985), for an extended discussion of how racial covenants influenced the demographics of suburbia. As the author notes, even legislative efforts to abolish racial covenants conceded their ongoing influence: "covenants, which were legal provisions written into property deeds, were a common method of prohibiting black occupancy until . . . *Shelley v. Kraemer*. . . . Even then, it was not until 1949 that FHA [the Federal Housing Authority] announced that as of February 15, 1950, it would not insure mortgages on real estate subject to covenants. Although the press treated the FHA announcement as a major advancement in the field of racial justice, former housing administrator Nathan Straus noted that 'the new policy in fact served only to warn speculative builders who had not filed covenants of their right to do so, and it gave them a convenient respite in which to file'" (208).

4. Ibid., 206-207.

5. Ibid., 213.

6. For a thorough study of the ways both public policy and private enterprise and speculation served as central factors in the shaping of the emerging suburban environment, see Mark Gottdiener, *The Social Production of Urban Space* (Austin: University of Texas Press, 1985), esp. chapter 7, 229-262.

7. Charles Abrams, *Forbidden Neighbors: A Study of Prejudice in Housing* (New York: Harper & Bros., 1955), 144; 149.

8. W. Dennis Keating, *The Suburban Racial Dilemma: Housing and Neighborhoods* (Philadelphia: Temple University Press, 1994), 8.

9. In "The Limits of Democracy in the Suburbs: Constructing the Middle Class Through Residential Exclusion," in *The Middling Sorts: Explorations in the History of the American Middle Class*, ed. Burton J. Bledstein and Robert D. Johnston, 256-266 (New York: Routledge, 2001), Theresa Mah compellingly points out that postwar suburbanization, in that it defined and made highly visible a white, middle-class, American majority, coincided with a powerful, if tacit, process of "racialization" (259). See Mah's article as well for a discussion of the so-called Freedom of Choice Initiative put forth as a referendum in California in 1951 in the wake of *Shelley v. Kraemer*, a move Mah describes as "one of many such attempts" across the United States to skirt the ban on racial covenants instituted by this court decision.

10. Valerie Babb, *Whiteness Visible: The Meaning of Whiteness in American Literature and Culture* (New York: New York University Press, 1998), 16. While Babb focuses her interesting study on the developing ideology of whiteness from the colonial period through the early twentieth century, one could argue that the mass migration to suburbia was marked by more than a noticeable racial/demographic move. In addition, if we consider the imaginative construction of suburban space in such popular culture outlets as magazines, advertising, and television, we see that it was heavily coded with—and helped to further define and reinforce—an ideology of whiteness.

11. Samuel Kaplan, *The Dream Deferred: People, Politics, and Planning in Suburbia* (New York: Seabury, 1976), 99.

12. Robert Fishman, *Bourgeois Utopias* (New York: Basic Books, 1987), 201-202.

13. Notable exceptions to this trend such as *Beulah*, which debuted in 1950, *The Nat King Cole Show* (1956), *I Spy* (1965), and *Julia* (1968) all featured African Americans in starring roles.

14. William Sharpe and Leonard Wallock also note this point, arguing that the presence of the character Will "signals to viewers how out of place black families seem in this rarified milieu" (19). See Sharpe and Wallock's insightful essay, "Bold New City or Built-up 'Burb? Redefining Contemporary Suburbia," *American Quarterly* 46 (March 1994): 1-30, for a discussion of the persistence of stereotypical suburban imagery in contemporary television and film.

15. Shelby Steele, "I'm Black, You're White, Who's Innocent?" in *Voices in Black & White: Writings on Race in America from Harper's Magazine*, ed. Katharine Whittemore and Gerald Marzorati, 213-228 (New York: Franklin Square, 1993), 221.

16. Jacquie Jones, "The New Ghetto Aesthetic," in *Mediated Messages and African-American Culture: Contemporary Issues*, ed. Venise T. Berry and Carmen L. Manning-Miller, 40-51 (Thousand Oaks, CA: Sage, 1996), 51.

17. My thanks to Michael Rogin for suggesting this film as an allegory of the racial paranoia driving "white flight" to the suburbs. Other films have depicted in comic manner the suspicion of ethnic "otherness" in the suburbs. A good example of this thematic concern can be found in the 1989 Tom Hanks vehicle *The 'Burbs*, in which much of the comedic plot centers on the suspicions members of an all-white, ethnically nondescript suburb harbor toward a mysterious and noticeably "ethnic" new family, the Klopeks, whose move into the neighborhood sparks both the surveillance and the ire of neighbors.

18. James Blackwell and Philip S. Hart, *Cities, Suburbs and Blacks: A Study of Concerns, Distrust and Alienation* (Bayside, NY: General Hall, 1982), 3. This book presents a useful, if now dated, analysis of issues related to African American suburbanization.

19. "The Battle of the Suburbs," *Newsweek,* November 15, 1971, 61-64.

20. Jack Patterson, "The Wall of Zoning," *Commonweal,* May 28, 1971, 283. Peter Muller, in *Contemporary Suburban America* (Englewood Cliffs, NJ: Prentice-Hall, 1981), refers to exclusionary zoning as a "suburban filter," arguing that discriminatory uses of zoning have "persisted essentially unchanged since zoning was first introduced after World War I" (96). See Muller's chapter 3, "The Social Organization of Contemporary Suburbia and its Human Consequences" (61-117), for an extended discussion of suburban segregation, highlighted by case studies.

21. The decade of the 1970s saw a flood of newspaper and journal articles, as well as books, calling for the opening up of the suburbs. See, for example, Dennis P. Sobin, *The Future of the American Suburbs: Survival or Extinction?* (Port Washington, NY: Kennikat, 1971); Anthony Downs, *Opening Up the Suburbs: An Urban Strategy for America* (New Haven, CT: Yale University Press, 1973); John J. Tarrant, *The End of Exurbia: Who Are All These People and Why Do They Want to Ruin Our Town?* (New York: Stein and Day, 1976); and Muller, *Contemporary Suburban America.*

22. R. J. Johnston, *Residential Segregation, the State and Constitutional Conflict in American Urban Areas,* Institute of British Geographers Special Publication, No. 17 (London: Academic Press, 1984), 100. See as well Michael N. Danielson, *The Politics of Exclusion* (New York: Columbia University Press, 1976), for a discussion of the Mt. Laurel case.

23. In *The Politics of Exclusion,* Danielson argues forcefully that "local governments generally are silent partners in the web of racial discrimination which characterizes the private housing market" (13). For a thorough study of homeowners' associations and their influence, see Evan McKenzie, *Privatopia: Homeowner Associations and the Rise of Residential Private Government* (New Haven, CT: Yale University Press, 1994).

24. For a discussion of steering and its impact, see Roger Witherspoon and Sheryl-Lee Hilliard, "No Trespassing!" *Black Enterprise* 15 (May 1985): 37-40.

25. For a useful review of middle-class black suburbanization in recent decades, see David J. Dent, "The New Black Suburbs," *The New York Times Magazine,* June 14, 1992, 18-25.

26. Susan Rafter, *Blacks in Suburbs: A Bibliography.* CPL Bibliography No. 133 (Chicago: CPL Bibliographies, 1984), i.

27. Thernstrom and Thernstrom, 212.

28. Constance Perin, *Belonging in America: Reading Between the Lines* (Madison: University of Wisconsin Press, 1988), 103.

29. Robert W. Lake, *The New Suburbanites: Race and Housing in the Suburbs* (New Brunswick, NJ: Rutgers University Press, 1981), 3.

30. Indeed, the very visibility of racial "otherness" in the predominantly white suburbs further complicates questions of assimilation and racial community. As Wilson Jeremiah Moses argues in *The Wings of Ethiopia: Studies in African-American Life and Letters* (Ames: Iowa State University Press, 1990), the "ultimate test" of the "ethnicity" model of African American identity is whether blacks "are capable of vanishing into the suburbs, where other ethnic groups cease to be [ethnic] . . . and become . . . just plain American" (4). The dubious reward of African American "disappearance" into the landscape of suburbia proves the central concern of Naylor's *Linden Hills.*

31. Homi K. Bhabha, "On the Irremovable Strangeness of Being Different," *PMLA* 113 (January 1998): 35.

32. Angels Carabi, "Interview with Gloria Naylor," *Belles Lettres* 7 (Spring 1992): 41-42.

33. The first extended discussion of the Dantean parallels in *Linden Hills* was offered by Catherine C. Ward in her essay "Gloria Naylor's *Linden Hills*: A Modern Inferno," *Contemporary Literature* 28.1 (Spring 1987): 67-81; for another excellent, close analysis of Naylor's uses of Dante's *Inferno*, see Margaret Earley Whitt, *Understanding Gloria Naylor* (Columbia: University of South Carolina Press, 1999).

34. At least one critic, Mary F. Sisney, positions the novel squarely within a tradition of "black novels of manners," while arguing that Naylor "is taking the novel of manners in a new direction." See Mary F. Sisney, "The View From the Outside: Black Novels of Manners," in *The Critical Response to Gloria Naylor*, ed. Sharon Felton and Michelle C. Loris, 63-75 (Westport, CT: Greenwood Press, 1997).

35. Virginia C. Fowler, *Gloria Naylor: In Search of Sanctuary* (New York: Twayne, 1996), 69.

36. W. E. B. Du Bois, *The Souls of Black Folk* (New York: Modern Library, 1996), 5.

37. Gloria Naylor, *Linden Hills* (New York: Penguin, 1986), 2. Subsequent references will be indicated parenthetically in the text.

38. Keith A. Sandiford, "Gothic and Intertextual Constructions in *Linden Hills*," *Arizona Quarterly* 47.3 (Autumn 1991): 121.

39. Ibid., 122.

40. Jerome E. Thornton, "The Paradoxical Journey of the African American in African American Fiction," *New Literary History* 21.3 (Spring 1990): 735.

41. The name Norman gives this mysterious, recurring disturbance is "the pinks," as it causes him to suffer the hallucination that he is being attacked by a "pinkish slime"; his violent reaction invariably finds him harming himself physically and destroying the couple's furnishings and possessions. Virginia Fowler has taken an interesting interpretive position on this strange element of the text, arguing that since the phrase "pink" is sometimes used as slang for a white person—indeed, though Fowler does not note this, at one point Lester Tilson refers to a white woman as a "pink job"—Norman's reaction to attacks of "the pinks" can be read metaphorically in racial terms; as Fowler suggests, "The pinks thus constitute a powerful trope for the sickness underlying African Americans' embrace of white values" (75).

42. Fowler, 60.

43. In addition to portraying the artificiality of Linden Hills society, the section of the text chronicling Winston's wedding suggests the pervasive control over sexual identity in this society. For an extended discussion of the connections between narrowly defined sexual roles and the class structure in this novel, see Kimberly A. Costino, "'Weapons Against Women': Compulsory Heterosexuality and Capitalism in *Linden Hills*," in *Gloria Naylor's Early Novels*, ed. Margot Anne Kelley, 39-54 (Gainesville: University Press of Florida, 1999).

44. The extended subplot of Willa Nedeed and the connection she discovers to her predecessors provides ample justification for Fowler's claim that "*Linden Hills* represents, in fact, Naylor's most incisive critique of male patriarchy" (60).

45. Grace E. Collins, "Narrative Structure in Linden Hills," in *The Critical Response to Gloria Naylor*, ed. Sharon Felton and Michelle C. Loris, 80-87 (Westport, CT: Greenwood, 1997), 86.
46. See Sandiford for an extended discussion of Naylor's use of the gothic mode.
47. Karen Ross, *Black and White Media: Black Images in Popular Film and Television* (Cambridge: Polity Press, 1996). In noting the persistent use of the urban milieu by black filmmakers, Ross argues, "The preoccupation with ghetto contexts and the violence they necessarily connote may circumscribe, by their very success, the possibility of other black voices being heard. While such films are valuable in providing insights into the experiences of young black men, they are largely desolate in their conclusions. It is still open to question whether such films function to force an examination of the condition of African American communities or whether they simply/also pathologize black communities for the voyeuristic pleasure of the majority white audience" (82). Ross's excellent study examines both American and British film and television. For works focusing specifically on the racial dynamics of American film and television, respectively, see Ed Guerrero, *Framing Blackness: The African American Image in Film* (Philadelphia: Temple University Press, 1993), and Sasha Torres, ed., *Living Color: Race and Television in the United States* (Durham, NC: Duke University Press, 1998).
48. Donald Bogle, *Toms, Coons, Mulattos, Mammies, and Bucks: An Interpretative History of Blacks in American Films*, new 3rd ed. (New York: Continuum, 1997), 337.
49. Repeating symbolism links Pops to the class identification of Sharane's family: Like Sharane's father, he drinks "Dick Gregory" shakes, and he watches the same television programs as they do.
50. Richard Dyer, "Is *Car Wash* a Musical?" in *Black American Cinema*, ed. Manthia Diawara, 93-106 (New York: Routledge, 1993), 102.
51. Catherine Jurca, in *White Diaspora: The Suburb and the Twentieth-Century American Novel* (Princeton, NJ: Princeton University Press, 2001), makes a comment concerning the naturalistic setting of Richard Wright's 1940 novel *Native Son* that applies equally well to the omniscient eye of white authority in this 1990 film: "Segregation is associated with the absolute mobility of whites and the violation and invasion of public and private black space" (109). While invasion of privacy is, in one form or another, a staple of suburban fiction and film, in Hudlin's socially heterogeneous cityscape, the invasiveness of the omnipresent police becomes a trope for a highly regulated, exclusionary landscape.
52. Tommy L. Lott, "A No-Theory of Contemporary Black Cinema," in *Cinemas of the Black Diaspora: Diversity, Dependence, and Oppositionality*, ed. Michael T. Martin, 40-55 (Detroit, MI: Wayne State University Press, 1995), 46.
53. Guerrero, 190-191.

CONCLUSION

1. Dick's *Time Out of Joint* offers a fascinating take on 1950s' suburbia as a contrived and entrapping environment, all the more prescient in that it was written and published in 1959, in the midst of the great suburban boom. Dick's protagonist, Ragle Gumm, lives an idiosyncratic existence in what seems to be an utterly typical suburban town of the late 1950s. Always sensing that his world seemed a little too

ordinary, Gumm eventually discovers that the present is actually 1998, and he has been living in a make-believe time and place, a town fully constructed and populated to resemble suburbia in the 1950s. The influence on *The Truman Show* is unmistakable; in a broader sense, Dick anticipated the oft-repeated perceptions of suburbia as an artificial place.

2. *Far From Heaven* marks the second adaptation of Sirk's *All That Heaven Allows*. The first was German director Rainer Werner Fassbinder's 1974 film *Ali: Fear Eats the Soul*.

3. Frederic Jameson, *Postmodernism: or, The Cultural Logic of Late Capitalism* (Durham, NC: Duke University Press, 1991), 287.

4. See, respectively, James Howard Kunstler, *The Geography of Nowhere: The Rise and Decline of America's Man-Made Landscape* (New York: Simon & Schuster, 1993), and Daniel Lazare, *America's Undeclared War: What's Killing Our Cities and How We Can Stop It* (New York: Harcourt, 2001). Both authors lament the physical and philosophical ramifications of suburban sprawl.

5. This population estimate comes from Edward J. Blakely and Mary Gail Snyder, "Fortress Communities: The Walling and Gating of American Suburbs," *Nation's Cities Weekly*, October 2, 1995, 1ff. For a fuller discussion of the impact of gated communities in the United States, see Blakely and Snyder's *Fortress America: Gated Communities in the United States* (Washington, DC: Brookings Institution Press, 1997).

6. See Kennedy's fascinating argument, "Residential Associations as State Actors: Regulating the Impact of Gated Communities on Nonmembers," *Yale Law Journal* 105 (December 1995): 771.

7. Peter Calthorpe, *The Next American Metropolis: Ecology, Community, and the American Dream* (Princeton, NJ: Princeton Architectural Press, 1993), 37.

8. Todd W. Bressi, "Planning the American Dream," in *The New Urbanism: Toward an Architecture of Community*, ed. Peter Katz, xxv-xlii (New York: McGraw-Hill, 1994), xxx.

9. For a brief overview of the components of a New Urbanist development in the Duany/Plater-Zyberk mold, see their short essay "The Neighborhood, The District, and The Corridor," xxv-xlii in Katz's *The New Urbanism*; for a fuller enunciation of the pair's New Urbanist philosophy, see Duany, Plater-Zyberk, and Jeff Speck, *Suburban Nation: The Rise of Sprawl and the American Dream* (New York: Farrar, Straus and Giroux, 2000).

10. Vincent Scully, "The Architecture of Community," in Katz, ed., *The New Urbanism*, 221-230; 226.

11. Tom Martinson, for example, in *American Dreamscape: The Pursuit of Happiness in Postwar Suburbia* (New York: Carroll & Graf, 2000), balks at Duany and Plater-Zyberk's zeal for community via landscape design, suggesting that "[t]he notion that [the suburbanite] exists to docilely populate some gentry designer's stage set is simply beyond reality" (43). Martinson goes on to point out that, however lofty its original goals may have been, Seaside has "matured into a pretentious cartoon of its original small-town ideal" (149). This point is difficult to dispute, especially on sunny summer days, when Seaside becomes flooded with visitors vying to get a look around the town. As tourists' cars occupy every available parking spot and line both sides of the one highway leading into and out of town, one gets the sense that Duany and Plater-Zyberk's small-town vision has proven to be a bit elusive.

12. Andrew Ross, *The Celebration Chronicles: Life, Liberty, and the Pursuit of Property Value in Disney's New Town* (New York: Ballantine, 1999), 317-318. As Ross notes, "most advocates of New Urbanism will say that planners are simply not in a position to address the major social ills of America in their designs" (317).

13. D. J. Waldie, *Holy Land: A Suburban Memoir* (New York: W. W. Norton & Co., 1996), 6. Waldie refers here to Peter Blake, *God's Own Junkyard: The Planned Deterioration of America's Landscape* (New York: Rhinehart and Wilson, 1964).

14. Waldie, 6.

15. Sharon Zukin, *Landscapes of Power: From Detroit to Disney World* (Berkeley: University of California Press, 1991), 141.

16. Margaret Marsh, in *Suburban Lives*, notes that museum curators have expressed interest in preserving a Levitt house as a cultural artifact, while conceding that they would first have to "strip away the 'improvements'" to restore it to its original state. As Marsh concludes, "The middle-class residential suburb . . . has become an historical artifact. . . . It is not farfetched to think that Levittown, or a community like it, might become the Colonial Williamsburg of the twenty-second century" (188).

17. See O'Rourke's "I Hate the Suburbs—Sort of. . . . But What I Really Hate Is Myself" *Rolling Stone*, September 30, 1999, 35ff.

18. Peter Calthorpe, "The Region," in Katz, ed., *The New Urbanism*, xii.

19. The phrase "centerless cities" comes from Kenneth Jackson's *Crabgrass Frontier: The Suburbanization of the United States* (New York: Oxford University Press, 1985); "edge cities" from Joel Garreau, *Edge City: Life on the New Frontier* (New York: Doubleday, 1991); and "technoburb" from Robert Fishman's *Bourgeois Utopias* (New York: Basic Books, 1987). See also Mark Gottdiener and George Kephart, "The Multinucleated Metropolitan Region: A Comparative Analysis," in *Postsuburban California: The Transformation of Orange County Since World War II*, ed. Rob Kling, Spencer Olin, and Mark Poster, 31-54 (Berkeley: University of California Press, 1991).

20. Robert Fishman, in *Bourgeois Utopias*, argues that the increasing decentralization of not only housing but also industry, services, and jobs represents "not the culmination of 200 years of history of suburbia, but rather its end. Indeed, this massive change is not suburbanization at all but the creation of a new kind of city, with principles that are directly opposed to the true suburb" (183).

Index